AN ABOLITIONIST ABROAD

Sarah Parker Remond, undated photograph. Portrait Photograph Collection. Courtesy Phillips Library, Peabody Essex Museum, Salem, Mass.

AN ABOLITIONIST ABROAD

Sarah Parker Remond in Cosmopolitan Europe

SIRPA SALENIUS

UNIVERSITY OF MASSACHUSETTS PRESS
Amherst and Boston

Printed in the United States of America

ISBN 978-1-62534-245-4 (hardcover), 246-1 (paperback)

Designed by Sally Nichols
Set in Arno Pro
Printed and bound by Sheridan Books, Inc.

Cover design by Sally Nichols
Cover art: Cityscape view looking toward cathedral,
Florence, Italy, ca. 1890. Library of Congress,
https://www.loc.gov/item/2001700798/.

Library of Congress Cataloging-in-Publication Data

Names: Salenius, Sirpa, author.
Title: An abolitionist abroad : Sarah Parker Remond in cosmopolitan Europe / Sirpa Salenius.
Description: Amherst : University of Massachusetts Press, 2016. | Includes bibliographical references and index.
Identifiers: LCCN 2016031024| ISBN 9781625342461 (pbk. : alk. paper) | ISBN 9781625342454 (hardcover : alk. paper)
Subjects: LCSH: Remond, Sarah Parker, 1826–1894. | African American women abolitionists—Biography. | African American abolitionists—Biography. | Remond, Sarah Parker, 1826–1894—Travel—Europe. | American Anti-Slavery Society—Biography. | African Americans—Intellectual life—19th century. | African American intellectuals—Biography.
Classification: LCC E449.R319 S25 2016 | DDC 326/.8092 [B] —dc23
LC record available at https://lccn.loc.gov/2016031024

British Library Cataloguing-in-Publication Data
A catalog record for this book is available from the British Library.

For Marcello

Contents

Acknowledgments

THE RESEARCH FOR THIS BOOK STARTED IN 2012 when I was organizing the sixth workshop of the Nineteenth-Century American Writers Study Group of the European Association for American Studies (EAAS) in Florence, Italy. The topic I had chosen for the event focused on African American women—writers and travelers—and their identity construction. On this occasion, Sarah Parker Remond became the object of my interest. The stimulating discussions with colleagues—in particular with professors Farah Griffin (Columbia University), Asunción López-Varela Azcárate (Universidad Complutense de Madrid), and Marie-Claude Perrin-Chenour (Paris X / Paris Ouest Nanterre-La Défénse)—during the workshop motivated me to continue my quest for further information on Remond. After my workshop presentation on "transatlantic Remond," her fascinating, progressive life inspired me to write an academic essay, and, as new material kept surfacing, Remond grew to become the central figure of the present book.

Although much of the material that make up this volume was waiting to be discovered in the archives in Florence, my research would not have been possible without the work of those who shared their findings in publications that appeared decades before, starting with Dorothy B. Porter's study from 1935, which came out in the *Journal of Negro History*. Therefore, I am grateful for the biographical notes, essays, articles, and dissertations published by Dorothy B. Porter, Ruth Bogin, Sibyl Ventress Brownlee,

Carla Peterson, Angelita Reyes, Marilyn Richardson, Jean Fagan Yellin, Teresa Zackodnik, and others, which have been extremely useful for my own inquiries into Remond's life and activism. Likewise, I wish to thank Stefano Luconi for his suggestions on publications that deal with Giuseppe Mazzini, the unification of Italy, and the British and American responses to the Italian Risorgimento movement. In addition, I am grateful to the editorial team at the University of Massachusetts Press for working on this project with me, and wish to thank the anonymous referees for the time they invested in reviewing the manuscript and for offering me insightful suggestions that allowed me to improve an earlier draft.

I am, moreover, grateful to the archivists Anita Israel and Christine Wirth at the Longfellow House–Washington's Headquarters National Historic Site Archives, Cambridge, Massachusetts, for unpublished journals they located in their archives. Other archivists I wish to thank for their invaluable assistance with this project include Amanda Thursfield, Nicholas Stanley-Price, and Ornella Forte at the Non-Catholic Cemetery for Foreigners in Rome for information concerning the burial of Remond and Gertrude Agnes Putnam; Christopher David Burns at the University of Vermont's archives for his help in accessing George Perkins Marsh correspondence; and Anne L. Busteed at Hamilton Hall for the unforgettable experience of visiting the Remonds' residence on Cambridge Street in Salem, Massachusetts.

In addition to the above mentioned sources, I have gathered material from various archives and libraries both in the United States and Italy, including the New York Research Library, Schomburg Center for Research in Black Culture, Library of Congress, Massachusetts Historical Society, Boston Athenæum, Salem Peabody Essex Museum Archives, Salem City Hall, the Fondo Archivistico di Santa Maria Nuova, Bedford College University of London Archives, Biblioteca Nazionale Centrale di Firenze, and the library of Scuola Normale Superiore di Pisa. It is with great pleasure and gratitude that I acknowledge the valuable work of many archivists with whom I have been in contact who have been extremely helpful in assisting me with this project, sharing their knowledge, time, and enthusiasm. They made me believe in the enlightened world that Remond envisioned. I also wish to thank my family and friends for their support and encouragement, and, finally, my gratitude goes to Sarah Remond herself for her inspiring and empowering example of womanhood.

My article on Sarah Parker Remond appeared in *CLCWeb: Comparative Literature and Culture*: Sirpa A. Salenius, "*Negra d'America* Remond and Her Journeys," *CLCWeb: Comparative Literature and Culture* 14, no. 5 (2012), http://docs.lib.purdue.edu/clcweb/.

AN ABOLITIONIST ABROAD

Sarah P. Remond, undated photograph. Portraits of American Abolitionists, photograph number 81.448. Courtesy Massachusetts Historical Society.

Introduction

Sarah Remond and the Black American Grand Tour

Why is it that in so many of the States neither freedmen nor their friends find any longer suitable protection? . . . There is but one answer, and one source from which all these difficulties emanate—slavery in the past and its hateful remnants in the present. The Southerners and their Northern allies are determined that the black race shall not be recognized, shall not receive justice. They are determined to prevent the consummation of emancipation, to make freedom almost nominal. Reconstruction cannot be permanently settled until hatred of the coloured race is kept in check or exterminated. No one who has kept pace with the history of the coloured race can hope to re-educate a nation at once: therefore the only remedy is to check this hatred, made up of fashion, prejudice, and intense ignorance.

—*Sarah Parker Remond*

RACIAL INJUSTICE IN THE RECONSTRUCTION ERA HAD its roots in slavery, argued Sarah Parker Remond in September 1866.[1] The African American Remond, who was born free to a committed abolitionist family in Salem, Massachusetts, on 6 June 1826, was a pivotal figure in the fight against racial discrimination and slavery, two fundamental problems in the new American nation.[2] She received her education in Salem; Newport, Rhode Island; London; and Florence, Italy, and she became one of the most gifted and eloquent antislavery orators of the nineteenth century. Her cultural and political contributions to black emancipation can be connected to what scholars have defined as "an immensely self-aware transatlantic radical black political tradition which transcends a narrow nationalism."[3] Similarly to such activists as Frederick Douglass, Remond assumed an important role in the transnational radical black emancipation movement that changed the conceptualization of black identity and black presence in society.

An Abolitionist Abroad: Sarah Parker Remond in Cosmopolitan Europe examines the activism and transatlantic travels of Remond, who triggered a transformation in black awareness of self, control, and power when she placed herself in the center of controversies concerning the social, political, and educational rights of African Americans and women. Moreover, she challenged white patriarchal norms and questioned American conceptions of citizenship. She defied the restraining race-gender expectations that constructed African American women as powerless when she became one of the first and few antebellum women to take the lecture pulpit. She further rejected society's expectations of her as subservient when, like nineteenth-century American artists, she embarked on her Grand Tour of Europe to receive an education that was unavailable to her in her native country. "My strongest desire through life has been to be educated," she wrote in an autobiographical essay that appeared in London in 1861.[4] She departed on her journey to Europe, and thus joined American Grand Tourists, the majority of whom were white intellectuals, artists, and writers.

With determination Remond transcended racial and gender barriers and in Europe obtained schooling that permitted her to embark on new professional endeavors. She became a nurse in London, completing her studies at one of Europe's most prestigious medical schools, the Santa Maria Nuova hospital school in Florence, where she graduated as an obstetrician. In Europe she found an ideal environment for pursuing her education and cultivating international relations and interracial networks of activism. In London she collaborated with white British abolitionists and women's rights advocates, and she helped create a new black standard—one of agency and success—against which to measure racial justice. Her presence was in the core, not in the margins, of transatlantic women's emancipation and antislavery movements. She contributed to social and political change by participating in international gender and race activism and by assisting the Italian revolutionary Giuseppe Mazzini achieve his ambition of Italian unification. In Florence and Rome she joined a polyglot, cosmopolitan society that welcomed her without prejudice. Similarly to white Americans who met Remond in Florence in the 1860s—such as Henry Wadsworth Longfellow, who by then was a celebrated translator, scholar, and poet, and the art collector James Jackson Jarves—the black American female doctor became part of a cultured and intellectual Old World cosmopolitan society. This book, then, is about Remond, the transatlantic world she influenced, and the world that, in turn, shaped her.

Remond first articulated her political agenda in the United States where she raised her voice for empowerment and showed how America could live up to its ideals. The oppression Remond struggled against—slavery and discrimination—were fundamental problems of the 1800s, a century of radical sociopolitical change that took place on both sides of the Atlantic. American and British abolitionists were the most conspicuous activists addressing the issue of slavery and speaking about it with the loudest voices, although the institution existed, and was eradicated, in other countries and territories as well. In the United States slavery, as the historian Arthur Riss points out, distorted the nation's ideals: political identities were defined and rights granted on the basis of race, gender, and even religion, thus blocking the ideals of freedom and equality expounded in the Declaration of Independence.[5] Consequently, then, since the American nation was born around racism yet founded on idealistic ambitions to guarantee freedom and equal rights to all, such aspirations remained unfulfilled promises to those who were excluded on the basis of their race or gender.

Remond's politically and socially informed reflections focused on the antagonism of white and black America as she campaigned to transform the nation's empty promises into a reality that would include black Americans and women. Her inquiry on injustice raised questions concerning slavery, discrimination, and segregation, and addressed racial and gendered subordination as well as the unwarranted robbing of constitutional rights including that of citizenship to America's black population, and she was particularly concerned about the situation of African American women.

In the United States, the experiences of black and white women differed greatly in several ways. The scholar Hazel V. Carby notes that "the hierarchical structuring of the relationship between black and white women" was not only the norm in American society but also characterized the bonds of interracial sisterhood.[6] "To be a black woman in nineteenth-century America," the historian Dorothy Sterling points out, "was to live in the double jeopardy of belonging to the 'inferior' sex of an 'inferior' race."[7] Moreover, black women were excluded from the consideration in the dominant cult of true womanhood that described the parameters used to define women because they were perceived and defined as inferiors but paradoxically also rejected because of their strength and independence. If white women often felt themselves to be prisoners of this cult of true womanhood, which made them dependent on men, black women in slavery and in the northern free districts, instead, had to rely on themselves for survival. As Sterling argues, black women had no alternatives but to develop skills and rely on their own initiatives and strength.[8] Although black men were publicly acknowledged as leaders in free black communities, women shouldered responsibilities, worked outside their homes, organized women's societies, established educational associations, and campaigned against slavery. Already in the early decades of the nineteenth century, African American women were demonstrating their abilities as entrepreneurs and professionals, thriving in business ventures, and caring for the members of their communities as school teachers or founders and editors of newspapers.

The active professional women included Remond's sisters—Nancy Shearman, Susan H., Caroline Remond Putnam, Maritcha Juan, and Cecelia Remond Babcock—who were successful entrepreneurs like their father, John Remond; they were among the pioneers who took action to fully express themselves privately and professionally. They successfully managed a hair salon, worked as hairdressers and manufacturers of wigs, and ran a bakery. Other, more widely known nineteenth-century black women who achieved international success and fame included the sculptress Edmonia Lewis, who competed with white American men and women artists for commissions in Rome, and the concert singer Elizabeth Taylor Greenfield, who toured in the northern United States and England.[9]

In addition, many women, including those in the Remond household, participated in advancing a political program of black emancipation. Remond's mother, Nancy Lenox, for instance, applied her entrepreneurial and radical vision of the future to establishing a pioneering black women's antislavery society in Salem in addition to working in her husband's catering business. Similarly, the family of Caroline Remond's husband, Joseph Putnam, included women who were active in promoting social reform. Caroline's mother-in-law, Jane Putnam, was involved in black liberation and social integration, and she dedicated her time to finding ways to enlarge educational opportunities for African Americans through racial integration of Boston schools. Moreover, already in the early 1830s, she had established a Boston temperance society with other black women activists and social reformers.[10] In addition, African American women were among the first to deliver speeches publicly, addressing mixed audiences that were both biracial and mixed gendered years before the more frequent appearance, and acceptance, of women on the lecture pulpit. Hence, women were working in African American communities as well as in transatlantic circuits as artists or businesswomen, forming networks, and founding associations to serve as organized forums for promoting racial and gender emancipation. These black women used their professional and private endeavors to advance the cause of racial equality and empowerment.

The Remond women were intellectual political leaders committed to the ideology of racial uplift within the Salem black community. They found various ways to articulate their talent and commitment to gender and racial progress. In formal emancipation movements such as abolitionism, women's rights, or freedpeople's relief organizations that were active before, during, and after the Civil War, black women joined forces, as Sterling notes, "with the most progressive white women of the country, sometimes forging lasting friendships." According to Sterling, black women fought "to win acceptance from whites and, at the same time, hold on to their own identity."[11] However, rather than struggling to win the acceptance of white women, black activists were striving for racial equality and were eager to collaborate with white Americans toward realizing common goals: abolition of slavery, elimination of race discrimination, and emancipation of women.

Indeed, in addition to slavery, the "Woman Question" characterized nineteenth-century societies in the United States and Europe, uniting progressive-leaning women who grew increasingly frustrated with the gendered power asymmetries that dictated their lives, options, and liberties.

In 1840, women from both shores of the Atlantic gathered together for the first international meeting on abolitionism: the World's Anti-Slavery Convention, which took place in London. Although officially women were not allowed to participate in the meeting, it provided an opportunity for American representatives to form alliances with British women.[12] Lucretia Mott, a Quaker activist from Pennsylvania who participated in the convention, met there Elizabeth Cady Stanton, who was on her honeymoon.[13] After their return to the United States, Mott and Stanton committed themselves to organizing a women's rights convention in their native country. It signaled the beginning of a formal American women's rights movement, which stemmed from a transatlantic antislavery event and was one of the first attempts to consolidate an international alliance. In 1848, the women's rights movement formally separated from abolitionism at the Seneca Falls meeting, where the focus of discussions shifted from the liberation of slaves to contemplating ways to improve women's situation. There were no black women present at the meeting, but, Sterling explains, "they participated in similar woman's rights meetings thereafter."[14] Women, then, took action against bigotry, worked toward dismantling racial and gendered inequality in education and society at large, shouldered the responsibilities of being professional career women, and acted as pioneers in international activism.

During the century, women's associations grew in number and membership as they developed into powerful organizations where both white and black women figured prominently as members and leaders. The actions of progressive women resonated transnationally and their examples empowered other women both nationally and internationally. Many women, white and African American, were proactively taking charge of their lives and becoming models of female independence.

Remond was an astounding example of such autonomy. After starting her career as an antislavery orator in the United States, where she lectured between 1856 and 1858, Remond joined the increasing number of women who traveled to Europe for various reasons, some more conventional (for example, recreation or health), some more innovative or motivated by ideological and political concerns. Although traveling abroad was uncommon for them, especially in the first part of the century, "black and white women," as the scholar Jennifer Bernhardt Steadman has argued, "could and did travel and lay claim to agency by moving beyond these confining definitions of womanhood, blackness, and class."[15] However, overseas destinations were accessible mainly to privileged white women who had the means to travel. Hence, the rarity of opportunities available for African American women was even more pronounced than for nineteenth-century middle- or upper-class white females.

And yet, both white and black women traveled, moving across the United States as well as abroad, to such faraway places as Jamaica or Russia (the destinations of the African American Nancy Prince), to Egypt (which was popular among white women in the 1870s), and to various parts of Europe. The black sculptress Lewis established herself permanently in Rome; the ex-slave Ellen Craft, together with her husband, William, chose England as their home after their escape from slavery; the journalist and anti-lynching advocate Ida B. Wells toured in England and Scotland in 1893–94, lecturing to wide audiences; and the fugitive slave Harriet Jacobs crossed the Atlantic to visit England as many as three times: in 1845–46, as the nanny of the author Nathaniel Parker Willis's daughter Imogen; in 1858, when she went looking for a British publisher for her autobiography; and finally in 1867–68, when she traveled together with her daughter Louisa Matilda to raise funds that would enable her to build an orphanage and old people's home in Savannah, Georgia. Similarly, Remond left her native country for Europe: she first toured in England, Ireland, and Scotland lecturing against slavery, promoting women's rights, raising funds for the Italian unification movement, and studying languages before she enrolled at All Saints University College Hospital in London, graduating as a nurse before permanently moving to Florence, where she became an obstetrician. In Florence her knowledge of French, Latin, and Italian enabled her to connect with the multilingual, international high society and to forge strong social and cultural ties that were transatlantic in nature. African American women, then, could and did travel, moving across national frontiers on their mission of self-discovery and exploration.

These (few) African American women insisted on their rights to equality, independence, and citizenship as they moved away from the United

States, where the "racially exclusive conceptions of national identity from which blacks were excluded as either non-humans or non-citizens" prevailed.[16] Steadman has suggested that "traveling black women directly challenge nineteenth-century and even present-day definitions of black experience."[17] To be sure, black women such as Remond reassessed their identity and claimed authority, letting hope and determination triumph over prejudice. For these women, travel entailed freedom and autonomy but also the potential for social, cultural, and economic advancement.

As women moved, physically and metaphorically, they abandoned the safety of their domestic walls and reinvented new models of womanhood that were less conventional and more adventurous. The literary scholar Mary Suzanne Schriber contends that gaps in gender ideology were opened when women demonstrated their capacity to cross oceans fearlessly and comfortably. "Constricting definitions of 'woman's sphere' were challenged," Schriber notes, "and the roles of women in the public arena were expanded by a powerful surge of activities: women's quest for public rights of citizenship early in the century; women's work for causes such as abolition and their discovery of their own strengths in the process; women's press for suffrage in the aftermath of 1848 and the Seneca Falls women's convention; women's union in numerous voluntary associations such as Sorosis and the WCTU; and women's entrance into colleges, the professions, and the workplace."[18] Although Schriber is discussing white, mainly middle- or upper-class women, she also recognizes that black women challenged the same limitations as well as fought against race discrimination. The growing alternatives for self-improvement that "rendered white women more mobile and bold as the century progressed," Schriber suggests, "found a parallel in the activities of African American women who organized, participated in abolitionist groups, and sought education and professions."[19] During the nineteenth century, then, women, including Remond, became involved in activities that concerned abolition, women's suffrage, and education, and they took advantage of the increased opportunities for learning and careers that took them outside the confining walls of their domestic environments.

For women, crossing the ocean meant leaving limiting gender and race restrictions behind and gaining confidence with asserting their rights to public and political action, be it a choice in professional careers or participation in reform activism. In Europe, where Remond participated in a social life free of racial discrimination, she realized her dreams of self-fulfillment, thus taking individual action toward breaking the color line. With other women, she moved beyond white patriarchal parameters into an international space where her activism resonated transnationally. In Britain, Remond continued her relentless campaign aimed at abolishing slavery and participated in women's fierce demands for suffrage and full participation in social and political decision-making.

Remond was a remarkable example of a black woman who not only collaborated with white British abolitionists but also with women's rights advocates, holding leading positions in antislavery and women's rights organizations, thus helping to create international networks of transatlantic alliances. She personally helped to build transatlantic bridges of collaboration and activism as she worked both with abolitionists and radical women's rights advocates, many of them white.

Common for many women's reform movements was the interracial nature of the formal associations and meetings; especially in Britain, abolitionists worked together without race segregation. This stance differed to some extent from the attitude that prevailed in the United States, where even liberal activists who were committed to racial equality tended to treat their black colleagues with patronizing attitudes. In Europe, instead, race prejudice existed to a lesser degree and African Americans—at least the well-known and eloquent abolitionist orators—were accepted on equal terms in all social circles. They were warmly received at high society gatherings, and representatives of the middle and upper classes welcomed the contributions of their overseas colleagues to furthering their mutual goals of gender and racial liberation. Moreover, British and Irish working classes were eager to hear their message concerning the liberation of the oppressed. Remond, whose activism crossed oceans that confined nations and traversed barriers that defined gender, class, and race expectations, also networked with one of Europe's leading revolutionaries, Giuseppe Mazzini, who was dedicated to liberating Italy from Austrian rule.

Starting from the 1840s, Italy's various states were protesting against their foreign oppressors. The Austrians controlled the Kingdom of Lombardy-Venetia, the Duchies of Parma and Modena, and the Grand Duchy of Tuscany, whereas the southern Kingdom of the Two Sicilies was under the rule of the Spanish Bourbons but nonetheless linked to Vienna. Only the Kingdom of Sardinia (Savoy, Piedmont, Liguria, and Sardinia) was under domestic reign, independent from Austria.[20] Around the mid-nineteenth century, people on the peninsula were determined to achieve liberty, fighting for its unification from separate states into one nation, with Mazzini and Giuseppe Garibaldi as the leading figures of the new Risorgimento movement. The first war aiming at independence was fought in 1848–49, followed by a second attempt to unify the country in 1859. The two alternatives for unification were the radical republican and more moderate monarchical solutions. Mazzini's program was a popular insurrection that, in his vision, would lead to a unified nation. The Kingdom of Sardinia, instead, advanced its unification plans by forming an anti-Austrian alliance with France to acquire Lombardy, Parma, Modena, Tuscany, and the northern section of the Papal States in 1859. The first phase of Italy's unification was completed a year after, in 1860.[21]

Turin became the first capital of the unified nation in 1861, after which Florence assumed the administration of the country from 1865 to 1870. Italy, allied with Prussia, acquired Venetia in 1866, and the conquest of Rome completed the national unification in 1870, with Victor Emmanuel II, who proclaimed himself king of Italy, as the leader of the monarchy.[22] Following the last territorial conquests, Rome was named the capital. Although many Italians were satisfied with the new nation, especially in the northern parts of the peninsula, large sections of the country resisted the political and economic integration into the kingdom.[23] The majority, however, celebrated, if not the unification, then at least their welcomed liberation from foreign rule. In 1866, when Italy was nearing the conclusion of its unification, Remond moved from London to Florence, which at the time was the capital of the newly established monarchy.

Remond had followed the Italian Revolution from England, where Mazzini was in exile and where Remond herself was pursuing her studies while simultaneously dedicating her time to various forms of activism. The people directly involved in the Risorgimento movement, the main protagonists of Italy's unification, were her friends and activists with whom she collaborated. One of the most influential of them was Mazzini, whom Remond met in London in 1861.

In 1866, Remond left London to continue her studies in Florence, carrying with her letters of introduction from Mazzini. Italy, one of the main destinations on Continental Europe, attracted Americans and other foreigners who traveled to profit from its cultural and artistic capital. Travelers, as the historian William W. Stowe argues, "were motivated by personal as well as cultural and social agendas."[24] American artists and writers gravitated toward Italy's cultural riches, which they used to develop their own expressions of national literature and visual arts. Indeed, the transatlantic crossing was pivotal to Americans who acknowledged the significant, formative role of Italy in the development of American national culture and identity. In this context, the Grand Tour of the Old World (as the tour of Continental Europe was commonly known) became instrumental in the process of acculturation, in acquiring a sense of history, culture, and sophistication that Americans perceived as characteristic of Europe, particularly pertinent to such countries as Italy. The tour rapidly turned into a mechanical journey with its established itinerary that commonly started from England, which was the first landing place for travelers crossing the ocean from New York to Liverpool, and from there continuing their journeys to their final destinations, France and Italy.[25]

Among the first widely known American authors to arrive in Italy in the late 1820s—a decade or so after the end of the Napoleonic Wars that had impeded Continental travel—were Longfellow and the novelist James Fenimore Cooper. The American dandy Nathaniel Parker Willis, who was a foreign correspondent for the *New York Mirror* and author of *Pencillings by the Way* (1835), followed in the 1830s, and the journalist Margaret Fuller arrived a decade later. After the Civil War, many pioneering American authors—among them Mark Twain (Samuel Clemens), Henry James, Constance Fenimore Woolson, and William Dean Howells—established themselves in Italy, where they started experimenting with a new form of literary expression: realism. The contribution of these writers to the nascent national literature was significant: they were among the first to create truly American literary works. They all resided in Florence, which at the time was a central gathering place for cosmopolitan globe-trotters of all nationalities.

The first Americans to join these cosmopolitan social circles were polyglot intellectuals. Their fluency in foreign languages and their cultural backgrounds facilitated their acceptance among other world citizens gathered in cities such as Florence, where the cosmopolitan group identity had its roots in the cultured intellectualism that the various members were expected to share. Much like what the historian Nico Slate has referred to as "colored cosmopolitanism," which allowed advocates of "colored solidarity" to "articulate an inclusive humanism that defied narrow, chauvinist definitions of race, religion, or nation," the cosmopolitanism of Italy embraced universal, international, and interracial humanism.[26] The society welcomed American and other foreign visitors without judging their cultural, racial, religious, or national differences. Since race was not a basis for discrimination in these gatherings where the literati united to discuss politics and social change, the intellectual, international salons welcomed such visitors as Remond and Lewis, who arrived when other Americans, mainly white artists and writers, had already introduced themselves into the ranks of Italian nobility.

The turbulent nineteenth century witnessed a rapidly increasing number of American travelers in Italy, flocking mainly in such cities as Rome, Venice, and Florence. The last, with its vast cultural heritage and cosmopolitan aristocratic gatherings, was the hub that drew Americans to experience the Italian *dolce-far-niente* lifestyle, that is, sweet leisure, and high-society sophistication as well as to admire original art works commonly known to Americans through copies, engravings, and etchings. The European continental tour soon became a stabilized, culturally framed experience but nonetheless invaluable for aspiring American artists and writers who arrived in Italy to work on purely American subject matters so as to contribute to the nascent canon of national cultural production. Generally, these Americans discussed themes that concerned their native country and tended to remain oblivious to Italian realities, hence their works were embedded in American controversies. Sculptors, in particular, chose the themes of slavery and women's emancipation for their colossal statues.

Such artists as Lewis and Hiram Powers are examples of Americans who chiseled blocks of marble to represent the liberation of the oppressed. In such statues as Powers's idealized *The Greek Slave,* which was so popular that the English poet Elizabeth Barrett Browning wrote a sonnet of the same title celebrating it, and Lewis's *The Freed Woman and Her Child* and *Forever Free,* slavery is linked to an idealized woman, paradoxically sculpted in white marble.[27] In addition to the abolitionist message, then, such sculptures made powerful ideological and political statements on women and race. According to the art historian Charlotte Streifer Rubinstein, Lewis said that in her work, "she was expressing her 'strong sympathy for all women who have struggled and suffered.'"[28] At times, indeed, slavery was associated with gender emancipation and expressed through a female figure being freed of the chains that had enslaved her. By contrast, Lewis's African *Hagar,* Rubinstein argues, symbolized "the alienation of black women in white society."[29] In this way, Americans in Europe were participating in an ongoing discussion on national identity while defining their identities individually and collectively, as artists and writers, as Americans and women. The tour had a significant impact on the creation of American visual arts and literature, in the formation of museums and libraries, and in the reinvention of national identities.

In Italy, African Americans found an opportunity to reassess their identities as they enjoyed liberties and social privileges denied them in the United States. In Rome, Lewis, who moved to Italy around the same time as Remond, became friends with European nobility, including the Marquis of Bute, who purchased her statues and commissioned new works. Since it was quite common for travelers in Italy to visit artists' studios—in Florence, those of Powers and Thomas Ball; in Rome, those of Lewis and William Wetmore Story—it is unsurprising to find commentaries in American fictional works and travel writing that served to promote the works of American sculptors and painters who were established in the creatively more fertile Italy.

Such publicity was important for artists in general, but for black women such as Lewis, praise of her work in widely circulated guidebooks and travel articles served to prove the potential and self-realization of women and African Americans as successful and talented sculptresses, as professional artists. The American author Levina Buoncuore Urbino was among those who visited Lewis's studio in 1868, when "Miss Lewis, the colored artist, was at work upon a Hagar. Her Marriage of Hiawatha," Buoncuore Urbino wrote, "is small and handsome; she had sold several; wished she could afford to make Longfellow a present of one."[30] A few years later, in 1870, the American future leader of women's temperance, Frances E. Willard, visited Lewis's studio in Rome where she found Longfellow's "fine, idealized bust" among "several excellent busts of Americans & a medallion of the Abbé Liszt, a friend of hers [Lewis's], whom she told me she often hears play, at his villa near Rome." Willard admired the woman artist, whom she found "cheerful & strong," with "genius to which many a wealthy traveler vainly aspires."[31] Remond received similar commendations from those who met her, and like Lewis, she was well-connected in Italian high society.

Praise from American white men and women, commissions from British nobility, and friendships with such famous writers of the time as Longfellow and the composer Franz Liszt bear testimony to the absence of prejudice that dominated black American life in the United States. Through their experiences, Lewis and Remond, among others, demonstrated the capabilities of women and African Americans when they were allowed to fully and freely express themselves personally and professionally.

Remond, who traveled at a transformative moment in history, joined white American artists and writers who crossed the Atlantic for education and tourism, to start their careers, or to cultivate cosmopolitanism and culture in such international centers as Florence. Some of them, including Remond herself, chose to establish themselves permanently in Europe. In this way, Remond's transatlantic travels can be placed within the nineteenth-century American Grand Tour tradition, which commonly has been associated nearly exclusively with the white intellectual elite of the United States. The tour, in other words, has commonly been defined in terms of race, class, and often gender. And yet, African Americans took their place among white Americans in the transatlantic crossings of borders and cultures. Similarly to white intellectuals, they traveled from the United States to Europe for increased educational and professional opportunities and acculturation as well as to obtain cosmopolitan sophistication. For African American travelers, however, the Grand Tour often was motivated by more collective goals such as speaking for their race and fully expressing and concretizing their potential in order to validate their racial identity and demonstrate black equality.

Relatively many African Americans left the United States for England, especially after the Fugitive Slave Law came into effect in 1850. The law rendered assisting fugitive slaves a federal crime and thus endangered runaway slaves who had established themselves in the northern states and now risked recapture. However, it also threatened the liberty of free African Americans who unexpectedly feared being kidnapped and sent to slavery. Hence, free and previously enslaved black Americans crossed the Atlantic for their personal safety, to avoid recapture, but also to raise money for black activities, to obtain education, to promote the cause of abolitionism, and to influence international opinion against American slavery and racial discrimination.[32]

Many fugitive slaves who had been forced to flee the country became antislavery lecturers hoping they could gain financial and moral support for their cause. They helped to build the international, transatlantic antislavery network that grew powerfully during the years between 1830 and 1860. The transatlantic antislavery lecture circuit included such celebrated African American orators as Remond and her brother Charles Lenox Remond; former slaves Douglass and William Wells Brown; and such fugitive slave women as Ellen Craft, who toured together with her husband, William, also a former slave. These black speakers, who first toured in the United States before continuing their activities in Great Britain and Ireland, talked about racial prejudice and slavery from a personal experience. The persuasiveness of their message against human bondage often triggered immediate emotional responses from their audiences.[33] They toured in England, Scotland, and Ireland campaigning for black liberation. At the same time, others, such as Sojourner Truth, continued to promote abolitionism and women's rights in the United States, where gender and racial politics were intertwined in women's activism within formally organized suffrage and reform movements that had an effect on women's emancipation worldwide.

The same decades that witnessed the forming of transatlantic abolitionist collaboration saw the building of international female alliances of women's rights activists. Such American white women as Mott, Stanton, and Susan B. Anthony believed, as the scholar Margaret H. McFadden has pointed out, that "women had no more political rights than slaves."[34] These central figures in the United States, who included Remond, fought for the emancipation of women, lectured against slavery, and networked internationally with others. Information promoting their causes circled in the form of pamphlets, books, articles, and correspondence, both public and private. In a similar way, people navigated in the transatlantic world where they participated in meetings and lecture circuits. Women entered into reform movements as public speakers and activists and formed networks that reached across the Atlantic. The international networks dedicated to the advancement of women's rights extended all over Europe as far north as Sweden and Finland, and the presence of women's emancipation movements was especially strong in such countries as France and Germany, in addition to England. As McFadden further explains, "The gradual building up of international relationships and contacts between women in Europe and North America, across borders of nations, languages, ethnic groups, and sometimes class, intensified throughout the nineteenth century."[35] Remond joined the multinational, multiethnic, interracial, and transnational networks that covered various reform movements: women worked together in the Atlantic community on abolitionism, temperance, and women's rights, discussing controversial issues that concerned race, gender, and class. In other words, women internationally were concerned for the oppressed. Peace and "white slavery," or international prostitution, were also on the agenda of many reform activists who campaigned for women's political and property rights.

These women who aspired for professional rather than domestic self-fulfillment often were seen as unwomanly.[36] However, despite the suspicion conventionally thinking men and more traditional women expressed when encountering independent, career-oriented New Women, these progressive pioneers boldly forged ahead toward their chosen goals, fighting to realize their ambitious personal and collective dreams. They set examples for others to emulate and thus, as Schriber has pointed out, rewrote history and culture "by writing women into them."[37]

Remond, as this book demonstrates, challenged the norms set by American white society and subverted nineteenth-century racial and gender ideologies by achieving success in her personal life and careers. She resisted prejudiced assumptions when she became one of the few nineteenth-century American women to lecture in public in the antebellum years, often to interracial audiences of both men and women. She participated in national and international debates on racial and gender emancipation, assuming an influential position as an antislavery lecturer and women's rights advocate first in the United States and then in Europe. She not only expected but demanded that her voice be publicly heard. When she traveled to Britain and from there to Italy, her desire was to leave bigotry and color prejudice behind. In Europe she found freedom, improved opportunities, and a possibility to reinvent her Self.

As she gained distance from the oppression of her native America, Remond demanded the recognition of her political and social rights. The exclusion of African American participation in national rights and responsibilities was a significant theme in nineteenth-century black protest. The historian Paul Gilroy, among others, has examined the ideas of nation, national belonging, and the relationships among race, culture, and nationality, observing that American citizenship was not extended to include African Americans. As he points out, racial classifications celebrated race-based conceptions of national identity that excluded America's black population whose humanity was questioned and whose rights and citizenship were denied.[38] Remond, for one, demanded that her national belonging be recognized and her right to an American passport be acknowledged. With such demands she challenged the restraining expectations constructed of African American women as powerless victims, as the "voiceless property of others."[39] Moreover, in contrast to dominant racial theories that insisted on black inferiority, Remond was accepted and warmly welcomed in white British activist sisterhoods as an equal. She resisted assimilation into the prominent primitive-civilized, or inferior-superior, classification of people that prevailed even in the seemingly more liberal British society. To quote Gilroy, "Notions of the primitive and the civilized which had been integral to pre-modern understanding of 'ethnic' differences became fundamental cognitive and aesthetic markers in the processes which generated a constellation of subject positions in which Englishness, Christianity, and other ethnic and racialized attributes would finally give way to the dislocating dazzle of 'whiteness.'"[40]

In addition, Gilroy's three points concerning black political struggles can be applied to underline how such women as Remond participated in a similarly complex and many-faceted strategy to liberate herself from color-defined oppression. She fought against slavery and struggled to obtain rights and liberties; she fiercely insisted on her quest for citizenship, which meant recognizing and granting her the same privileges that white Americans enjoyed. Moreover, she continued her pursuit of autonomy, of creating what Gilroy has suggested was a common goal of many black travelers: "An independent space in which black community and autonomy can develop at their own pace and in their own direction."[41] In Europe, Remond found a space in which she could grow and develop her capacities in a direction of her own choosing, released from stereotypical assumptions and confining prejudice.

Remond, like other members of the free black elite of northern states crossed the ocean from cities such as Boston or New York to such English ports as Liverpool, often traveling in first class. Remond, her sisters Maritcha and Caroline Remond Putnam, Caroline's son Edmund Quincy Putnam, and his wife, Gertie, all traveled—for leisure, education, and work. Similarly, Lewis and the daughters of William Wells Brown, Clara and Josephine, headed for Europe to complete their education. Many of them, including Remond, had studied foreign languages, which facilitated their integration into foreign societies. After departing on their Grand Tours, these African Americans chose Europe as their permanent home and lived in such cultural capitals as Paris, London, Florence, and Rome. Hence, not only was transatlantic travel available to black Americans but they had the means and courage to permanently remain in Europe where they joined the fashionable social circles of their less prejudiced adoptive homes.

In Europe, Remond and her family, in particular her sisters, participated in social activities that in the United States were either exclusively reserved for whites or were racially segregated. In London, Florence, and Rome, they mingled with foreign nobility and organized musical soirées where some of the most famous musicians of the time performed to racially mixed audiences. At the time, music was considered a form of communication and a distinguishing feature of social relations; as an artistic expression of a specific location and culture, it expressed the self-identity of a given social group. For African American travelers, it became a means to underscore their inclusion in transatlantic cosmopolitan society.[42] In England and Italy, Remond and her family members claimed their position among the prominent cosmopolitan hosts and hostesses and visiting Grand Tourists, and as with their white counterparts, they entered a polyglot high society where they participated in cultural and intellectual exchanges with Italians, other Europeans, and Americans. They joined progressive nineteenth-century men and women of various nationalities at aristocratic salons; in the company of European nobility they enjoyed such sophisticated entertainments as opera and concerts, and participated in intellectual *conversazioni* on equal terms. They felt welcomed and accepted by a high society that openly displayed their acceptance of difference and absence of race prejudice. As Remond and her relatives distanced themselves from American sexist and racist attitudes that insisted on their inferiority, they demonstrated that dominant norms were socially constructed to sustain assumptions of white supremacy and to empower white men. In Europe, black Americans felt liberated from such dictates as they bonded with activists and intellectuals of all races and nationalities.

An Abolitionist Abroad discusses the turmoil of the nineteenth century through the figure and experience of one person, one African American woman, Sarah Remond. This book participates in a conversation concerning race and its perception in the United States and Europe in the nineteenth century. It aims to examine the racial paradigm founded on the polarity of white supremacy and black inferiority, an idea that continues to resonate in contemporary societies. The existing discrimination that persists from the early nineteenth century and beyond to the so-called post-racial society of the United States continues to hinder racial mixing and prevent equality. Recent renewed racist attacks and police brutality can, perhaps to some extent, be seen as a reaction triggered by the election of a black president, Barack Obama, making an African American the most powerful person in the United States. Despite successful and influential black Americans, whose examples testify to the social and political advancement of the black population in the United States, racial prejudice undeniably still exists in contemporary societies. As the lawyer and historian F. Michael Higginbotham has pointed out, often it is expressed in more subtle ways through discrimination in housing, employment, "white flight" from neighborhoods with black residents, racial profiling, and, finally and more disturbingly, police brutality.[43]

The pervasive racial paradigm, Higginbotham explains, started during the birth of the American nation: "The false notion of white superiority / black inferiority ingrained through slavery led to whites separating themselves from blacks through Jim Crow practices," and the "blatant and subtle ways" racism continues in contemporary America where "unequal treatment" results in "missed opportunity."[44] One of the aims of this book, then, is to contribute to the tearing down of these false notions concerning race; it participates in ongoing efforts to eliminate the racial paradigm constructed on the notion of black inferiority. The inspiring example of Remond, her resistance to prejudice, her struggle against injustice, and her successful cross-racial collaborations and international interactions demonstrate that "black separation and white isolation" are unnecessary societal models.[45] As the following chapters demonstrate, Remond refuted notions of black victimization and instead embarked on her journey toward individual and collective success, transforming her dreams and ideals into reality.

This work is divided into four sections that focus on Remond's life in the United States, her activism in England, her participation in Italian unification movement, and her career and cosmopolitanism in Italy. The topics of the chapters that follow this introduction would each merit a more thorough and detailed discussion, which in some instances has already been done in other academic publications. *We Are Your Sisters: Black Women in the Nineteenth*

Century, edited by Dorothy Sterling (1984), Shirley J. Yee's *Black Women Abolitionists: A Study in Activism, 1828–1860* (1992), and *The Abolitionist Sisterhood: Women's Political Culture in Antebellum America,* edited by Jean Fagan Yellin and John C. Van Horne (1994), just to name a few of the many full-length books that address some of the topics here reintroduced in relation to Remond, demonstrate the decades-long interest in the experiences of black women activists. The present book is placed in conversation with these earlier publications and continues my previous research that focuses on nineteenth-century American writers and artists in Italy. Therefore, I am here interested in the thematics discussed in earlier publications to the extent that they enable me to contextualize Remond's experience in the United States, Britain, and Italy. I show that the nineteenth-century American travelers, the Grand Tourists—white and black, male and female, artists and activists—shared the aims and goals of their journeys, and common to them was the impact transatlantic travel had on transforming their worldviews and shaping their identities. The encounter with realities different from their own helped give new directions and dimensions to their lives, widening the scope of their interests and pursuits.

Initially Remond's concern for racial justice stemmed from the education given and example set by her parents, and at first her career as a reform activist was national, limited to influencing Americans. Predictably, the first two chapters of the book focus on the early career of Remond as an abolitionist and women's rights advocate in the United States. Her family, as well as the education she received formally at school and unofficially at home, influenced her ideological stance toward race and gender politics. Remond's early experiences in activism in her native country facilitated her participation and integration into the international abolitionist and women's rights networks in Britain where she actively took part in forming relationships and establishing reform societies with other women. It is in England, as discussed in chapters 3 and 4, where she developed her capacity to express her convictions through written and spoken word. She found her place among the leading figures of international reform movements through her participation in transatlantic networks of female advocates who were working to ensure the emancipation of slaves and women.

Moreover, through British abolitionists she made her first contact with Mazzini, which led to the dedication of her efforts to the liberation of Italians from the oppression of foreign rule.

Remond's universal approach to envisioning freedom beyond racial, gender, and national borders is the topic of chapter 5, which examines the instrumentalization of the Italian nationalist movement in promoting the cause of racial liberation. Together with other women, Remond assisted the advancement of the unification movement during her stay in London, where she befriended and worked with Mazzini. It was an informative experience for Remond, who came in contact with Italian realities through one of its leading revolutionaries; the encounter fueled her interest in pursuing medical studies in the cosmopolitan cultural capital of Florence.

Remond's studies, career, and contact with Italians as well as Americans living in or visiting Italy after the Risorgimento and the American Civil War are discussed in the last two chapters, which focus on Italy. The title of chapter 6, "Firenze 'La Bella,'" is how foreigners commonly referred to the city and how Remond herself defined the then capital of unified Italy when she first arrived there at the age of forty in 1866. Remond's purpose in moving to Florence was to continue her medical studies, which she succeeded in doing at one of Europe's leading hospital schools. While studying in Italy, her social life was active and she met many prominent Americans who arrived in Florence eager to connect with the cultured life of the cosmopolitan hub. This section discusses her friends and acquaintances, her participation in the salon of the Greek author Margherita Mignaty, and Remond's presence at the musical soirées at her sister Caroline's and nephew Edmund's residence in Rome. These chapters address the concept of cosmopolitanism and the ongoing debates concerning the definition and application of the term. In dialogue with such works as Paul Gilroy's *The Black Atlantic: Modernity and Double Consciousness* (1993), Ifeoma Kiddoe Nwankwo's *Black Cosmopolitanism: Racial Consciousness and Transnational Identity in the Nineteenth-Century Americas* (2005), Kwame Anthony Appiah's *Cosmopolitanism: Ethics in a World of Strangers* (2006), and Nico Slate's *Colored Cosmopolitanism: The Shared Struggle for Freedom in the United States and India* (2012), among others, I examine the Old World cosmopolitanism that characterized Remond's social experience in Florence. Finally, the coda introduces some conclusions regarding the various themes and topics the book addresses and raises questions for further study.

An Abolitionist Abroad: Sarah Parker Remond in Cosmopolitan Europe is based on archival documents that offer a new reading of nineteenth-century African American reality, one of education and social integration, of leisure and luxury. The letters Remond's nephew Edmund and his wife, Gertie, wrote to Madame Mignaty describe the fashionable sand treatments that the Putnam couple experienced during their vacation in Viareggio, a stylish resort for Florentines who enjoyed the quiet life of the seaside town and its sandy beaches. The letters also discuss Edmund and Gertie Putnam's travels to Lucerne, another vacation destination much in vogue especially among the English and Americans. The author Buoncuore Urbino reported in her travel book of Europe that during her visit there in September 1868, the "fine hotels of Lucerne were filled with strangers, many of whom were Americans."[46] Before the Putnams, Remond had been in Lucerne though merely passing through the city on her way to Florence in the summer of 1866. Hence, Remond and her family took part in trendy leisurely activities and explored the most fashionable European travel destinations where they mingled with the sophisticated upper classes.

In conclusion, the aim of this book is to provide an alternative vision of nineteenth-century African American experience through the example of Remond, an experience of black protagonism embedded in a transatlantic world in the cosmopolitanism of England and Italy. The book discusses, and surviving family letters testify to, the racial and class mixing that occurred in Florence where race prejudice and discrimination had no space in the social activities of the polyglot society. A similar atmosphere permeated Rome, where Remond and her family entertained high bourgeoisie and aristocracy with whom they enjoyed listening to the most sought-after musicians and composers of their time at racially mixed private receptions. The Italian sociopolitical ideology sanctioned Remond's striving for self-fulfillment and realizing racial justice and social equality.

Remond's transgression of racial and gender barriers, which became manifest in her transatlantic activism and self-assertion, found an enhanced expression in the life she created for herself across the vast ocean separating her from American prejudice. As this book demonstrates, Remond's transatlantic life was rich and nuanced; it was dedicated to ensuring equal treatment of black American women politically, legally, and socially. In addition, her geographical journey became a metaphorical adventure, an intellectual quest for self-realization. In Europe she claimed her position as a leading figure in formally organized struggle for emancipation. She reassessed her identity as an intellectual and professional woman and thus affirmed her place among the educated elite of her native country. Hence, she provided a new model of black womanhood. Moreover, writing Remond in the history of transatlantic abolitionist and women's rights movements means integrating marginalized voices in social change. As an insider in British activism and Italian cosmopolitanism, Remond participated in the making of transatlantic and transnational history. Through the efforts and example of Sarah Remond, an empowered black identity emerged from the margins of her nation.

CHAPTER 1

Remond and Antebellum Free Black Communities

THE AFRICAN AMERICAN SARAH PARKER REMOND WAS born free in Salem, Massachusetts, in 1826 into a relatively prosperous family of entrepreneurs and antislavery activists. She was fortunate to obtain an education in the humanities, and as an avid reader, she developed rhetorical skills that proved useful to her when she took the platform to speak against slavery. Remond was gifted, energetic, and ardent, and she possessed natural eloquence. She used her talents of persuasion to promote race and gender emancipation, becoming one of the most articulate and powerful antislavery orators of the century. The historians Ruth Bogin and Jean Fagan Yellin convincingly argue that "black female abolitionists developed new cultural forms out of their unique heritage and in response to the pressures of institutionalized racism and sexism both outside and inside the abolitionist movement."[1] Similarly, in addition to formal talks, Remond engaged in personal resistance to discrimination and segregation. By focusing on some of Remond's experiences, this chapter addresses the complexities and anxieties embedded in nineteenth-century racial politics. Like many other black women in the antebellum United States, Remond contested sexist and racist stereotypes, exactly as she had been taught to do by her parents, thus becoming an example of black female progress.

Remond grew up in a home where racial justice and freedom for African Americans formed the fundamental ideological core of the family's black protest. She was, as she wrote in her autobiographical essay, "the youngest but one of ten children of John and Nancy Remond."[2] Remond's essay and Dorothy Burnett Porter's "The Remonds of Salem, Massachusetts" are among the few published sources that refer to ten children; other sources mention eight: Nancy (b. 1809), Charles Lenox (b. 1810), John Lenox (b. 1812), Susan H. (b. 1814), Cecelia Remond (b. 1816), Caroline Remond Putnam (b. 1825), Sarah Parker (b. 1826), and Maritcha Juan (b. 1827).[3]

However, according to the records at Salem City Hall, Nancy Lenox and John Remond had not ten but eleven children; three of them died at an early age: Mary Remond passed away from lung fever on 30 April 1820 at the age of six months; one "son of John Remond" died on 26 October 1821 at the age of four of Cynanche Trachealis (an inflammation of the glottis, larynx, and upper trachea); and another "son of John Remond" died of "Pneumony after measles" on 2 November 1821 (his age is not indicated). All three children were buried in a cemetery referred to as "Hill," most likely the Broad Tree Cemetery located on a small hill at the end of Cambridge Street in Salem. It was the early burial place of the city and close to the Remond residence. The city hall register indicates that the three deceased children's place of residence was Cambridge Street, where the Remond family lived in a house called Hamilton Hall.[4] Other Remond family members are buried at the Harmony Grove Cemetery.

The Remond family belonged to a Salem community that included many mixed-race Americans. The Remond siblings all had relatively light complexions, and Caroline Remond's son Edmund (born 20 April 1847 in Salem) was registered in the 1855 Massachusetts census as "mulatto." The same census indicates that his household included George Putnam, who at the time was fifty and Jane Putnam, forty-eight; they were his grandparents. Other members in the family unit were Caroline E. Putnam (age 29); Joseph H. Putnam (age 29); and Caroline's sisters-in-law Georgiana F. Putnam (age 23), Jane W. Putnam (age 21), and Adelaide B. Putnam (age

18), all "mulattoes." Hence, both of Edmund's parents came from mixed-race families, resulting in his light complexion.[5]

The family Remond was born into had established itself in Salem, a town that she described as "one of the most healthy and pleasant of New England towns. It contains about 25,000 inhabitants who are characterised by general intelligence, industry, and enterprise, and few towns in the States can boast of more wealth and refinement than Salem."[6] Salem had a lively black community consisting of middle- and even upper-class educated professionals, such as the Remonds, who actively worked toward abolishing slavery and realizing racial equality.

Starting from the eighteenth century, as the historian Shirley J. Yee explains, "free black women and men had worked to build viable communities, in order to survive in a society that was growing increasingly hostile to nonwhites."[7] In Massachusetts, black Americans had been emancipated from slavery in 1783, and in the eighteenth century, schools in Salem were integrated.[8] However, being free was quite different from having access to the same rights and privileges as white Massachusetts residents. Starting from 1807, separate schools for white and black Salem students became the norm, a practice that persisted until 1843, and in church services black Salem residents worshiped in segregated sections.[9] Indeed, segregation was the norm, as Ruth Bogin confirms: "The railroad linking Salem with Boston maintained a separate 'colored people's car' " and education was, for the most part, "dominated by Jim Crow."[10] In order to secure good education, employment, and social respect, black Americans had to confront discrimination that insisted on their racial inferiority.

The question of slavery and oppression of free black Americans were, then, linked to social and political privilege and power, and race theories served to sustain such power structures and ideologies. In the South, pseudoscientific theories served to justify slavery; in the North, Americans interpreted social status and national rights in terms of race so that they could restrict African American access to schools and professions, and to privileges in general. Hence, as the scholar Matthew Frye Jacobson has suggested, both regions used scientific explanations about race to justify notions of white supremacy.[11] Likewise, Americans, whose society fundamentally was biracial, tended to think in dualistic terms.[12] It was against such dualistic thinking that such activists as Remond fought. She wished to refute the white supremacy / black inferiority paradigm.

In the nineteenth century, scientific inquiry into racial categorization regarded visual markers of physical appearance as evidence of racial difference and hierarchy. The perceived difference was then linked to presumed moral, intellectual, and cultural characteristics. Important in such theories, as historians have observed, was "the set of rights and privileges that accompanied the classification."[13] The black "races" were placed at the bottom of racial structures, whereas white Americans represented racial superiority and, thus, assumed power. Since these pseudoscientific racial theories aimed to validate white supremacy, they were built on prejudices and racist generalizations.

As the nineteenth century progressed, the three racial classifications—"white," "Indian," and "Negro and mulatto"—developed into a more complex ranking of the world's peoples.[14] It was the mixed-race American, in particular, who complicated existing race classifications and generated fear of racial degeneration among white social authorities. As the historian Werner Sollors suggests, a pervasive theme in U.S. history is "the deep concern about, and the attempt to prohibit, contain, or deny, the presence of black-white interracial sexual relations, interracial marriage, interracial descent, and other family relations across the powerful black-white divide."[15] Since interracial sexual relations, however, did occur, often as sexual abuse by white masters of their female slaves, mixed-race children were an undeniable reality, especially in the antebellum South. As a consequence, Sollors notes, "a whole science of drawing the color line and of 'reading race' emerged," and "many contradictory racial definitions coexisted."[16] Scientists used such "evidence" as skull size, and shape and size of nostrils, lips, or feet to determine a person's race, especially that of mixed-race Americans. In this context, the invention of the one-drop rule, according to which a person was black if he or she had even a single drop of "African blood"—an abstract definition and a quantity that was impossible to measure—served to discriminate against Americans who were born to black parents.

The mixed-race American was positioned in the crossroads of conflicted versions of national identity, belonging, and citizenship, epitomizing the arbitrary nature of racial definitions as well as raising questions relating to social and national inclusion and exclusion.[17] Later in the century, Nico Slate points out, "Jim Crow segregation held sway throughout the Southern United States, locking many Black Americans in a system of peonage all too similar to slavery. Blacks in the North and West faced equally insidious forms of racial segregation and inequality, enforced, as in the South, by the threat of violence."[18] Throughout the century (as well as before and beyond), then, these laws, pseudoscientific theories, and racist attitudes not only insisted on the inferiority of slaves but robbed even free black Americans of their rights to freedom, citizenship, and such civil liberties as education.

The majority of elite African Americans had social origins in the communities of free blacks, many of whom were racially mixed and had access to improved social and educational opportunities. In 1830, the number of free African Americans reached nearly 320,000; their presence was most numerous in northern cities.[19] They challenged the Anglo-Saxon articulation of national identity as representing internal homogeneity.[20] Many of the leading black figures involved in organized activism, including the Remonds, were, indeed, born free and they enjoyed relatively comfortable living in the rather large urban black districts of such cities as Boston, New York, and Philadelphia, or smaller cities, such as Salem, that had vibrant and cultured African American communities. In general, free African Americans of the North were relatively well to do. Many religious and educational leaders came from such free communities, as did some abolitionist lecturers who departed on intensive lecture tours, risking verbal and physical harassment from hostile audiences as they spoke out against discrimination.[21] Hence, had there not been an established binary construction of white versus black, they could have joined white social leaders, who formed a circle of financially and intellectually prosperous men and women in control of society.

The Remonds, who were cultured race leaders, originally came from cities, even countries, outside Salem. Remond's mother, Nancy Lenox, was the daughter of a black Revolutionary War veteran, a free-born African American who assumed an active role in fighting against discrimination and working toward abolishing slavery. She came from Newton, Massachusetts, "seven miles from Boston," as Remond wrote in her essay, "and her immediate ancestors were natives of that vicinity." In her brief autobiographical narrative, Remond described her mother in the following way:

> Nancy Remond is a woman possessing every characteristic which can adorn or ennoble womanhood, combined with the most indomitable energy. We were all trained to habits of industry, with a thorough knowledge of those domestic duties which particularly mark the genuine New England woman. With no private means, it was also most necessary. We were taught to knit and sew, and to cook every article of food placed upon the table. The most trifling affair was obliged to be well done. Her aim seemed to be to guard, and at the same time strengthen her children, not only for the trials and duties of life, but also to enable them to meet the terrible pressure which prejudice against colour would force upon them.[22]

Thus, Nancy Remond challenged black women's exclusion from domesticity, womanhood, and motherhood.

As Hazel V. Carby points out, womanhood "was denied the black woman" because she relied on herself, unlike white women who, for the most part, depended on men. Consequently, in the case of black women, the concept of dependency failed as a link between "the material organization of the household, and the ideology of femininity" because black women at times were heads of households.[23] "The image of the strong, nonsubmissive black female head of a household," according to Carby, was not a positive one. Black women, she continues, "had to confront the dominant domestic ideologies and literary conventions of womanhood which excluded them from the definition of 'woman.' "[24] Sexism and racism charged such negative perceptions of black women who reconciled their careers with motherhood, but as independent women they were ahead of their time.

Remond presented her mother as the central figure in the family, the one in charge of home discipline, the one who taught the children to take care of themselves, to be self-sufficient, to learn how to sew, knit, and cook, but also to confront color discrimination. To some extent, then, Nancy

Remond did correspond to the parameters defined by the cult of true womanhood and reflected the image of ideal motherhood, both concepts that were central tenets in nineteenth-century America where they defined white (middle-class) women.

According to the literary scholar Beth Maclay Doriani, the formulation of the ideal American woman—pious, pure, domestic, and submissive—was so powerful "that not only did white, middle-class women aspire to this standard but so did many black women."[25] However, since many middle-class black women were more self-sufficient than white women, they were hardly ever submissive; instead, they took an active role in society, working toward obtaining equality and respect, and they taught their children morality and value systems. Their actions corresponded to the concept of Republican Motherhood articulated by the historians Linda K. Kerber and Susan Castillo: "The discourse of Republican Motherhood enabled women to incorporate political values into domestic life, with mothers educating future (male) citizens and shaping their moral choices, thus participating indirectly in national life."[26]

Black mothers, however, also educated their daughters, influencing their moral development and encouraging them toward independence. Thus, political action started in the home where women, to quote the scholar Paula Baker, "combined political activity, domesticity, and republican thought through motherhood."[27] Moreover, mothers such as Nancy Remond were politically active not only indirectly in the domestic sphere but also through participation in public protests against segregation and discrimination. As discriminated and marginalized Americans, black women had learned, as Dorothy Sterling puts it, "the art of survival, acquiring vitality and independence that made them unique."[28] Remond's mother was one of the independent women who taught her children to be self-sufficient. Her insistence on performing even the smallest tasks with dedication testifies to her aspiration to encourage her children to excel in all endeavors, even when working on seemingly more insignificant or trivial tasks. She wanted her children to feel proud of their training, background, and achievements.

Sarah Remond's admiration for her mother comes across through the traits she foregrounded in her autobiographical essay: Nancy was ennobled and adorned with positive qualities of womanhood, charged with unremitting energy, caring for her children whom she prepared for the hardships they were bound to encounter as black Americans. In many ways, Remond's mother stood as a role model for her children, who would proudly and boldly transmit what they had learned at home to others of their race. And yet, despite the instructions and preparation Nancy Remond transmitted to her children, she was unable, as Sarah Remond wrote, to "fit us for the scorn and contempt which met us on every hand when face to face with the world, where we met a community who hated all who were identified with an enslaved race." Moreover, Remond continued, "While our mother never excused those who so unjustly persecuted those whose only crime was a dark complexion, her discipline taught us to gather strength from our own souls, and we felt the full force of the fact, that to be black was no crime, but an accident of birth."[29] In other words, her mother instructed Sarah and her siblings not to feel ashamed of the color of their complexion but to cultivate inner strength so they could combat discrimination and injustice. Nancy instructed them to consider the white supremacy / black inferiority paradigm as an arbitrary invention aimed at keeping black Americans socially and politically subservient.

Interestingly, Sarah Remond barely mentioned her father in the essay, which may indicate her desire to foreground the role women had in raising families and the responsibilities of mothers in preparing their children to forge ahead with pride and inner strength in the face of discrimination. She emphasized the role of mothers in forming future generations, transmitting values, and educating and instructing them to become independent. Remond's father appeared in the essay only in connection to the public sphere, defending his children when they risked expulsion from the school that proposed their transfer to an all-black institution. As Remond explained, it was her father who had "waited upon the school committee, and most earnestly protested against their proposed plan."[30] Unfortunately, John Remond was unsuccessful in fighting the school authorities, and the children were forced to leave the school, an order that disheartened his daughter. The children, similarly to their father, realized the importance education had in the march toward social and political equality.

Remond's father, who was a native of Curacao in the West Indies, had immigrated to Salem in 1798 with the purpose of obtaining schooling. On his arrival to the United States, his last name, which perhaps originally was Dutch, was recorded as "Vonreman" (from what may have been "Van Reman").[31] It seems that his mother was an African but of French origins and his father Jewish.[32] He was about ten years old when he became one of the approximately three hundred African Americans living in Salem at the turn of the nineteenth century. Soon after, he moved to Boston where he acquired skills at barbering, hairdressing, and catering; he also met Nancy Lenox, a talented caterer. At the time, it was quite common for black men to find work as servants, cooks, barbers, waiters, carpenters, and educators, whereas black women served as laundresses, dressmakers, or keepers of boardinghouses and oyster houses, or worked as cake bakers, shopkeepers, and confectioners.[33]

In 1805, John Remond was back in Salem working as the caretaker of the new local assembly hall, Hamilton Hall, where he also resided and kept a store; it was located on Cambridge Street. It was built in the early 1800s and was used as an important venue for prestigious dinners and meetings. At the age of nineteen, he became well known in Salem as the caterer in charge of socially prominent events organized at Hamilton Hall. He was a successful caterer and trader, especially in oysters, and he collected and sold fine wines and champagne, and prepared pickled lobsters. He had business activities in centrally located addresses, at 6, 8, and 14 Derby Square and 5 Higginson Square. In addition he worked as a hairdresser and barber.[34]

John Remond's business activities truly started to flourish when he and Nancy Lenox, a talented Boston baker and fancy cake maker, were married in the African Baptist Church in Boston in October 1807. In free black communities, according to Sterling, "marriages were based on mutual affection, with the husband taking pride in his wife's achievements."[35] Nancy now started to cook for the family catering company. When President James Monroe invited the Marquis de Lafayette to visit the United States, John Remond was in charge of the dinner organized at Hamilton Hall on 31 August 1824. The invoice for this dinner lists many items that the caterer sold in his own store, including oysters, wild birds, ham, turkey, milk biscuits, watermelon, grapes, peaches, brandy, cider, and wine; for the dinner he also took care of table linen, flowers, and cleaning. He was the most prominent caterer in Salem for nearly fifty years.[36] When he withdrew from his business activities, his eldest daughter Nancy's husband, James Shearman, who was John Remond's business partner, took over some of his undertakings, including the oyster trading, oyster bar, and ice cream parlor.[37]

The Remonds, then, were professionals who enjoyed relative economic affluence. One of the main advantages of being born free was the ability to acquire education, though even then, the opportunities for study were limited and depended on location. Scientific theories supporting racism emerged around the mid-nineteenth century to support segregation. They also served to deny black Americans access to quality education, employment, and political decision-making. Hence, for black men and women education, as Yee suggests, "constituted a form of overt resistance to racist practices."[38] It became a statement against prejudice and a political act toward equality. It played a vital role in the lives of African Americans and served to develop their capacities for constructing their chosen futures and advancing prospects for improved living. Education was a powerful means toward independence but also toward social and political progress, economic advancement, and citizenship. In other words, it was linked to progress and entailed rearticulating blackness; it emerged, to quote Gilroy, "as a major focus for political activity."[39] It was a force that served to generate an enlarged vision of opportunities, which had the potential to lead, first and foremost, to an increased sense of self-respect and subsequently to social ascent and political power. Consequently, many Americans of free black communities made repeated efforts to secure high-quality education for their children. Free blacks, however, had only limited access to educational institutions, while slaves were entitled to no schooling at all.

The Remond family was among the many who recognized that education was instrumental in the progress toward full citizenship. Charles Lenox articulated the commonly shared desire for learning that prevailed among African Americans: "I ask no man for his sympathy. I am simply asking of the majority because we are a minority, an opportunity to develop the facilities which the Creator has given us. I tell you my friends, if we were equal in numbers tomorrow, we should not ask your aid, into our own hands we would take the vindication of our rights."[40] The Remond children were among the privileged few who obtained relatively high-quality education, which they employed to work for racial progress.

In great part, education depended on the initiatives of individual families. Initially, the Remond children were given basic education at home, learning to read and write. One of Sarah Remond's favorite pastimes was, indeed, reading: "I found the most exquisite pleasure in reading, and, as we had no library, I read every book which came in my way, and, like Oliver Twist, I longed for more," she wrote in her 1861 essay.[41] For formal education, Remond's parents made recurrent attempts to place their children in a private school where they could have a quality education, but the children were repeatedly rejected by schools because of their skin color. Unlike in many other regions, the Salem public schools were not segregated, so the children entered one of the public primary schools. They remained only for a short while before Sarah and her sisters passed the entrance examination to one of the local high schools for girls.

Soon after their acceptance, however, the school committee expelled the Remond girls although their teacher found them "among his best pupils."[42] The expulsion took place right after the school committee started to contemplate the founding of another school that would be open exclusively for black children, thus transforming the existing high school into an all-white educational institution. Hence, Remond and her sisters were rejected and their studies were interrupted because of race discrimination. After she "only wept bitter tears" upon hearing that the committee had ordered her to leave the school, Remond's fighting spirit gained strength: "In a few minutes, I thought of the great injustice practised upon me, and longed for some power to help me to crush those who thus robbed me of my personal rights."[43] Hence, her determination to stand up for herself and fight against injustice started to take form when she was still a mere girl eager to gain knowledge. She recognized that learning was her right and presumed she could claim that right in the same way as white Americans. Years after, she remembered the incident, which, as she explained, was engraved in her heart "like the scarlet letter of Hester." "American prejudice against free-born men and women," she wrote, was "as deep-rooted as it is hateful and cruel."[44]

In 1835, the Remond family moved from Salem to Newport, Rhode Island, where the parents hoped the children could obtain an education in a private school in a less racist environment. Instead, they encountered the same difficulties that they had unsuccessfully avoided in Salem. The schools refused to accept black students, which forced the children to live through yet another bitter experience with discrimination. Consequently, some influential African Americans, who refused to succumb to such oppression, established a private school where Remond was admitted.[45] According to the *National Anti-Slavery Standard,* Remond subsequently had "the advantage of a liberal education in one of the best boarding schools in Boston."[46]

In addition to formal education in racially segregated or interracial schools, African Americans who lived in the northern free communities received informal education in literary societies often formed and conducted by women in cities such as New York, Philadelphia, and Boston. These societies materialized for the purpose of organization, mental improvement, and intellectual reformation of the black population. Libraries, reading rooms, and debating societies collected books and arranged lectures on literary and scientific subjects, and the societies also trained public speakers.[47] Through societies and churches black women were able to acquire organizational experience that they could employ to antislavery activities. Hence, the schools and churches, together with the press, were among "the most powerful institutions within the free black community," and "provided the greatest support for a gender ideology during the antebellum period."[48]

In addition, prominent, quite prosperous black families were involved in establishing black churches, founding schools and newspapers, and forming organizations to assist the poor, widows, children, and fugitive slaves. Leaders of these groups were respected in their communities, becoming role models others could emulate. The supportive net of the black community assisted its members, which consisted of both free-born African Americans and former slaves, in protest against white supremacy and black subordination.[49]

An example of such a community could be found in Newport where the Remonds lived for approximately five years. According to Remond, the black population was "of an elevated character, and for industry, morality, and native intellect, would compare favourably with any class in the community."[50] During the time there, Remond's father continued his business activities, now working at a "Perfumery and Dressing Room" located at 137 Thomas Street.[51] The Remonds formed pleasant relations with the cultured local African American society, and they had access to public libraries where they could find the best works of English and American literature. Remond avidly read novels but also daily and weekly newspapers. "These were resources of which *even* prejudice could not deprive me," she retorted.[52] Her parents, moreover, further enhanced the children's learning at home with the reading of fiction, newspapers, and antislavery writings. In this way, they prepared their children to appreciate literature, follow news, and attack color prejudice. Consequently, although Remond received some formal education at various schools, it was the home schooling that influenced her most and shaped her character.

In 1841, the Remonds were back in Salem, where John Remond resumed his business activities, becoming one of the town's best-known residents working as an entrepreneur—a hairdresser, caterer, and merchant-trader, retailing wines and specialty foods. He was "Salem's noted caterer," as the author Mary Harrod Northend described him in her study of *American Homes and Their Furnishings in Colonial Times*.[53] Northend also recalled him as famous for the "delicious suppers" he prepared.[54] One of the important functions John Remond had organized, in addition to the reception for Lafayette, was a dinner for President Andrew Jackson in 1833.[55]

The culinary interest of the father was a shared pursuit and talent in the Remond household, especially among the women. The work experience of black women differed from that of middle-class white women, who, as Yee points out, "did not need to earn a wage, but it was similar in many respects to that of poor white women." It therefore follows, Yee continues, "that both class and race were strong determinants in the formation of labor patterns in the United States."[56] However, black Americans such as the Remonds cannot be considered representatives of the poor, often uneducated lower classes. Instead, the family was cultured and successful in its various endeavors, both financially and socially. In the Remond household, Susan continued her mother's profession as a fancy cake maker. Working from home, she prepared cakes, bread, and desserts that she served in a small dining room. Her spotlessly clean kitchen was a gathering place for radicals, abolitionists, and female suffragists.[57] Her business endeavors, then, were closely tied to emancipation activism.

The other daughters—Cecilia, Maritcha, and Caroline—were also living as financially independent and successful businesswomen: they prospered as hairdressers and manufacturers of wigs, and they were well known for a medicated lotion against hair loss that they prepared. Caroline was especially famous for this formula, which became known as "Mrs. Putnam's Medicated Hair Tonic." As hairdressers for ladies and children, the sisters operated the Ladies Hair Work Salon and their wig factory, which was the largest in the state, from its location on 18 Washington Street in Salem.[58] All of the family's business activities were centrally located in the most fashionable shopping areas of Salem, at 175½ and 184 Essex Street.[59]

The parents, and subsequently their children, then, were well-established businesspeople and activists working in the Salem black community, many of them representatives of an educated middle class. In addition to running their successful business ventures, the Remonds were all active in promoting race and gender emancipation, joining other free black men and women who actively fought against the legalized discrimination of which they were targets, even in the more progressive northern states. Both Charles Lenox and his sister Sarah became sought-after abolitionist speakers, and as antislavery lecturers, they were examples of black protagonism, of African Americans who took their place among the most prominent figures in black liberation movements. In addition, Charles served as one of the black leaders of the Underground Railroad that secured the liberation of slaves and facilitated their escape toward freedom.[60] The family members were all involved in founding and leading organizations geared at racial justice, and they assumed responsibilities within associations and at various events. They were determined to change society.

Similarly, the Remonds' extended families included financially independent men and women who were promoters of social change. Remond's oldest brother, Charles Lenox, married twice, both times choosing independent women as his spouse. His first wife, Amy Matilda (Williams Cassey) Remond, was the daughter of a well-known abolitionist whose first husband, Joseph Cassey, had been a wealthy activist from Philadelphia. After Amy passed away in 1856, Charles married, in July 1858, Elizabeth ("Lizzie") Magee, who financially supported the family during her husband's lecture tours in the United States and England.[61] In addition to lecturing against slavery, Charles functioned as a recruiting agent and worked as a clerk at the Boston custom house.[62] Ruth Rice, the wife of Sarah Remond's brother John Lenox, was one of two women elected on a fifteen-member finance committee of the New England Colored Citizens' Convention, held in Boston in 1859.[63] Other family members, such as James Shearman, the husband of Nancy and John Remond's eldest child, Nancy, earned his living as an oyster dealer in Salem.

Another family of activists connected to the Remonds, the Putnams, shared selections of occupation, interest in education, and determination to fight against discrimination. Sarah Remond's sister Caroline married Joseph H. Putnam, the son of George Putnam, an African American hairdresser and barber. Joseph continued his father's profession but also worked as an assistant school teacher. The Putnams lived in Boston before moving to Salem in the summer of 1850. Joseph's sister Adelaide was a musician in Salem before moving to New York City to work as a music teacher, and his other sister, Georgiana ("Georgie"), worked as a teacher first in Salem, then in Brooklyn, where she became the principal of a grammar school. Before the family's move to Salem, George Putnam, Caroline Remond's future father-in-law, actively worked for abolitionism and school desegregation. His Boston home at 16 Belknap Street was a significant meeting place for Garrisonian abolitionists, among them the American artist Thomas Cole and Remond's brother Charles. The two men were close friends who shared the same goals and aspirations, and during Charles Lenox's tour in England and Ireland, Cole made sure that Charles's letters were published in the *Liberator.* White and black activists met at the Putnams to discuss activities that included plans for creating a college for young black men to offer them a possibility for education in the United States.[64]

George Putnam's wife, Jane, participated in temperance activism and had formed a temperance society in Boston with other African American women in the early 1830s. Moreover, she was among the black women who submitted a petition to the Massachusetts legislature reproving the law that prohibited interracial marriage. In 1843, to her great satisfaction, the legislature revoked the contested law.[65] In addition, Jane, who was involved in efforts to provide educational opportunities for African Americans, promoted integration of Boston schools. The Putnams, similarly to the Remonds, believed in desegregated educational institutions that would offer an opportunity for cross-racial interaction. Hence, early on, they realized that integrating black and white Americans, rather than physically and socially separating them, would improve chances for pacific cohabitation and would instruct Americans how to respect and embrace difference, thus rendering equality a reality.

However, like many white Americans, black Bostonians were divided over such fundamental issues as education, which created internal tensions within black communities. The most prominent African Americans in Boston were integrationists, who were opposed by those blacks who wanted to maintain the city's segregated black educational institutions. At the core of the controversy on whether African American children should be educated in racially segregated or integrated schools was the question of acceptance in American society and definitions of black identity, which consisted of "a combination of physical, cultural, and political variables."[66] The integrationists argued that the socializing influence of mingling with children of the socially prominent (white) group had a positive impact, whereas incompetent teachers, neglect, and abuse dominated in segregated schools. The counterargument concerned the presumed degradation that was associated with amalgamation. In 1855, the legislature silenced the separatists, making Boston the first major city with an integrated school system.[67] Sarah Remond was among those who supported social integration and sustained that separate churches and schools were nothing but a hindrance to African American elevation.[68]

Remond, Jane Putnam, and many other black women campaigned for racial integration, sectarian education, gender emancipation, and racial equality within various reform movements. Yee notes that "central to the experiences of black female abolitionists were community-building, political organizing, and forging a network of personal and professional friendships with other activists."[69] Black women were involved in founding abolitionist and intellectual societies, such as the Female Literary Association of Philadelphia, which commonly were located in important urban centers. This particular association operated in the city where the prosperous Forten family lived.

In 1853, when she was sixteen, Charlotte Forten, of the Philadelphia Forten family, temporarily moved to Salem where she joined the Remonds because private schools in her home town excluded black students and her father refused to enroll her in one of the segregated schools of Philadelphia.[70] The Forten family belonged to a circle of free black activists, and among other associations, the Forten women were members of the Philadelphia Female Anti-Slavery Society, a biracial organization founded in 1833.[71] When Charlotte moved in with the Remonds, she first lived with Amy and Charles Lenox; in 1857, she came to live with Caroline and Joseph, who shared their home with Joseph's mother, Jane, at the time an owner of a hairworks shop in Salem. Although Sarah Remond did not live with her brother or sister, she visited them frequently. Charlotte Forten, who soon became friends with Remond, found her "always attractive, without making any particular effort to be so."[72]

Forten continued her studies while living with the Remonds, first at the Higginson Grammar School where she enrolled from November 1853 to March 1855, and subsequently at the Salem Normal School. She became the first African American student to attend the racially integrated school, graduating in 1856.[73] She became a school teacher, and similarly to the Remonds, was dedicated to improving the situation for black Americans through education and activism. In her free time she studied French, German, Latin, European history, and literary classics, and together with the Remonds read poetical works by Alfred Tennyson, Samuel Taylor Coleridge, Lord Byron, Walter Scott, and her favorite poet, Elizabeth Barrett Browning, among others.

Sarah Remond, who owned a volume of Barrett Browning's poems that included "Casa Guidi Windows" (1851), the poet's vision of Italy's oppression which led to the Risorgimento, was equally fascinated with literature and cultural studies. As avid readers, Forten and the Remonds read biographies, including Thomas Moore's *The Life of Byron* (1830–31), and they studied literary criticism that included James Russell Lowell's *Fable for Critics* (1848). Eager to learn more about foreign countries, they read such travel narratives as Harriet Beecher Stowe's *Sunny Memories of Foreign Lands* (1854) and perused plays by Shakespeare, memoirs of Madame de Staël, and such early feminist works as Margaret Fuller's *Woman in the Nineteenth Century* (1843). Together with the Remonds, Forten visited museums, attended concerts, listened to opera, went to hear Lowell's lectures on "English Poetry," and attended Ralph Waldo Emerson's talks on "France" and "Beauty." They looked at pictures of Italy and listened to stories about Europe. In the evenings they played whist and chess, listened to music, played musical instruments and sang, and discussed women's rights and racial prejudice.[74] Their interests and pastimes were identical to nineteenth-century white intellectuals with the only difference being the constant presence of a shadow cast by racial discrimination.

To put her literary interests and language skills to use, Forten translated books from Latin and French. For instance, she worked on a translation of Madame de Staël's *Corinne, ou l'Italie* (1807), one of the most prominent works associated with Italy at the time, but she also wrote articles ("At the Home of Frederick Douglass"), poems ("Wordsworth"), and essays on various topics, such as "The Umbrian and Roman School of Art" on art history.[75] She knew the novelist Nathaniel Hawthorne's sister and was a friend of the American poet John Greenleaf Whittier, who described Forten as "a young lady of exquisite refinement, quiet culture and ladylike and engaging manners, and personal appearance."[76] In addition to her translation activities and studies, Forten promoted the cause of racial equality by educating African American children, and, decades later in 1896, she became a founding member of the National Association of Colored Women. Charlotte Forten, then, like Remond, was interested in literature, knew languages, had pleasant manners and appearance, and dedicated her energies to black empowerment.

In sum, Charlotte Forten and the Remond women, as well as many other African American women in free black communities, had many interests, were eager to cultivate their cultural vocations, and applied their talents to profitable endeavors. Many of them worked outside their homes, managed their own business activities, and generally shared equal responsibilities with the male members of their families, with men only occasionally assuming dominating roles. These women, who in addition took care of their domestic duties, also fervently participated in black activism. The black community that sustained itself had strong female support networks, and women were active initiators in establishing antislavery associations and dedicated their time to promoting the liberation of slaves. Family and community ties were strong in the free black neighborhoods where the process of community-building led to the "politicization of African-American activists."[77] While living with the Remonds, Forten frequently attended antislavery meetings with her host family and came into contact with such leading abolitionists as William Wells Brown, Lydia Maria Child, John Greenleaf Whittier, and William Lloyd Garrison.[78] Antislavery lecturers and writers, as some scholars have argued, "contested versions of race and nation at one of the most critical turning points in the drama of American self-definition."[79]

The 1850s, which brought a change in the situation of African Americans, was a crucial decade for racial and national identity discourse in the United States, partially due to the passage of the new Fugitive Slave Law. Slaveholders, as Susan Castillo writes, "were allowed to recapture runaway slaves, even in free states," and those who tried to assist or rescue runaways could face fines and even imprisonment.[80] The new law, then, became a threat not only to escaped slaves but also to freedmen, transforming them into potential slaves. In fact, when the Fugitive Slave Law was first enforced in 1850, the first man doomed to slavery under the new law was a free man, Adam Gibson. Others followed: according to William Craft, four of the first eight people sent into slavery under the new act were free African Americans.[81] According to the historian Barbara McCaskill, "there were mounting cases of the disappearances of freeborn African Americans—especially women and children—who had been seized by bounty hunters and whisked summarily into slavery, without any opportunity to establish their true identities."[82] As a consequence of this threat to the liberty of the black population, the Unitarian minister Theodore Parker prepared handbills that circulated in Boston warning about the kidnapping of African Americans, former slaves as well as free blacks.

Another change occurred in 1857, when Chief Justice Roger Taney's *Dred Scott* decision declared that African Americans "had no rights which the white man was bound to respect."[83] In 1857, Castillo explains, a Missouri slave, Dred Scott, petitioned for his freedom on the grounds that he had lived in free states where slavery was illegal.[84] In the case known as *Dred Scott vs. Sanford,* the Supreme Court ruled against Scott, denying people of African ancestry the rights of white Americans.

In her autobiographical essay, Remond addressed the injustice inherent in the decision and its grave consequences for black Americans: "The Fugitive Slave Law, and the Dred Scott decision, are most keenly felt by all the coloured race;—the Fugitive Slave Law, which returns into bondage every slave who seeks an asylum in a free State from the slave hunters and their bloodhounds, who in many instances have kidnapped free persons of colour; the Dred Scott decision, which declares that 'black men and women have no rights which white men are bound to respect,' completely annihilating the citizenship of every coloured American."[85] According to her testimony, kidnapping of free African Americans was a real threat and cause of anxiety to America's free black population in the 1850s when Remond started lecturing against slavery; the *Dred Scott* decision, instead, had a long-lasting impact on the lives of African Americans.

In addition to organized activities, the fight against discrimination continued in the private lives of African Americans, and many, including the Remonds, whose parents had prepared them to confront prejudice, refused to succumb to hostile treatment of white authorities. One example of such resistance comes from Remond, who with her behavior brought attention to the injustice of racial segregation.

In 1853, Remond had bought tickets to sit in a box at a local Boston theater, the Howard Athenaeum, with her sister and the black author William Cooper Nell, a close friend of the Putnams who seems to have been attracted to Sarah Remond.[86] Instead of being allowed to enjoy the performance of the opera *Don Pasquale* as planned, they were forced to leave because they refused to sit in a segregated area designated for the black audience. As they were forcefully pushed out, Remond's dress was torn and her shoulder injured.[87]

Information about the incident appeared in local papers but also traveled across the ocean all the way to Scotland, where the *Dundee Courier* of Angus published a notice on the subject in its 8 June 1853 issue, ironically appearing under the title "American Equality":

> The question whether coloured women can sit in boxes has come up for consideration and adjudication in the Police Court, Boston, Massachusetts—Mr Justice Russell on the bench. It appears that Mrs Caroline Putnam and Miss Sarah P. Remond, very handsome, intelligent, and respectable coloured persons, sisters to a well-known abolitionist Charles Lennox, of Salem, having previously procured box tickets, visited the Howard Athenaeum. They delivered their tickets to the doorkeeper, and passed into the lobby. Here they were recognized as coloured persons, and were informed that they could not occupy seats in the boxes. They persisted in their right to sit in the box in which they had purchased seats. It was stated to them that coloured persons were admitted to the gallery only and that if they did not choose to sit there, their money would be refunded. They refused to listen to any compromise, whereupon the manager gave orders that they be removed from the lobby. This order was executed by officers Philbrick and Palmer, and they were ejected. Mrs Putnam prosecuted Messrs Philbrick and Palmer for assault and battery. Justice Russell, in his decision, did not admit the plea of custom in excluding persons of colour from the house, but held that the manager, in failing to state in his advertisements that they would be excluded, was bound to furnish them with seats. Palmer was fined one dollar and costs, Philbrick one dollar without costs. From this sentence the parties appealed, and gave bail for trial.[88]

Refusing to be pushed around or intimidated, the Remond sisters stood their ground, unwilling to accept a compromise that would have prohibited them from enjoying the performance from the seats they had chosen. After her forcible expulsion from the Athenaeum, which resulted in an injury to her arm, Remond took the case to court and, according to some sources, was awarded five hundred dollars by the First District Court of Essex.[89]

That same year, Remond was asked to leave an exhibition hall at Franklin

Institute in Philadelphia.[90] At another time, her sister Caroline was refused entry in Philadelphia at two ice cream saloons. Since she would not leave without reacting, Caroline Putnam "told one of the people some wholesome truths, which cannot be soon forgotten."[91] When about a week later Caroline was ready to return home to Salem, she was denied admission to the railway car she wished to enter and was, instead, directed to the "colored car," which she refused to board. Consequently, she was denied access to the train and was forced to wait for a later one.[92] On another occasion, Mrs. Jane Putnam and her daughters were refused admission to a museum after they had purchased their tickets, merely on account of their complexion. "Insulting language was used to them," wrote Forten in her diary. "Of course they felt and exhibited deep, bitter indignation; but of what avail was it? none, but to excite the ridicule of those contemptible creatures, miserable doughfaces who do not deserve the name of men."[93] These women, then, publicly denounced discrimination both in their speeches and during episodes in their private lives, speaking equally powerfully against racist and misogynist thoughts.

In addition to the example they offered through their private protests and actions, these women entered the public sphere to promote black empowerment, working as teachers, lecturers, and entrepreneurs, and by advancing in their chosen professional careers. In addition, through their participation in various reform activities, such black women as Remond, her sisters, and relatives were deeply involved in shaping the future of African Americans and women. They responded to bigotry and fought against prejudice. Moreover, they acquired organizational skills and gained self-confidence, which they used to advance societal reform. They believed that in elevating their race through experience and education, they would eliminate racism.

CHAPTER 2

Early Activism in the United States

WHEN SHE WAS IN HER THIRTIES, SARAH Remond started lecturing against slavery in the United States. The lecture tours and conferences she participated in were forums for intellectual exchange, and women who were active in them operated not only in national but also transnational settings. The interracial interactions in which she engaged, however, at times revealed underlying racial tensions and gendered rivalries, which surfaced in conflicting ideological views. Moreover, despite the discrimination she encountered and risks to her personal safety on her speaking tours in the United States, where anti-abolitionist, racist, and sexist mobs attacked lecturers, Remond continued to promote the causes she believed in, even, or perhaps especially, when it meant confronting prejudice and defying conformity. Indeed, regardless of the obstacles, as she wrote in her autobiographical essay, she was "quite determined to persevere."[1] She was unwavering in her campaign to raise awareness of the horrors of slavery, lecturing in front of large audiences that at times were openly hostile toward her, a black woman who readily took the platform to speak in public on behalf of her race. Consequently, her presence on interracial lecture tours drew attention to her gender and race, turning them into powerful political statements.

In Salem, which was a dynamic center for abolitionism, activists closely collaborated and networked with other white and black abolitionists who were contributing their time and resources to fighting against slavery in nearby cities such as Boston. For white women, who could not participate in political life, could not vote, and whose property was controlled by men, involvement in abolitionism "gave rise to increased political awareness about the limitations of their own situation."[2] Although white women were under patriarchal control, the situation for black women was different: black men, as Hazel V. Carby reminds us, "have not held the same patriarchal positions of power that the white males have established."[3] Moreover, social and political limitations were not restricted to property or voting rights but affected all aspects of African Americans' lives. Therefore, for black more than for white women, protest against power inequality meant self-affirmation. For black Americans, racism, slavery, and freedom inevitably were far more important than for white abolitionists.

By 1830, fifty antislavery groups were working toward abolishing slavery; several of them were active in Boston, New York, and Philadelphia, and one in New Haven, Connecticut.[4] Since the early days of activism, women had pioneered in the public sphere by taking courageous action to promote their views. The first woman to deliver a political speech in public, Maria W. Stewart, was a Bostonian from a middle-class black district where she attended school before starting her public lecturing career and working as a teacher. As early as 1831, she addressed an audience, known at the time as "promiscuous," consisting of both African American and white men and women.

In her public political talks, Stewart spoke in defense of African Americans while also promoting women's rights. She gave her first lecture specifically aimed at women at the Afric-American Female Intelligence Society in Boston in 1832. She also spoke of topics that concerned the black community such as "literacy, self-determination, abolition, economic empowerment, and racial unity," but according to the historian Beverly

Guy-Sheftall, "she admonished black women in particular to break free from stifling gender definitions and reach their fullest potential by pursuing formal education and careers outside the home, especially teaching."[5] According to Stewart's black feminist agenda, black women should express their full potential, pursue formal education and professional careers, and "assume leadership roles within their communities."[6] Her early publications included a pamphlet that came out in 1831, some religious meditations published in 1832, and her public lectures, which appeared in the *Liberator;* a volume of her collected works was published in 1835.[7] During the 1830s, when Nancy Remond and Jane Putnam became actively involved in changing society, Stewart offered them and other women who followed, including Sarah Remond, an empowering example as she addressed controversial issues and introduced revolutionary ideas both in her publications and her talks. She, like Remond after her, never hesitated in publicly voicing her convictions, even when it meant having a detrimental reputation among conservative Americans.

Stewart's proto-feminist lectures also addressed the persecutions she endured as a woman on the platform. Her appearance in the lecture pulpit was such a radical novelty that, according to the scholar Joycelyn Moody, she was rejected by both races. To render her message acceptable to prejudiced audiences, Stewart, like many early activist women speakers, appealed to her audiences' religiousness and moral sense of justice. In addition to her talks, as Moody points out, "Christian evangelicalism, literary sentimentalism, and black nationalism converge" and surface in all of her writings.[8]

Soon after Stewart started her public lectures, Lydia Maria Child published *An Appeal in Favor of that Class of Americans Called Africans,* which appeared in Boston in 1833. In her publication, she insisted that slaves and blacks were Americans and "therefore entitled not only to freedom but to *all* the rights of Americans."[9] Her demands were not limited to liberating slaves but extended to claiming for blacks the same political and social rights and privileges enjoyed by white Americans; these rights included education and citizenship.

Other publications that entwined slavery with other political agendas included Angelina Grimké's *Appeal to the Christian Women of the South* (1836) in which the author argued that slavery was sinful and the campaign against slavery was a crusade against sin. Like many other women activists, Grimké used religious rhetoric to justify her political activism; the biblical references served "to legitimize women's political involvement in the crusade against slavery, characterizing it as a deeply moral course of action."[10] The historian Rodney D. Coates has pointed out that white feminists "such as Elizabeth Cady Stanton and Angelina Grimke Weld, recognizing a common plight with enslaved Blacks, joined in with White-led antislavery societies that agitated the nation in the 1830s."[11] The Grimké sisters, Angelina and Sarah, were Quakers and fervent abolitionist daughters of a slave owner, John Faucheraud Grimké, who belonged to the wealthy elite of South Carolina. The Grimké sisters, as Ruth Bogin and Jean Fagan Yellin note, "became the earliest female agents for abolitionism in the United States."[12] Angelina Grimké started her lecturing career in 1836, speaking at the American Anti-Slavery Society's women's sewing and parlor meetings in New York. From the more intimate sewing circles and parlors, the meetings moved into larger spaces such as churches.

Following the example of Maria Stewart and Angelina Grimké, then, many wives and daughters in Salem and its vicinity joined forces to create organized forums and establish formal organizations for abolitionist crusade. The Anti-Slavery Society of Salem and Vicinity was established in January 1834 and its sister organization, the Salem Female Anti-Slavery Society, in June of the same year. The organizations were local chapters of a parent association, the American Anti-Slavery Society, formed by William Lloyd Garrison in 1833. Its members consisted mainly of representatives of middle-class and professional Salem residents.[13]

The Salem Female Anti-Slavery Society was among the first black female organizations formed in the northern states. Its aims were to immediately abolish slavery, encourage black Americans to remain in the United States, and acknowledge black Salem residents as equals. Remond's mother, Nancy, was one of its founders, and the Putnams and Remonds held leading positions in local and national antislavery movements. For instance, John Remond was a member of the Massachusetts Anti-Slavery

Society starting from 1835; his son Charles Lenox was the first black lecturer of the society; and John and Nancy's daughters were members of the Salem society, which later became racially mixed.[14] In 1855, Charlotte Forten joined the Salem society and Amy Remond was elected its vice president that same year. In 1859, Caroline Remond Putnam assumed the responsibilities of the president of the society. In May 1865, together with Abigail (Abby) Kelley Foster, Caroline replaced Maria Weston Chapman and Anne Warren Weston on the board of managers in the Massachusetts Anti-Slavery Society.[15] In the same month, Caroline was chosen as one of the vice presidents of the Salem Anti-Slavery Society's anniversary event. The activities of the society included providing a range of assistance to fugitive slaves as well as propagating the abolitionist message and recruiting supporters. The members of the Salem society raised funds, held bazaars, helped fugitive slaves in Canada, and organized antislavery lecture series.

The bazaars and sewing fairs women activists organized raised money for antislavery speakers, agents, and literature (pamphlets, newspapers, petitions). Women quite efficiently arranged the rapid circulation of material and funds, thus becoming petitioners and organizers who expanded their political activities and awareness, justifying their actions by referring to their moral duty to become involved in antislavery campaigns. The fairs were often organized in hotels, meeting halls, or other public places, thus taking women outside of their domestic realm. Moreover, the abolitionist sewing fairs became social events and venues for class and racial mixing that served to raise awareness of slavery but also to recruit others to join the cause of abolitionism. "In working for the fairs, women were both educating themselves and organizing their communities," suggests the scholar Barbara Bingham Van Broekhoven.[16] Although sewing was considered an acceptable activity for women, the antislavery sewing circles were highly political. At these meetings one member would read aloud from antislavery publications while others knitted, sewed, or prepared articles for sale at fairs. The chief organizers of the first Boston Fair of 1838 were Child and Chapman. Others followed their example, and antislavery fair activities continued and increased between 1840 and 1860.[17]

Similar fairs and charity bazaars were organized in other northern cities in which women often sold British articles, including engravings, embroidery, and lace, thus transforming them into events of transnational collaboration. At the same time, these bazaars became social events that gathered together women interested in overseas products and fashion. "The great antislavery bazaars in Boston, Rochester, and Philadelphia in the mid-nineteenth century," the historian F. K. Prochaska asserts, "often displayed the latest London fashions."[18] Generally, men were less involved in the bazaars, which became directly associated with women. Thus, these bazaars contributed to expanding women's influence in philanthropy, and with their inherent political intent, they became instrumental to twentieth-century suffragettes.[19]

In addition to fairs and bazaars, one of the main activities of the Salem Female Anti-Slavery Society, which dissolved in 1866 when its members concluded that their primary goal, abolition of slavery, had been accomplished, was to sponsor abolitionist lectures. These were given by such well-known orators as Frederick Douglass and included such prominent speakers as Lucy Stone and Charles Remond. Traditionally the lectures were held on Sunday evenings, perhaps so that the active entrepreneurs of the community could also attend.[20]

Following the example of the black women of Salem, a group of women in Boston established the Boston Female Anti-Slavery Society, whereas women in Philadelphia, as Bogin and Yellin explain, "attended the founding meeting of the American Anti-Slavery Society in December 1833."[21] Such women as Lucretia Mott, Grace Douglass, and Margaretta, Sarah Louisa, and Harriet Forten were among the women committed to the cause of emancipation who organized the Philadelphia Female Anti-Slavery Society.[22] Scholars have pointed out that it was "the female society of greatest longevity and stability in membership," which cultivated ties "with more remote and weaker groups."[23]

Antislavery lecturing became more challenging as the abolitionist movement in the United States started to show signs of weakening following an ideological division concerning organizational tactics. Since the 1830s, African Americans at black national conventions had wrestled with opposing ideas and divided leadership. Issues for debate included the movement's association with white abolitionists, black leadership, segregated schools, the black national press, emigration, and black nationalism. The larger questions concerning emancipation and full citizenship for free African Americans were also on the abolitionist agenda at national and regional organizations established in the northern and western states. In 1837, those opposed to slavery started to differ in their views concerning how to eradicate it, which led to the division of existing societies into rival organizations split over the question of tactics: whether to promote moral suasion or political action.[24]

Although the convention movement was a powerful voice that served to project new ideas and kindle hope for the future, it was weakened, as the scholars Jane H. Pease and William H. Pease have argued, "by the divisiveness of ideological controversy and the shattering consequences of personal rivalry."[25] Consequently, black opposition to slavery had divided agendas and separated the movement into William Lloyd Garrison's radical abolitionism, which combined other reform causes, including that of women's rights, into its program, and a more moderate and political approach to abolitionism promoted by the American and Foreign Anti-Slavery Society. Both Remond and her brother Charles supported the Garrisonian vision in which race and gender emancipation were intertwined. In addition, both Remond siblings were personal friends of Garrison.

In addition to tactics, another motive that led to the division of the societies, then, was the question of women's rights, particularly whether women should be granted the right to vote equally with men in the national antislavery societies. A schism led to the formation of rival societies. The newly formed Massachusetts Abolition Society became the counterpart for the Massachusetts Anti-Slavery Society, while the national American Anti-Slavery Society found its rival in the American and Foreign Anti-Slavery Society after its split in 1840. The latter, formed by Lewis Tappan and other opponents of Garrison, ceased its activities in the 1850s, whereas the American Anti-Slavery Society was active even after the Civil War. Douglass, for one, supported the Garrisonian nonpolitical action until 1851, when he changed his views and joined the political activists without, however, considering his position antagonistic to the Abolition Society. Charles Remond, instead, continued to consider political action and party doctrines as hindrance to the progress of the antislavery movement.[26] Although abolitionists disagreed over integration and segregation, inclusion of other reform movements, and tactics, they persevered in their struggle for black progress by simultaneously reconstructing ideas of black selfhood and identity. Their aim was to liberate the concept of black identity from prejudice and social injustice.

Black abolitionists from all backgrounds joined forces in antislavery societies, vigilance committees, and black churches. The new leadership of the 1840s included many who had experienced slavery firsthand, for example, Douglass, William Wells Brown, Martin R. Delany, Henry Highland Garnet, Samuel Ringgold Ward, and Jermain W. Loguen. Many of them became professional abolitionists who lectured, published newspapers, and actively assisted fugitive slaves escaping by way of the Underground Railroad.

African American men and women were the predominant leaders of these prevalently black organizations, in charge of their societies and activities. By assuming leadership positions, these African Americans defied white patriarchal society's ideological expectations and norms, which were set to subjugate America's black population. However, most of the antislavery organizations welcomed both black and white activists, who in racially mixed societies tended to have unequal power relations: white members often assumed the leadership positions. In addition, organizational fragmentation could, at times, be class-based and thus reveal not only race prejudice but include discrimination on the basis of class.

With others, Sarah Remond fought against segregation, participating in the organized activities of antislavery societies that often were nonsectarian. The membership of biracial women's societies included many young, unmarried women like Remond. In addition to lecturing against the institution of slavery, female activists wrote pamphlets that objected to gender inequality.[27] Many white but also some black women and men who participated in the racial and gender liberation campaigns shared a relatively high educational background and came from the middle and upper classes.

White Quakers (members of the Society of Friends) were among the first to join organizations dedicated to protesting against racial inequality. The Quaker Abby Kelley (later Foster), for instance, inspired women first at the Female Anti-Slavery Society of Lynn, which she joined in 1837, then at the National American Anti-Slavery Society Convention in New York City where she served as a delegate. She became a friend of Remond and Sarah Douglass, who was a prominent black educator and activist.[28]

The American Anti-Slavery Society, for whom Remond became a lecturer in 1856, grew rapidly. By 1838 its racially integrated membership had reached 250,000 activists consisting of fugitive slaves, free blacks, Quakers, and others. Kelley was present in its network of lecturers, together with Remond, the Grimké sisters, Sarah Douglass, Lydia Child, and Lucretia Mott. It was to Kelley Foster that Remond wrote in December 1858 that "my only regret is that I did not sooner begin to do what little I might, in this particular field of labour. I feel almost sure I never should have made the attempt but for the words of encouragement I received from you."[29] Kelley, then, was fundamental in encouraging Remond to start her public lecturing career, and the relationship of the two women seemed based on equality and support.

The other women who toured with Kelley and Remond had contributed to the progress of black emancipation in many ways. Child was known among abolitionists for her *Appeal in Favor of That Class of Americans Called Africans* (1833), and, together with Mott, she became one of the most prominent white women to campaign for abolishing slavery and dismantling inequality. Mott was a dedicated reform activist whose campaigns covered a range of issues including abolitionism and women's rights but also temperance, peace, prison, and education reform. She was instrumental in creating the transatlantic web of collaboration between American and European women, which, to a great extent, was the result of her European tour of 1840. She established an extensive network of contacts in England, Ireland, Wales, and Scotland, creating a matrix that was, according to Margaret H. McFadden, "a structure of friendships, acquaintances, ties, and cross-linkages" and "the precondition for mature feminist internationality."[30] Her contacts included women of various nationalities across classes and religions. The international network that (white) women formed and Remond consolidated was dedicated to transnational efforts that ranged from women's emancipation to moral reform.

In the United States, the interracial collaboration networks established for a common cause—elimination of slavery—welcomed both white and black speakers. The influential black women on the antislavery lecture circuit included the former slaves Sojourner Truth and Harriet Tubman, and the free-born novelist Frances Ellen Watkins Harper, who, together with Sarah Remond, Barbara Steward, and Mary Ann Shadd Cary, were professional abolitionists working as lecturers, antislavery poets, newspaper publishers, and conductors of the Underground Railroad during the 1850s.[31] Hence, the presence and contribution of black women were significant, while representatives of both races united their efforts in promoting social change.

Watkins, who became one of the prominent figures dedicated to emancipation around the same time as Remond, was born in Baltimore in 1825 to free black parents, members of the city's extensive middle-class black community. As with so many other black abolitionists, she came from a middle-class background, from a community of free African Americans. She was, however, orphaned at the age of three and raised by her aunt and uncle, Henrietta and William Watkins. Her uncle was a known abolitionist who practiced medicine and served as a preacher and shoemaker. In addition, he had organized a black literary society and established a school, the Watkins Academy, in 1820. In her twenties, Watkins started her career as a poet by publishing her first collection under the title *Forest Leaves* (1845). Subsequently, she became a teacher at Union Seminary, a school for free blacks in Ohio, established in 1847. Although she placed importance on education, she abandoned teaching to take up lecturing for the cause of abolitionism. The Maine Anti-Slavery Society hired her as a speaker, and she toured the United States addressing audiences that brought together both white and black Americans. After touring for about a year and a half, traveling all the way to Canada, she was hired by the Pennsylvania Anti-Slavery Society in 1857.

Similarly to Remond, in her speaking engagements Watkins "refused to limit herself to issues considered suitable for women."[32] She publicly started promoting women's rights in 1866, joining such others as Mary Ann Shadd Cary, Sojourner Truth, Harriet Tubman, Ida B. Wells, Josephine Ruffin, and Mary Church Terrell, who lectured at suffrage conventions and participated in committees of women's organizations, most of them run by white women. When Watkins joined the Philadelphia Anti-Slavery Society, it was forging ahead in interracial collaboration and on women's rights under Mott's leadership. Its black female members included Charlotte and Margaretta Forten and Sarah Douglass. Soon after, Watkins started working for the Pennsylvania Peace Society and its national affiliate, the Universal Peace Union, whose goals were abolition of the death penalty, justice for Native Americans, and an end to lynching. She remained in Pennsylvania and Ohio for the rest of her life, participating in reform movements that were largely white.[33]

In addition to Watkins and Remond, others who influenced the American emancipation scene included Cary, a black teacher and lawyer, who became the chair of a Committee on Female Suffrage, promoting women's rights and equal employment opportunities. She was one of the first African American women to support the American Woman Suffrage Association, and in 1871, as Dorothy Sterling explains, "she was one of sixty-four District women who attempted to register to vote."[34] Moreover, she was one of the founders of a Colored Woman's Progressive Franchise Association, whose aims included the founding of newspapers, stores, and banks directed by women.[35] Like Remond and Watkins, she advocated women's emancipation.

Far from being voiceless and passive as white America would have them, African American women spoke and acted for themselves and for others of their race, claiming agency and voice. Women lecturers, who addressed interracial audiences of men and women, spoke against slavery and racism, and became central facilitators in organized proto-feminist activities. The Remond women, who had been participating in the building of a formal organizational structure for antislavery activism since the 1830s and whose home had become a gathering place for black and white opponents of slavery, were among the early courageous black pioneers.

Since the 1830s, the support for black emancipation had increased in the United States. White and black abolitionists established national and regional societies that grew from 60 societies in 1834 to over 2,000 in 1840 with a membership of 200,000.[36] The national American Anti-Slavery Society (AAS), established in 1833, was followed by other societies in the Northeast, Ohio, and Michigan. Both men and women, black and white contributed their time and energy in the organization of all-black and racially mixed antislavery societies. At the same time, the 1830s also witnessed increasing hostility toward the northern free black population because of their social progress, improved education, and the growth of the antislavery movement.[37]

The racial and gender mixing within these organizations triggered hostility from those who held an opposite view of how the American nation and society should be formed. In antebellum America, it was not uncommon for anti-abolitionist and anti-black rioters to attack meetings, harass abolitionists, and destroy homes of members of free black communities.[38] The aggression was a reaction to intensified antislavery activism, demand for black liberation, and women's radical claims for gendered power equality. Both men and more conservative women were particularly hostile toward women who publicly expressed their views and became involved in the country's politics. Violent mobs attacked antislavery women, for instance, in Boston in the 1830s, when such activists as Chapman and Angelina Grimké violated the norms of customary female behavior. Antislavery women in such cities as New York and Philadelphia as well as in smaller towns in Massachusetts, Pennsylvania, and Maine were victims of mob attacks throughout the 1830s. According to Bogin and Yellin, the "mobbing of the 1838 convention and the burning of Pennsylvania Hall marked the zenith of the violence that forever distinguished the experience of antislavery women from that of other organized women."[39]

One of the most notorious incidents of protest against abolitionists and women speakers occurred at the Second Anti-Slavery Convention of American Women, held in Philadelphia in 1838, where Abby Kelley addressed a "promiscuous" audience. The local community reacted with violence. They protested against racial and gender mixing but also the fact that women were at the podium. The mob that gathered to remonstrate burned down the meeting hall and threw rocks at the fleeing participants.[40] Hence, activists were not only verbally abused but also physically attacked by those who held opposing views. In a similar way, but with less aggression, female pioneers who had placed women's suffrage as the priority on their political agendas—Elizabeth Cady Stanton, Lucy Stone, and Susan B. Anthony—recalled at the first international Women's Convention in Washington, D.C., in 1888 that in the early years, "the audience greeted us with rotten eggs and not with flowers and applause."[41] Such hostility toward progressive women and abolitionists was quite common in the early days of protest against inequality but it also persisted throughout the nineteenth century and beyond. Awareness of such harassment of white women never discouraged black women such as Remond from joining abolitionist lecture tours that involved traveling in racially segregated states. Indeed, such courageous activists as Kelley Foster and Anthony, who were joined by Remond, continued their public efforts toward abolishing slavery, and they insisted on their right to speak in public.

Despite the violent obstruction, determined and dedicated Americans continued their activism, fighting against color prejudice within formal organizations and in their private lives. These early pioneers paved the way for others, including Remond, to continue the fight against prejudice and segregation. In 1837, the Anti-Slavery Convention of American Women convened in New York. It was one of the three conventions that year that could be seen as national gatherings of American antislavery women, bringing together both black and white women including Mott, the Grimké sisters, Sarah Douglass, Maria Stewart, and Child. Although the gathering was racially mixed, the majority of the women present, however, were white.[42]

Women's activism continued both nationally and internationally. As their organized activities became more gender conscious, geared also toward women's rights and interests, women, Bogin and Yellin argue, started "acting consciously *as* women."[43] As they entered the public sphere conventionally reserved for men, they started to underscore their femininity and propriety while enlisting members and establishing new societies. Mott and Stanton were among the women who gathered at the 1840 London Anti-Slavery Convention, which resulted in their determination to organize women in the United States into a formal women's rights movement. In increasing numbers women wrote pamphlets and interacted with other women to promote their common goal.

Women's rights conventions that were held in the United States included the groundbreaking Seneca Falls Convention of 1848, which formally separated women's rights from abolitionism. The meeting attracted approximately three hundred participants. During the convention, organized substantially by Stanton and Mott, the participants drafted the "Declaration of Sentiments," which contained a resolution concerning voting rights for women. The rhetoric used to articulate the declaration echoed that of the Declaration of Independence.[44] According to the scholar Diane Barnes, since it was considered "too radical by most of the men and some of the women attending the convention, the resolution faced failure until [Frederick] Douglass spoke in its favor."[45] Although abolitionism at the meeting was organizationally separated from women's rights campaigns, in practice antislavery activists were closely connected with the growing women's movements, involved in advancing women's rights but also promoting temperance efforts, assisting fugitive slaves, fighting for black Americans to have access to education, and campaigning against racial segregation and racist laws. In all fronts and while dedicated to various causes, activists fought back when confronted with the realities of the racially charged and prejudiced America.

Around the same time, other important women's rights conventions were organized in Rochester, New York, in 1848; Worcester, Massachusetts, in 1850 and 1851; Akron, Ohio, in 1851; and Syracuse, New York, in 1852.[46] Many of these areas were progressive political centers with influential antislavery feminist circles. The meetings served to attract attention, and some of the goals were achieved as a consequence of mobilizing public debate.

The activist campaigns continued after the Civil War. In 1866, American feminists changed the Women's Rights Convention into the Equal Rights Association, and universal suffrage formed their primary social and political agenda as they struggled against oppression. In 1869, the National Woman's Suffrage Association, instead, completely divorced itself from the question of black suffrage. However, despite the organizational separation, Frederick

Douglass continued to support women's emancipation and their right to vote, firmly believing in universal equality.[47]

In addition to local and national events, women acted transnationally. Stanton and Anthony, who realized the importance of transatlantic collaboration between feminists, were among the first prominent American suffrage leaders to network with other women internationally. Such transatlantic networks were fundamental in introducing African American orators, including Remond and such fugitive slaves as William Wells Brown and William and Ellen Craft, to British audiences. Later in the century, Stanton and Anthony were involved in establishing a transnational women's organization, the International Council of Women, which originated from the American National Woman Suffrage Association's meeting held in Washington, D.C., in 1888, with women participating not only from various parts of the United States but also from numerous European countries.[48] By then, slavery had been abolished but discrimination based on racial and gender difference continued. Such discrimination had its roots firmly ingrained in slavery and the antebellum United States.

Several women's antislavery organizations, as Bogin and Yellin point out, "offered equal membership to both black and white women. By rejecting segregation, the women in these socially mixed societies created a gender-specific organizational structure that posed an institutional challenge to American racism."[49] Often, however, prejudice and patronizing attitudes characterized the racially mixed societies. It was common, especially in the initial phases of organized activism, to find only white activists holding leadership positions; white abolitionists commonly wished to keep black activists in subservient positions within the movements. In other words, even white abolitionists had difficulties visualizing the integration of blacks into American society, and they tended to believe that a racially mixed social reality was impossible. Consequently, black women had to resist both racism and sexism even from white men and women operating in antislavery societies.[50]

One of the many associations whose goal was equality was the American Equal Rights Association (ERA). Active from 1866 to 1869, it fought to obtain suffrage for black men and women under the leadership of Lucretia Mott. Its activities, however, ceased due to a dispute concerning the right to vote.

The prioritization of suffrage either on the basis of gender or race became an issue that divided activists in many abolitionist and reform movements. As debates circulating around suffrage intensified, such white radical feminists as Stanton and Anthony, according to the historian Margaret Hope Bacon, revealed their racism, arguing that women should be granted the vote before "ignorant negroes" or "Sambos."[51] Hazel V. Carby confirms that both women "acceded to racist, exclusionary practices in order to court potential white female supporters in the Southern states."[52] Remond, for one, testified that white Americans who united with their black sisters and brothers in their efforts to advance gender and racial acceptance in practice tended to sustain the century's arbitrary theories of racial hierarchy, believing in the notions of black inferiority and white supremacy. As she argued in a lecture she gave in England on 8 January 1861: "The American people have never recognized the black man as a brother, nor the black woman as a sister."[53]

In antislavery and women's organizations, then, the concept of interracial sisterhood was an ideal based on the theoretical aspiration of women bonding around a common cause, which did not always correspond to reality. The collaboration did not necessarily result in emotional "sisterly" ties between white and black women or a homogenized group identity, two idealistic assumptions often associated with an unrealistic expectation characterizing racially mixed sisterhoods. Instead, interracial sisterhood based on equality remained a utopian concept as women's lives were embedded in rivalry and divided by class, race, and ideological views.

The historian Michael Kammen has pointed out that in antebellum America, abolitionists "harbored profoundly ambivalent feelings about people of color, and most of their countrymen continued to do so long after the Civil War and Reconstruction."[54] These patronizing attitudes, the historian Alan Rice argues, "encoded their deep distrust of blacks rising above their station."[55] Often, indeed, white abolitionists wished to discourage black activists from taking on leadership responsibilities, gaining social and political power, and moving beyond or rising above what white Americans deemed the appropriate social position of blacks. In other words, the more prejudiced white activists wished to anchor their black colleagues into a position of inferiority.

White women, Carby argues, "stand in a power relation as oppressors of black women."[56] Indeed, there were white abolitionists who shared the prevailing assumption of black inferiority. For instance, Elizabeth Buffum Chace, who was one of the founding members of the Female Anti-Slavery Society of Fall River, reported in her diary that some white members of the society, who were committed to promoting abolitionism and racial equality, wished to avoid association with blacks. Although some of the white members of the society had no objection to black women attending the meetings, they found it improper, or unacceptable, for blacks to become full members. In other words, African American women could passively sit in at the meetings but they were neither expected nor allowed to formally or actively participate in the organization's activities. Thus, Buffum Chace "raised such a storm among some of the leading members" when she invited some "very respectable young colored women" to join the society she had been involved in forming. The incident nearly led to the society being dissolved.[57]

Despite the resistance from the other white members of the society, Buffum Chace and her sister Lucy Buffum Lovell, however, stood their ground, and the black women they had invited to join were accepted as members. Thus, the interracial sisterhood failed to materialize collectively, but the idea was sustained and manifested through actions taken by such individuals as Buffum Chace and her sister, daughters of Arnold Buffum of Rhode Island, the first president of the Massachusetts Anti-Slavery Society in 1832.[58] These two white women belonged to a group of individuals who truly believed in, worked for, and sustained racial equality.

Abolitionists were creative in founding mediums to condemn slavery and discrimination. In addition to promoting social mixing in societies, the speeches of orators and writings of white and African American abolitionists all advanced social and political change, including a move toward black independence, and improved educational and professional opportunities. In addition to circulating ideas, lecturers, and antislavery pamphlets, men and women disseminated fictional texts and autobiographical fugitive slave narratives that spoke against slavery. Antislavery and sentimental literature, as Arthur Riss suggests, were "crucial in the humanizing of the Black slave during the antebellum period."[59] Such widely circulated texts as Harriet Beecher Stowe's *Uncle Tom's Cabin* (1852) played a "central role in the cultural process of 'personifying' slaves."[60] Its author, as is well known, was a white woman who both challenged and endorsed degrading racial stereotypes of African Americans.[61]

In addition to fictional antislavery novels, autobiographical narratives written by fugitive slaves appeared in print in the 1840s and included Brown's *Narrative of William W. Brown, a Fugitive Slave,* which came out in 1847. The slave narratives obtained transnational success, gaining immense popularity, for instance, in Britain, where they became a significant part of the propaganda employed to win international support for the antislavery cause. The many editions that were printed testify to their popularity. Many texts, indeed, appeared in print in their American and British versions but were also translated into other languages. Brown's story, the historian R. J. M. Blackett notes, "went through three British, two American, one French, and one German edition."[62] Moreover, many former slaves who wrote about their escapes also spoke in public. Following the publication of his narrative, Brown lectured in Massachusetts and Connecticut and then in Europe around the same time as Remond.These slave narratives and abolitionist lecturers persuaded both national and international audiences.

A few years earlier Douglass, who had escaped from bondage in Maryland in 1838, started writing his *Narrative of the Life of Frederick Douglass.* He published three versions of the story of his escape, the first of which appeared in 1845. That same year he started publishing a weekly antislavery newspaper, the *North Star,* together with Martin R. Delany in Rochester, New York. In this way, Douglass added a black newspaper dedicated to racial uplift and denouncing racial discrimination to the sources that kept Americans informed on the situation of the African American population, whether free or slave. Some years later, toward the end of his 1845–47 lecture tour in England, Douglass purchased his freedom with the help of British supporters, who assisted him in collecting the approximately six hundred dollars needed to pay for his freedom. By then, he was internationally celebrated as an abolitionist orator and writer.

The Swedish novelist and women's rights advocate Fredrika Bremer met Douglass in Rochester during her antebellum tour of the United States in 1850. She had already read Douglass's *Narrative* and was impressed by his "strong and profoundly sensitive spirit."[63] His autobiography, in Bremer's view, was "one of the most interesting books which any one can read," and the author was maintaining himself "as a literary man, always working for his great object—the emancipation of the slaves and the improvement of the free colored people."[64] Bremer's travel book, *The Homes of the New World: Impressions of America* (1853), in which she described her antebellum tour and reported of her meeting with Douglass, brought attention to the condition of slaves and re-introduced Douglass, whose autobiographical book already was known to her Nordic readers. Moreover, Bremer's comments revealed how rapidly and widely antislavery narratives circulated in the transatlantic world.

African American women who were former slaves also wrote about their experiences in bondage. Women's autobiographical stories that were based on their trials in slavery included Harriet Wilson's *Our Nig* (1859) and Harriet Jacobs's *Incidents in the Life of a Slave Girl* (1861). The number of fugitive slave narratives that appeared in print increased during the 1850s and 1860s, coinciding with the threat posed by the new Fugitive Slave Law created to discourage slave escapes.

Fearing recapture many fugitive slaves who had built new lives for themselves in the North escaped to Canada. In a speech entitled "Why Slavery Is Still Rampant," Remond accused "professing Christians" for "sustaining or defending slavery," and the "whole army and navy of the United States" for pursuing and shooting down "the poor fugitives, who panting for liberty fly to Canada, to seek the security of the British flag."[65] From Canada the escaped slaves crossed the ocean to Europe where they joined the already existing abolitionist lecture circuit and contributed with their fugitive slave narratives to the transatlantic circulation of information and autobiographical as well as fictional antislavery texts. The ocean, then, as Alan Rice has suggested, stood both as a marker of "dehumanizing realities and of the possibility of mobility to freedom."[66] The bold and ingenious escape carried out by the Crafts is an example of such mobility and transatlantic crossings of people, texts, and information but also of the ways in which the stories were told, and retold, through different mediums and genres.

The Crafts, who subsequently toured in England around the same time as Remond was lecturing there, repeatedly told the story of their escape to incredulous audiences before they decided to publish it in book form. Ellen Craft, who was nearly white, had been the property of her father, James P. Smith of Clinton, Georgia. Her mother was a mixed-race slave, Maria, who worked on Smith's plantation. When still a girl, Ellen, whose physical likeness to the Smith family was evident and apparently embarrassing to the wife of Smith, was given as a wedding gift to Smith's white daughter, Eliza, who moved to Macon, Georgia, after her marriage to Robert Collins, a wealthy landowner. At the time, William Craft was working in Macon as a carpenter. The two slaves met, fell in love, and decided to claim their freedom. The Craft couple weaved an intelligent plot for their escape: the white-looking Ellen traveled as a young Mr. Johnson, whose illness required "him" to cover his face with bandages and whose inflammatory rheumatism on the right hand prevented him from signing hotel registers. In this way, the invented illness served to justify the covering of Ellen's smooth face and the pretended rheumatism to hide the fact that she was illiterate.

The couple executed the ingenious plan successfully, and by January 1849, the Crafts had arrived in Boston where they settled in the free black community. There they met Brown and Samuel J. May, a Unitarian minister, also a friend of Remond. William Craft soon established a thriving furniture business, while the abolitionists were eager to present the couple to packed audiences gathered at Tremont Temple and Faneuil Hall.[67] When the Fugitive Slave Law threatened their liberty, the Crafts left the United States for Liverpool, where they arrived in December 1850.

The autobiographical narrative of William and Ellen Craft demonstrates, as Barbara McCaskill has argued, "the complex, contradictory ways in which fugitives such as the Crafts composed, manufactured, packaged, sold, and even resold themselves to middle-class nineteenth-century black and white audiences."[68] Their story was received with great enthusiasm by a public that was thrilled about the originality of their escape plan. Ellen

Craft's gender and racial "passing" would become an imitated literary device in subsequent narratives.

Since autobiographical slave narratives brought attention to personal experiences in slavery, they were powerful tools that humanized slaves and worked against the institution of human bondage. The texts raised awareness of the brutality with which slaves were treated, the conditions in which they lived, and the violence with which even white southern women treated slaves who were stripped of their humanity: they were considered property of plantation owners and perceived as human merchandise, bought, sold, and mistreated. The texts of former slaves were highly popular and reached both national and transatlantic audiences. The narratives, together with their authors and other former slaves who became abolitionist lecturers, were highly effective in promoting the message of racial liberation, equality, and justice.

African American men and women, both in national and international settings, searched for social justice, which was an arbitrary idea, as the black author Pauline Elizabeth Hopkins argued in her fictional story *Winona: A Tale of Negro Life in the South and Southwest* (1902): "Social equality does not exist because it is an artificial barrier which nature is constantly putting at naught by the most incongruous happenings. Who is my social equal? He whose society affords the greatest pleasure, whose tastes are congenial, and who is my brother in the spirit of the scriptural text, be he white or black, bond or free, rich or poor."[69] Hopkins was one of the empowering black women who used fiction and journalism to promote black emancipation and raise awareness of political and racial issues that were central to African Americans. In her view, social justice was an arbitrary invention similar to nineteenth-century racial notions based on a polarity between white and black "races." Black women confronted race discrimination and challenged male authority, both black and white, in their attempt to liberate themselves from color and gender prejudice. Encouraging others with their example, such women as Hopkins and Remond strived to move toward self-realization, both professionally and privately.

Remond, whose strong character at times collided in stormy disputes with her equally stern sister Caroline's, became a successful antislavery lecturer in the United States: she represented the American Anti-Slavery

Society, but she was also an active member of the Salem Female Anti-Slavery Society, the Essex County Anti-Slavery Society, and the Massachusetts Anti-Slavery Society.[70] In 1856–58, she toured in New York State with her brother Charles Lenox, Wendell Phillips, Parker Pillsbury, Stephen Foster as well as May, Kelley Foster, and Anthony. They traveled through New York City, Rochester, Utica, and Montreal, then New England, Michigan, and Ohio.

In December 1856, Remond was in Ogdensburg, New York, where she was denied entrance to the Webster's Boarding-House. Consequently, Anthony refused to remain without Remond and her brother.[71] In February 1857, the American Anti-Slavery Convention in Rochester elected Remond as vice president and a member of the finance committee with Anthony.[72] During her stay in Rochester in 1857, Remond stayed with the abolitionist Amy Kirby Post, who was also a dear friend of the fugitive slave and author Jacobs. Garrison wrote to his wife, Helen, from Rochester on 9 February 1857 that he as well as the Remond siblings were staying with Isaac and Amy Post: "Charles L. Remond and his sister are here also, and in good health and spirits,—though they have had a hard time of it for the last two months."[73] Touring in segregated states with white activists, speaking in public, and encountering hostile audiences protesting against black and women speakers must have been challenging. Fortunately, such supporters as the Posts invited Charles and Sarah Remond to rest in their home. They were expecting Anthony to come by that afternoon.

Ten days later, on 19 February, Garrison wrote his wife that he had just arrived in Albany from Utica, together with Charles and Sarah Remond, who were staying at William H. Topp's, while Garrison and Anthony were guests of Lydia Mott's.[74] In September 1857, Sarah Remond was in Ohio speaking at the anniversary of the Western Anti-Slavery Society with Charles, Parker Pillsbury, Kelley Foster, and Lucy N. Coleman.[75] The tour served to train Remond and make her a confident speaker. As Garrison wrote from Syracuse on 12 February 1857, "Sarah spoke but once in our meetings, but acquitted herself admirably. She only needs a little more confidence and a little more practice to make a good lecturer."[76] She continued her training in the United States before boldly addressing packed audiences in Europe.

Later in February 1857, Remond was in Salem, delighted with her tour, which had included a visit to Niagara.[77] Upon her return to Salem, Anthony joined Remond on a visit to Boston.[78] In March, Remond gave an enthusiastic account of her tour to her friend Charlotte Forten, who wrote in her diary: "Am afraid much of envy stole into the pleasure with which I listened to Miss R[emond]'s animated account, for the friendship of a great, a truly noble *genius* has, since childhood, been one of the most fondly cherished of my many dreams."[79] She considered Remond a possessor of great talent, a "genius," which made Charlotte slightly envious of her friend for the life she led and the success she obtained.

A year later, in April 1858, May arranged for Remond to join her brother Charles in Plymouth, Massachusetts, and Pawtucket, Rhode Island. The abolitionists were capitalizing on Remond in her role as a black woman on the platform. As May wrote to Buffum Chace: "Sarah is quite a pleasing speaker, and the novelty of a young colored woman appearing as a speaker will be likely to be attractive."[80] In 1858, Remond, whose career as a public speaker advanced rapidly, made an appearance at the National Woman's Rights Convention in New York.

In September 1858, Remond had just returned to Salem from attending an antislavery convention in Cape Cod, at Harwich, where she participated in eight meetings, all well attended, with a "closely packed audience."[81] As Remond observed after her travels in a letter to a British abolitionist:

> Only think of it, in the nineteenth century, a nation which years ago declared the slave trade piracy, endeavoring to legalize traffic in bodies and souls of men and women. Is it not enough to make one's heart sick? It is true the traffic in slaves has always been carried on, but now there will be an attempt made to throw around this infamous crime the sanction of law. "And why not?" I may ask, "When the Supreme Court of the United States has declared that men and women with a dark complexion 'have no rights which white men are bound to respect.' "[82]

In other words, even before her departure for England in 1858, she had started promoting her abolitionist and feminist agenda in her native United States, rapidly moving from addressing local audiences to campaigning as a representative of national organizations. In addition, she had reached across the Atlantic to connect with supporters of the cause of equality. Her strong character, determination, and dedication to her ideals resulted in her continued advancement despite the fact that she repeatedly was confronted with discriminatory attitudes and probably also attacked by protesting mobs.

In November 1858, the *Liberator* published a letter written by Sarah Clay, whose guest Remond, her brother, and Pillsbury had been during their tour, in which she brought attention to Remond's lecturing skills. Her every word, according to Clay, had "waked up dormant aspirations which would vibrate through the ages." Clay further noted that Remond was not well known to the public: "I do not recollect of having seen, even in the *Liberator,* any particular notice of her as a lecturer, aside from the regular advertisements," Clay wrote. "She certainly possesses a mind of no ordinary culture, and a heart deeply imbued with every high and noble sentiment; seems perfectly familiar with history, especially that relating to human rights, and some of the very best authors of the age are occasionally quoted by her in most beautiful and illustrative appropriateness." Clay further announced Remond's decision to sail for England.[83]

Remond was ready to join the few black women who traveled abroad in the nineteenth century. On 28 December 1858, Garrison wrote from Boston of Remond's plans to leave for England: "To-morrow, Samuel J. May of Syracuse, (a cousin of Samuel May, jr.,) and Sarah P. Remond of Salem, intend embarking for the old world, in the Liverpool steamer, from this city."[84] May, Garrison informed, had plans to immediately continue his journey from England to Italy with his son who was in Paris. Instead, Garrison wrote,

> Miss Remond goes forth on her own responsibility, not representing any society, but identified by complexion and destiny, by sisterly sympathy and generous philanthropy with the millions in this country who are punished worse than white criminals for the color of their skin. . . . She is much esteemed and beloved by all who know her. . . . I can easily imagine how unutterable must be her feelings on finding herself, for the first time in her life, in a land where this dreadful spirit of case is quite unknown; where she can travel on terms of equality with others, with no liability to insult or ostracism; where she will be estimated according to her moral worth and intellectual force. . . . I have had no conference

> with her in regard to her transatlantic journey, and therefore do not know how far she thinks of attempting to lecture abroad on the subject of slavery. She is comparatively new in the lecturing field, but only needs practice to become a pleasing and impressive public speaker. Her appeals are to the conscience and the heart, and always made with dignity and earnest conviction. She is capable of gracing any circle, and will be her own best recommendation wherever she travels. She has been so long interested in the anti-slavery movement that she is thoroughly posted upon all matters pertaining to it, and I doubt not will be able to remove many unfounded prejudices against it and its advocates, as she shall have opportunity.[85]

As a successful public figure Remond became an empowering role model for many black abolitionists.

Together with her brother Charles, Remond became a transatlantic activist when she joined the black men and women who left the United States for England, where many of them traveled with the same goal: to gather transnational support for eliminating slavery and to escape the racism permeating American society. In addition, some black Americans crossed the ocean with the intent of raising money for abolitionism, and for building churches and schools in their own country, or they chose England as a residence because they could receive education that had been denied them in the United States. Moreover, Britain attracted American antislavery activists because it had taken a strong position against the international slave trade and had a very powerful abolitionist movement.[86]

Already before her departure, Remond had rejected society's expectations of her as submissive by entering the public sphere, a space traditionally reserved for men only. She traveled abroad after she had obtained some experience and success in the United States as a public speaker, and she bravely crossed the ocean to England, where she continued her crusade against American slavery. In addition, one of the strongest motivations for Remond's departure was her fervent desire to leave color discrimination behind.

CHAPTER 3

England, 1858–1866

SARAH REMOND CONTINUED TO PROMOTE SOCIAL PROGRESS, whose advancement, as many abolitionists agreed, would be more rapid and its impact more significant when carried out through collaborative transatlantic efforts and by joining international networks. As the scholar Amanda Claybaugh asserts, reformers crossed and re-crossed the ocean, "paying visits to one another, going on lecture tours, and attending Anglo-American conventions against slavery and for temperance or world peace." The Atlantic was also traversed "by writings about reform, including pieces by corresponding societies; reform petitions and 'Friendly Addresses'; as well as pamphlets, periodicals, and novels."[1] The transatlantic abolitionist message, then, circulated through personal contacts as well as in oral and printed forms; it was disseminated through lectures, speeches, journalism, fiction, drama, poetry, and correspondence.

Activism intertwined with self-invention especially in black American experiences of transatlantic abolitionism. For Remond—who permanently remained in Europe after her first and only Atlantic crossing—traveling to England also entailed reassessing her identity in a foreign environment that was, at least seemingly, devoid of the earlier pressures and limitations caused by prejudice and hostility. Her autonomy increased during her tour of England, Ireland, and Scotland, and her role in activism shifted to the core of international reform movements and transatlantic networking. Indeed, rather than remain in the margins, Remond became one of the protagonists in transatlantic activism. Europe offered her opportunities for self-exploration and expression, and provided liberation from political, gendered, and racial oppression. She not only approached but entered European society as a fully recognized and warmly welcomed member. Such female agency offered a new, distinct model of blackness, one of empowered and elaborated identity. In Europe, Remond reinvented herself as a representative of female versatility, activism, and black acculturation.

The independent women who traveled, such as Remond, not only embarked on geographical voyages but also, and more importantly, on sociological expeditions and metaphorical journeys. For women who were eager to travel in the Victorian period, "questing for self meant traversing boundaries of cultural propriety as well as negotiating definitions of cultural identity."[2] Redefining and promoting a new sense of identity was important for many nineteenth-century Americans visiting the Old World, but it was particularly central to women and within the African American experience of Europe.

William W. Stowe has argued that "American travelers used the experience of Europe to help them think about questions of race and gender, about ways of relating to their country, their compatriots, and the wider world as African Americans, former or current slaves, slaveholders, abolitionists, independent or dependent women, and marginalized or actively engaged men." Travel formed a site "of female empowerment" and more importantly, of the "assertion of power by dominant races, classes, and nationalities."[3] And yet, such black Americans as Remond, who joined Europe's most fervent antislavery circles in Britain, were able to rearticulate and reenact their goals in a transatlantic context through contributions to and responsibilities within international organizations. Remond helped form and direct reform activities in such cities as London, which was in many ways, as Paul Gilroy points out, "an important junction point or crossroads on the webbed pathways of black Atlantic political culture."[4] Her British colleagues in women's societies whose aim was to express female solidarity toward the oppressed accepted Remond as an influential member. The transatlantic sisterhoods, moreover, were a demonstration of how women organized their activities with the aim of creating larger international and interracial communities geared to resist and fight unequal power relations, racism, and slavery.

The transatlantic ties between the United States and England that were formed with the aim to end slavery dated back to the eighteenth century: in the 1760s, a group of Philadelphia Quakers "appealed to the British government to abolish slavery in the colonies," thus creating an Anglo-American connection that characterized the antislavery movement until the very end.[5] Although slavery existed in other countries as well, American abolitionists made concrete and conspicuous efforts to bring attention to the inhuman conditions of slaves living in bondage in their own country. They actively promoted awareness of the slavery question, and unlike nationals of other countries who suffered more silently, American abolitionists, together with the British, cried out over the injustice of human captivity.

The collaboration between British and American antislavery groups intensified during the 1830s when the British and American Anti-Slavery Leagues were founded. This transatlantic cooperation included forming ties between leaders but also making contact through personal encounters. Hence, in 1833, William Lloyd Garrison crossed the Atlantic to London. He traveled to meet the president of the British Anti-Slavery League, who then headed for Boston the following year. The transatlantic connections built around suffrage were equally significant, if somewhat less institutional.[6] Remond, who traveled in the late 1850s, joined the already existing and by then well-established web of networks that reached over the ocean, connecting the United States with England.

Remond's plans to leave the United States were ready by midsummer 1858 and put into practice in December when she sailed onboard an English steamer that left Boston for England.[7] To quote Remond: "I shall take passage from Boston in an English steamer. . . . Parker Pillsbury will write to a friend of his to meet me at Liverpool, and I shall hope to get along very well."[8] Remond, who traveled alone, left her native country on 29 December 1858 with "an intense desire to visit England, that I might for a time enjoy freedom, and I hoped," she wrote, "to serve the anti-slavery cause at the same time."[9] In addition, she felt "in need of a good English education," which she successfully obtained in London.[10] Her main objectives, then, were to serve the antislavery cause, enjoy freedom, and improve her education. "I hope to reach London before winter," she informed, "but I dread starting for many reasons. I do not fear the wind nor the waves, but I know that no matter how I go, the spirit of prejudice will meet me."[11] Instead, British antislavery activists received her with warmth and kindness.

On 12 January 1859, she arrived in Liverpool where William Robson, a prominent English abolitionist whom Remond had earlier met in Boston, greeted and welcomed her to his Lancashire home. Subsequently, according to the *National Anti-Slavery Standard,* abolitionist and women's suffrage activist Mattie Griffith, among others, "opened the way for her into the highest and selectest order of social and literary aristocracy."[12] Thus, Remond was warmly welcomed by abolitionists with whom, as she had hoped, she had an opportunity to contribute to the evolving feminist abolitionist message.

Although scholars have argued that it was uncommon for women in the nineteenth century to travel without being accompanied by a male protector—a husband or a brother—Remond, for one, made her 1858 transatlantic crossing alone. Although Reverend Samuel J. May from Syracuse was onboard the same steamer, *Arabia,* which crossed the ocean to Liverpool via Halifax, Remond was independently in charge of her voyage. She also seems to have traveled by herself on her many visits from England to Continental Europe—to France, Switzerland, and Italy. On 24 January 1860, for instance, the *New York Times* reported that she was on her way from London to Paris, and six years later Giuseppe Mazzini noted that she was traveling from London to Florence, passing through Switzerland.[13] Remond's sister Caroline, instead, made repeated transatlantic crossings, at times together with her son or, in 1872, in the company of a female friend, Christine Keadie "Kitty" Sargent, an artist with whom she traveled and lived in Europe.

It is evident that African American women were independently exploring the transatlantic world despite the fears and anxieties often associated with travel and encounters with the foreign. They joined white women who traveled abroad in increasing numbers, "furthering the transformation of women," as Mary Suzanne Schriber asserts, "from receptacles into creators of politics and culture."[14] As they journeyed, boldly and self-reliantly, women claimed independence that surpassed the gender-specific expectations set for them. Fearlessly they moved on without letting the anxiety associated with encountering the unknown decelerate their advancement. Not even the turbulent social and political events that changed the transatlantic world hindered the advancement of black American travelers, who were determined to enjoy their freedom and journey toward self-realization.

Remond's sister Caroline, who followed approximately a year later, also traveling from Boston to Liverpool, was less fortunate on her transatlantic crossing: she faced American prejudice onboard the English steam-vessel *Europa.* The captain refused her and her family places at the public table because American passengers had objected to being associated with people of "color."[15] The *Western Daily Press* and *Lloyd's Weekly Newspaper* of London ran a story about the discrimination, titled "Coloured Persons and Cunard Steamers," in July 1860. The introduction to the description of the incident was written by a Commissioner Hill and Reverend Edwin Chapman, who had heard of it directly from Sarah Remond. By that time, she had established herself in the prominent social circles of London. In their letter to the owner of the Cunard vessel, Hill and Chapman clearly indicated that should the reply be unsatisfactory, they intended to publish the correspondence in various newspapers, which they ultimately did; Sir Samuel Cunard's response had been merely to communicate to them that his decision was not to interfere in the matter.[16]

All of the correspondence on the situation, which the local newspapers subsequently published, included a brief introduction, followed by a letter of Hill and Chapman, and excerpts from a letter written by Caroline Putnam, together with a letter she had received from the U.S. representative of the Cunard company before her departure informing her that she and her party were denied access to the vessel's dining room. As Hill and Chapman pointed out, "the Europa is a British mail steamer, and Sir Samuel Cunard, her owner, is an Englishman, who, for his public services, has been rewarded with a baronetcy," and therefore, he should "adopt measures to prevent a recurrence of these acts of social oppression." In the letter addressed to Cunard, dated 11 June 1860, the gentlemen brought attention to his earlier promise, made in 1847 and now broken, "that no more offences such as that committed against Mr. F. Douglass should take place on board your steamers."

The gentlemen continued with an explanation of how they had heard of Putnam's mistreatment directly from Remond:

> It only remains to say that some weeks since Miss Remond, sister to Mrs. Putnam, a highly intelligent and most estimable person, now studying at the college for ladies in Bedford square, London, was present at an anti-slavery gathering at the house of one of the subscribers to this letter, and there laid the case before the persons assembled, who, feeling themselves implicated in the unworthy and most inhospitable treatment which American passengers had experienced in one of her Majesty's mail packets receiving the subsidy of the nation, and sailing under official colours, requested us to take such measures as should be necessary for preventing a recurrence of such disgraceful injustice.

Once again, Remond had taken immediate action to resist discrimination. As the letter demonstrates, she determinedly fought against bigotry, discussing the incident in public. Such publicity drew attention to the racist attitudes of the white passengers but simultaneously attested to the propriety of the black travelers. The letter also testified to, and underscored, Remond's respectability: she had enrolled in a fashionable London college where she was studying together with English ladies. At the time, Remond had been accepted in British upper-class society, which fiercely supported her and acted on her behalf.

The two authors of the letter expressed their shame concerning the incident, especially because the vessel represented "her Majesty" and sailed "under official colours" of a nation that, at least formally, had banned racial discrimination. At the same time, their attack was aimed at Americans because it had been the Boston representative of the Cunard line who had prohibited the Putnam family from joining the vessel's white first-class passengers. Like other British abolitionists, Hill's and Chapman's goal was to disgrace the United States for its discriminatory attitudes toward black Americans. As R. J. M. Blackett suggests, white Americans were aware "that blacks and their British allies had traditionally used every opportunity to embarrass their country. American refusal to grant passports to blacks and ships that restricted black passengers to the steerage class had long been publicly condemned in Britain."[17]

Following the published appeal to Cunard were extracts from Caroline Putnam's letter, written in London upon her landing there on 29 November 1859:

> We purchased tickets as first-class passengers on board the steamer Europa, Captain Leich, our party consisting of four—C. E. Putnam, Sarah L. Smith, Henry G. Cassey, and my son, Edmund T. Putnam. A few days before the steamer sailed, I received the enclosed letter from Mr. Bates, the agent of the Cunard company. Upon its reception, I called upon the gentleman, asking him why we were denied the privileges which are granted to every one until they prove themselves unworthy of them. He said American ladies and gentlemen would object to sit down by the side of coloured persons. I told him we were obliged to sail in the steamer, and I thought there would not be the least trouble, as we were able now to travel in the northern states of America without any, and were treated well at some of the best hotels, and I expected on board an English steamer I should receive good treatment, as persons living under her government were not judged by the colour of their skin but their conduct only; and I hoped we should be allowed our seats at the table. On the 2nd day of November we started, and when we had been on board about two hours one of the servants told us he wished to speak with us if we would follow him. We did so, and were shown into a very small room, and told by him that the captain wished us to take our meals there by ourselves. We told him that we should prefer going to the table, and that we should be rather uncomfortable, as the room was in the extreme stern part of the boat, and one of our party was an invalid, and had left home on that account. He said he had received his instructions from the captain, and there was no alternative. . . . During the whole voyage we were not allowed a seat at the table. . . . And during the last few days of our voyage we were obliged to sit in the ladies' cabin by ourselves, and servants bring us food as if we were criminals, when we had conducted ourselves with the strictest propriety. The captain committed a great wrong in submitting to the dictation of an American agent.—Yours, &c., C. E. Putnam.[18]

It was a well-written letter that clearly stated the events that had taken place before, during, and after the transatlantic crossing. Putnam evidently expected equal treatment with white first-class passengers, a request rejected by Cunard Line.

The letter Caroline Putnam had received from the Cunard Boston office had explained that "a separate table will be provided for yourself and party on board the Europa, hence to Liverpool, where everything will be furnished you that first cabin passengers are entitled to." The reason for such an arrangement, the Cunard representative informed, was that "the person who applied for your tickets did not state the fact that the party were coloured." He proposed two alternatives: having their meals in separate quarters or having their tickets refunded. Hill and Chapman concluded their public display of the correspondence by voicing their indignation concerning the way the entire episode had been handled, conveying their disappointment: "So we suppose we must continue to endure the shame and humiliation consequent upon the toleration, in the greatest line of British mail steamers of a hateful feeling of prejudice against the African complexion and race."[19] Such statements served to appeal to shared national pride, now replaced with "shame and humiliation" at being British. The two gentlemen publicly wished to embarrass Britain, and simultaneously the United States, for their unjust treatment of black travelers.

The publication of the correspondence in prominent newspapers demonstrates that Remond had been welcomed into British society, whose members were eager to instrumentalize the incident to voice their concerns about racial discrimination in their own country and in the United States. News about the incident appeared in the *Liberator,* and as a consequence of the publicity, on her return voyage to the United States onboard the *Arabia,* Putnam and her party "were admitted to all the rights and privileges of first-class passengers, without opposition on the part of any one, even though slaveholders were on board."[20] The publicity had served to improve the treatment of black travelers.

Many influential people in England who assisted Remond had previously formed personal contacts with her brother Charles, who had introduced his sister to such prominent American abolitionists as Maria Chapman of the Boston Female Anti-Slavery Society. Chapman, who had lived in Europe since 1848, provided Remond with letters of introduction to British activists. At her home in Paris, Chapman received such abolitionists as Mary Estlin and Richard Webb, while she repeatedly crossed the channel to visit the

Estlins in Bristol and to speak at antislavery meetings. She left Europe in 1855 having consolidated a network of friends and fellow activists.[21]

Commonly black abolitionist speakers arrived carrying letters of introduction with them, written by prominent activists, or were introduced to their British colleagues before they even crossed the ocean. Letters of introduction worked as instruments that contributed to the building of transatlantic cooperation; they reached such antislavery activists as the ophthalmologist Dr. John Bishop Estlin in Bristol, who willingly assisted fugitive slaves upon their arrival in England. The Estlin family welcomed, for example, the Crafts, who subsequently were introduced to social reformers Lady Noel Byron and Harriet Martineau, among others. In addition to connecting Sarah Remond with Chapman, Charles had connected his sister with May with whom Remond remained in contact after moving to England.[22] Moreover, as Blackett suggests, Charles "was directly responsible for establishing contacts between American and British abolitionists where they had not previously existed and rekindling interest among those who had withdrawn because of the 1840 schism."[23] He was especially successful in consolidating the Irish-American connection and also participated in the first World Anti-Slavery Convention, which took place in London in June 1840. The meeting, the historian Douglas H. Maynard explains, "marked the beginning of the sustained movement toward international organization which has led to today's extensive network of world conferences and international agencies."[24] Moreover, the meeting provided one of the first forums for transatlantic interracial collaboration between England and the United States.

Although officially women were excluded from the convention, many of them followed the discussions from the visitors' gallery. The meeting aimed at strengthening and enlarging the campaign against slavery. There were altogether 409 delegates, about 40 of them from the United States, 6 or 7 from France, and the rest from the United Kingdom and its colonies. Most of the American delegates came from New England, New York, and Pennsylvania; four were from Ohio. They all participated in the discussions, which lasted for ten days.[25]

The convention was an international joint effort that principally combined British and American forces. The historian Clare Midgley argues that it had "lasting repercussions on the future form of the British anti-slavery movement," which from then on focused primarily on slavery in the United States.[26] "As a joint Anglo-American enterprise," Maynard notes, "the meeting also represented one of the hidden and unofficial ties joining the two countries at a time when official relations were severely strained."[27] As an international alliance, the first of its kind, it was a great success.

Other international meetings followed in 1843 that included the second World's Anti-Slavery Convention and the first World's Peace Convention. Around the same time, temperance reformers started planning their own international gatherings.[28] In Europe especially, antislavery men and women were eager to sustain the ideal of racial equality through international networks and interracial societies whose agendas often included women's empowerment.

The organized women's suffrage movement in England originated from the first national women's rights convention organized in Worcester in 1850 with Frederick Douglass attending. Many black men, including William Wells Brown, Charles Remond, and Douglass promoted women's rights in addition to racial emancipation, but their attitudes changed in the Reconstruction era when antagonism increased between white women and African Americans on the question of suffrage. The stance of activists differed among prioritizing the rights of women, black men, or the universal right to vote.[29] In England, the National Union of Women's Suffrage Societies (NUWSS) was formed as late as 1897.

In England, Sarah Remond was able to forge alliances with white abolitionists and proto-feminists who, like her, were striving for political participation. Such bonding increased her independence, confidence, and self-esteem. To be treated without discrimination, to be accepted on equal terms, and to be welcomed in international, interracial sisterhoods had an impact on women in general but African American women in particular, whose realities were shaped by racial and gender inequality. For black Americans who landed in England, American discrimination appeared more forceful when compared to British liberty and the acceptance there of racial equality.

Antislavery networks and bridges of collaboration were built across the ocean starting from the 1760s, and the cooperation intensified during the 1830s and 1840s, when African Americans escaped the legalized bigotry of the American South and the sustained social segregation of the North to come to the more welcoming environment of England. The task of black lecturers in Britain was, as scholars have observed, "to inform international opinion about the nature of American slavery and discrimination in the hope that informed world opinion would somehow persuade America to grant blacks the full rights of citizenship."[30] Charles Remond, who was among the first to travel to England and Ireland, started his intense tour of the British Isles during the summer of 1840. At times, he spoke as many as twenty-three nights out of thirty against slavery, race prejudice, and colonization. He "laid the foundations for the emergence of blacks as the principal spokesmen for the American slave on the international scene in the 1840s."[31] The black men and women who followed him joined an already established web of abolitionist collaborators, contributing to the transatlantic effort to secure international condemnation of slavery. Among his many achievements, Charles Remond "reconfirmed free-black opposition to colonization."[32] He was among the first celebrated activists to appear on the extensive lecture circuit that subsequently included Douglass and such women speakers as Sarah Remond and Ellen Craft, who arrived when the United States was already heading toward civil war.

The scholar Teresa Zackodnik has observed that "black women such as Remond and Craft were effectively internationalizing black feminism through the transatlantic network."[33] As Remond contended, the international community had to listen and "render a verdict in behalf of her suffering countrymen and women."[34] In addition to Remond, such fugitive slave speakers as Douglass were especially successful in gaining international support against human bondage and race and gender oppression.

Douglass first lectured in England and Ireland between 1845 and 1847. During his speaking engagements, he spoke against slavery but also delivered speeches on temperance and women's rights. However, he emphasized that slaves and the abolition of slavery were his primary concerns even when, for instance, during his visit in Cork in 1845, his talks addressed "American Prejudice against Color" or "Intemperance and Slavery."[35] He also spoke of the importance of education, which was one of the first things many fugitive slaves, including William and Ellen Craft, sought after their arrival in England. They met Lady Byron, who was instrumental in assisting them.

As Martineau noted in an article published in the *Atlantic Monthly* (and later republished in Harriet Beecher Stowe's *Lady Byron Vindicated*), Lady Noel Byron was devoted to charities. She had opened one of the first English industrial schools in Middlesex in 1834 and a girls' school on her Leicester property in 1840. At Bristol, she bought a house for a reformatory for girls. She was interested in political movements and social change, and was known for her support for "the Sicilian cause" or Italy's unification, antislavery, and "her kindness to William and Ellen Craft."[36] With the help of Lady Byron, the Crafts enrolled in the Ockham School in Surrey, where they studied for three years. In addition, Ellen actively worked in antislavery organizations and assisted the newly emancipated slaves in the United States by making garments for them. Moreover, she contributed to the family finances with her salary obtained from her employment as a teacher. The Crafts lived comfortably outside London in Hammersmith, where they purchased a small house and their children attended some of the best schools. The Crafts, who were former slaves, and free-born Americans like Remond thus demonstrated what black Americans could achieve when they were granted an opportunity to study: financially independent and comfortable, middle-class lives.

For Douglass, the Crafts, and Remond, the freedom in Europe to voice their concerns and realize their personal emancipation was manifold. Black lecturers, as Blackett observes, were "lionized," and for the first time in their lives, "were treated as equals by most of those they met."[37] Their warm reception in Europe provided them with an invaluable opportunity to reassess their identities, and one form of empowerment was working together with white colleagues as equals. Although opposition to abolitionists and women activists was also a reality in Britain, black Americans were convinced that racist attitudes belonged to the United States more than to what they perceived as an enlightened Europe.

It was a common reaction among black Americans in England to notice the absence of color discrimination. Alan Rice has observed that "veneration of Britain and its freedom-loving propensities is a constant theme of African diasporan discourse and can be traced back to the eighteenth century and such figures as Phyllis Wheatley, whose trip across the Atlantic in 1773 begets the miracle of racial toleration."[38] Since black Americans often were blind to the existence of discrimination in Europe, their perception of black identity and social reality dramatically changed through travel and mobility. The more liberal European environment allowed them "to dream of real freedom at home."[39] They tended to create a utopian European space, which they compared unfavorably with their native United States.[40]

In addition to Remond, Douglass was among those who gave testimony to the difference between the nations, comparing the United States to Europe. He attested in his 1881 essay "The Color Line" that in Europe, the "malignant prejudice, as we know it in America, does not prevail" because "character, not color, is the passport to consideration; where the right of the black man to be a man, and a man among men, is not questioned; where he may, without offense, even presume to be a gentleman." During his two years in Europe, Douglass remained impressed by the racial mixing that occurred within the ranks of the upper classes, stirring black visitors' class consciousness. In the United States, he observed, the black man was "the trammeled victim of a prejudice, well calculated to repress his manly ambition, paralyze his energies, and make him a dejected and spiritless man," whereas in Europe, he found no color prejudice, "except among Americans who reside there." Furthermore, Douglass observed,

> In England and on the Continent, the colored man is no more an object of hate than any other person. . . . During the two years which the writer spent abroad, though he was much in society, and was sometimes in the company of lords and ladies, he does not remember one word, look, or gesture that indicated the slightest aversion to him on account of color. His experience was not in this respect exceptional or singular. Messrs. Remond, Ward, Garnet, Brown, Pennington, Crummell, and Bruce, all of them colored, and some of them black, bear the same testimony.[41]

It is interesting to note that Douglass pointed out a perceived difference between a "colored" and "black" American, testifying to the categorizations of

African Americans into representatives of various shades of complexion ranging from blacks to "mulattoes" to "octoroons," each with an associated set of discriminative attributes, attitudes, and destinies. He provided a long list of African Americans who had been to Europe to experience a sense of freedom from injustice based on the color of one's complexion, and he communicated to his readers the accompanying feeling of a reinforced positive sense of identity that came from his inclusion among the lords and ladies of British high society. In the United States, he argued, a black man was "the slave of society" rather than of an individual owner.[42] Color prejudice, he concluded, was a moral disease and an American phenomenon, not a European one.

In Douglass's view, class and racial acceptance characterized European society, while the color line stemmed from the depths of American slavery.[43] His statement testified as to how freedom for fugitive slaves was inseparable from movement and relocation. Their mobility was not only physical but also social: their journey started from slavery, where they were considered "merchandise" and "property," and advanced toward liberty, which allowed them to secure their personhood and become independent. In England, their social ascent continued as celebrities who joined "lords and ladies." They also connected with other black lecturers such as Charles and Sarah Remond. Like cosmopolitan globe-trotters, these black activists found a new home abroad where they felt at ease interacting with others of different nationalities.

The African American professor William G. Allen also noticed the racial acceptance that seemed to characterize life in Europe. He wrote in a letter published in the *Liberator* on 22 July 1853 that in London, "the colored man feels himself among friends, and not among enemies;—among a people who, when they treat him well, do it not in the patronising (and, of course, insulting) spirit, even of hundreds of the American abolitionists, but in a spirit rightly appreciative of the doctrine of human equality."[44] Allen's letter bears testimony to the color prejudice that also others such as Remond experienced among white Americans, even slavery's opponents, whose patronizing attitude he found insulting.

Allen, who was a professor of Greek and Latin, had personally experienced white hostility in the United States when he had wished to marry a Miss King, one of his white students at New York Central College in McGrawville in February 1853.[45] He was the second African American to hold a professorship at a predominantly white college, and he was one of three African Americans employed at the New York Central College, which was established by abolitionists. The other two were Charles Reason and George B. Vashon.[46] Like the Remonds, these educated professionals had achieved social advancement and respect through their prominent careers but nonetheless continued to suffer social marginalization and politically inflicted injustice.

The social and political equality that Allen perceived as typical of English society was an idealized vision. As Rice points out, "racism was a harsh reality for many blacks in Britain."[47] For example, James Watkins, a black traveler, complained in 1851 that he was unable to obtain employment in Britain and was treated with contempt by some people he had approached. Others went so far as to accuse him of dishonesty because, as an escaped slave, they argued, he had robbed his master of the amount he could have obtained had he sold Watkins at a slave market.[48] Other testimonies of discrimination come from the fugitives John Brown and Zilpha Elaw, who noticed the "prejudice against colour in England," and William Wells Brown, who encountered a black American whose poverty testified to his unsuccessful search for employment in England.[49] Such stories reveal the existing discrimination that privileged African Americans like Brown himself often were unable to detect underneath the warm welcome they received from British abolitionists.

In addition to racial prejudice, which perhaps existed in Europe to a lesser degree than in the United States, other forms of discrimination based on differences in class and gender were a reality, and British society was not nearly as liberal as Douglass and Allen believed: the British held strongly prejudiced views and tended to discriminate people on the basis of class. In many European countries, members of the upper class judged people by their social status and rigorously enforced class divides. This phenomenon was particular pertinent to British society's strict separation of classes, which was in such cities as London also physical. It advanced to a point where rich and poor in major cities literally inhabited separate worlds.

Furthermore, the divisions among the classes were not only economic and topographical but also political, moral, and even linguistic.[50]

However, such class-based discrimination was often not apparent to the celebrated African American orators who, unlike many British, directly interacted with representatives of both the upper and lower classes at their talks. In addition, black visitors formed an idealized impression of social equality, which stemmed from their acceptance in European upper class gatherings where they witnessed harmonious racial mixing. To such black Americans as Allen it was a surprise to see that "in parties given by the 'first people' in the kingdom may be seen persons of all colors moving together on terms of perfect social equality."[51] The hosts and hostesses of European cosmopolitan gatherings who invited representatives of different nations to take part in their meetings created an atmosphere that emanated acceptance.

The environment of Italy was perhaps even more tolerant than Britain, at least according to *Harper's Bazaar:* in 1879, it reported that the African American sculptor Edmonia Lewis, when asked if color was prejudicial to her in Rome, stated, "Never; I never hear of it there. Why, I am invited every where, and treated just as nicely as if the bluest of blue blood flowed through my veins. I number among my patrons the Marquis of Bute, Lady Ashcroton [*sic*], and other members of the nobility."[52] The blood running in her veins, as she pointed out, was not considered "black" in Europe but was deemed no different from "the bluest of blue." With such a statement she claimed her equality with British aristocracy and brought to mind America's arbitrary one-drop rule used to discriminate against black Americans.

Lewis was also proud of her achievements as a woman and an African American: "I have a bust of Longfellow in the college library at Harvard, a monument to Lynch Blaire at the Graceland cemetery at Chicago, and another monument to Dr. H. K. Hunt in the Mount Auburn in Boston. I am the *only woman* who has a monument in either cemetery."[53] In this context, Lewis foregrounded her gender rather than race when she pointed out her privileged position in receiving commissions and achievements. In other words, as an artist, in this particular instant, it was more important to her to be recognized as a pioneering woman than as a groundbreaking African American. As Lewis pointed out, she had achieved more than other women because of her talent and determination but surely also because she had been able to work without discrimination that would have otherwise obstructed her creativity. With such statements she affirmed her position among white American artists competing with her in Rome, who may have shared her political views and goals of gender and racial equality but whose words and actions, according to the art historian Charmaine A. Nelson, "often revealed an ambivalence in the social occurrences of cross-racial interaction."[54] However, Lewis received encouragement from many visiting Americans, and her social acceptance in Europe increased her confidence, self-esteem, and her productivity.

Consequently, black Americans achieved remarkable results in their careers, personal lives, and for the antislavery cause in the seemingly tolerant Britain, which was known for its efficient and organized antislavery activities, which included transatlantic and interracial collaborations. In addition to London, which was the center for reform activism in general, such cities and towns as Cork in Ireland or Warrington in Lancashire, England—which became a center of Garrisonian abolitionism in 1859—had active participation in the antislavery movements run by both men and women, locally and nationally.

At the time of Sarah Remond's stay in England, other African Americans who were lecturing there on abolitionism included the Crafts, Brown, and Douglass, who, unlike Remond, were all former slaves. They often participated in various events together, covering topics in their speeches that ranged from slavery, freedom, and reform to activism. Douglass, for instance, at times lectured with others, including Garrison, but his views, according to Blackett, "were given the place of prominence in local newspaper reports."[55] In a similar way, the Crafts, who arrived in England in 1850 and worked for the London Emancipation Committee supporting Garrisonian abolitionism, soon connected with other American fugitive slave speakers, including Douglass, Henry "Box" Brown, William Wells Brown, and others who were on the antislavery lecture circuit.

The Crafts appeared with William Wells Brown on platforms with an established program in which each had a specific role. According to Blackett, the Brown-Craft team was "by far the most popular" performance in this period.[56] During their performances, they followed a routine according to which Brown first introduced William Craft, who told the adventurous story of the couple's escape from slavery. Following Craft's talk, Brown delivered an hour-long speech after which he introduced Ellen, who then had an opportunity to add a few words to what had already been said. The presence of Ellen, who appeared white, efficiently persuaded the public to condemn slavery because, as Blackett suggests, "it was one thing to enslave a black person but enslaving a white woman was totally reprehensible."[57] Together the three former slaves toured, as the historian Barbara McCaskill notes, "such northern English factory cities as Liverpool, Manchester, Birmingham, and Leeds; resorts and ports like Bath and Bristol; Glasgow, Edinburgh, and Aberdeen, Scotland; and, framing the whole progress, the bustling capital of London."[58] In August 1859, William Craft gave a talk after Remond had delivered her lecture on "American Slavery" at the Essex Town Hall.[59] In addition to town halls and music halls in various towns and cities, London's Crystal Palace in Hyde Park was an established venue that hosted many antislavery events as well as the Great Exhibition. Many black lecturers were present at the exhibition, strolling together with their white friends.

Despite the apparent absence of race discrimination, mixed-race women with lighter complexions, such as Remond, more easily tended to correspond to antebellum white standards of femininity. Ellen Craft, for one, had such a pale coloring that she could easily have passed for a white woman. Moreover, as she was intelligent and had pleasant manners, she was welcomed into the best London society among other representatives of Victorian womanhood.[60] Local newspapers described Ellen as "a gentle, refined-looking young creature of 24 years, as fair as most of her British sisters, and in mental qualifications their equal too."[61] Prejudiced subtext comes across, though, through the praise of her "mental qualifications," which were linked to her apparent whiteness, associated with "gentle" and "refined" looks. In this way, her acceptability appeared intertwined with the newspaper's racial categorization of her as white, both because of her skin color and the associated notions of presumed intellectual and cultural characteristics. In addition to reflecting the standards of white women physically and intellectually, she also was a dedicated mother to her five children, thus epitomizing the period's ideal of (white) womanhood and motherhood, concepts that in the United States had excluded her and other black women.

American fugitive slaves lectured in large cities as well as small towns where their popularity often relied on sensationalism as they displayed neck chains, whips, and other objects of torture that slave owners had used to punish their "property."[62] Their antislavery lectures became a form of entertainment for contemporary audiences. Gruesome events, melodrama, and sentimentalism especially appealed to a public searching for sensational experiences. The Crafts' experience in slavery catered to such audiences and readers: "I have often seen slaves tortured in every conceivable manner. I have seen them hunted down and torn by bloodhounds. I have seen them shamefully beaten, and branded with hot irons. I have seen them hunted, and even burned alive at the stake," reported the Crafts in their autobiographical narrative.[63] Catering to their audiences' perhaps morbid curiosity, black abolitionists effectively informed Victorians about the abuse and destruction of families under slavery.

As McCaskill has observed, the black orators "exploited a national obsession. The nineteenth century was a time when spectacle was everything, and a time when droves of spectacles—minstrel shows, world's fairs, Wild West productions, jubilees, Dime Museums, fugitive slave exhibits—not only entertained and shocked viewers, but also projected their fears, prejudices, hostilities, and other anxieties."[64] The shows and fairs, among them wildly popular freak shows, traveled nationally and internationally, stopping at villages and larger cities, displaying abnormalities to astonished audiences. The scholar Harriet Ritvo suggests that the curiosities were mainly related to non-European human races, whereas Europeans were usually exhibited only when their talents or physical anomalies were exceptional. According to Ritvo, the monstrosities appealed to people from all social groups, and both the advertisements and the public's readiness to pay to view them were indications of the fascination and popularity they held.[65] Former slaves, who often appeared together, took advantage of the Victorian audience's attraction to tragic and appalling tales. Moreover, African American activists realized that by performing together, they could reinforce the impact of their lectures.

At times Remond appeared together with Douglass, often addressing current controversies. On 16 January 1860, the *New York Times* published a report of the annual meeting of the Leeds Young Men's Anti-Slavery Society, which was held on 22 December 1859 in the Music Hall. The *Leeds Times* of 17 December had reported that both Douglass and Remond would speak at the meeting, and the latter would give another talk the following evening, again at the Music Hall.[66]

According to the *New York Times* article, the main orator was Douglass, who spoke of John Brown's raid at Harper's Ferry, which had taken place in October 1859 when Brown and his companions tried to seize weapons from the federal arsenal to give to slaves who could then have employed them in an armed insurrection. According to the article, "Miss Sarah Remond also addressed the meeting" that had "a numerous attendance." The *New York Times* provided no indication of the topic of Remond's speech, whereas the *Liberator* reported that Remond concluded her speech, in which she had accused America of being an oligarchy, "by an eloquent tribute to the memory of John Brown."[67] Both Remond and Douglass also gave talks about slavery at the antislavery meeting in Wakefield, where "not less than 1,500 people [were] present."[68] Although Douglass may have been the most sought-after speaker, Remond also received significant attention for the bold talks that formed her antislavery campaign and for her efforts on behalf of equal rights for African Americans.

In England, Remond utilized the transatlantic abolitionist network, which her brother and such women as Lucretia Mott had established in the 1840s, and her tour included many of the same places where Mott had lectured in 1840–41. In 1893 and 1894, Ida B. Wells would likewise utilize Mott's contacts to organize her anti-lynching campaign in Britain.[69] The existing transatlantic collaboration web facilitated the spread of the abolitionist message aimed at reaching the international community that, in Remond's view, should hear the facts and act on behalf of "her suffering countrymen and women."[70] Black abolitionists were aware of the antagonism that existed between the United States and Britain, and recognized the British influence on American culture and opinion. Hence, speakers wished to persuade British audiences to support their crusade to end slavery and promote black advancement. William and Ellen Craft denounced "the Americans, as a people, [who] are notoriously mean and cruel towards all coloured persons, whether they are bond or free," and Remond's ambitious goal in Britain was to engage the sympathy of the entire nation toward abolitionism in the United States.[71]

The African American speakers drew large audiences throughout the thirty-year period between 1830 and 1860 that marked an elevated British concern for abolitionism. Charles Remond, whose eighteen-month visit to England had started in the spring of 1840, was instrumental in building the antislavery network, and as one of the first professional abolitionists, he set many of the conventions that others who arrived after him could follow. He was triumphant in Ireland, where he formed local groups, and he organized fundraising bazaars in northern England. Although the late 1840s and the 1850s were the peak years of antislavery activism, Sarah Remond, for one, attracted as many as two thousand people who came to hear her in Edinburgh in 1860 when the interest in abolitionism had already started to decline.[72] In the United States, instead, the intensifying racial tensions that led up to the Civil War were dramatically changing the lives of black Americans in both the North and the South.

Many black lecturers returned to the United States after the Civil War to participate in "race uplift," which meant employing their skills to assist emancipated slaves to become educated and independent citizens. The Crafts, for example, established a school near Savannah for African Americans who had been freed from slavery.[73] Thus, they continued to partake in the march of black Americans toward freedom, citizenship, and equality. Remond, instead, remained in Europe.

Almost immediately upon her arrival in England, Remond became influential in gender and race emancipation, and she took action to instigate the formation of new antislavery societies. In February 1859, the *Derbyshire Times* and *Chesterfield Herald* of Derbyshire informed that "there has been an Anti-Slavery Society established at Warrington, at the instance of a Miss P. Remond, a coloured lady of great powers of speech, who lately arrived from America, and has addressed crowded meetings in Liverpool and Warrington, on the subject of Slavery. We believe the lady intends to make a tour of this country in order to arouse public opinion on behalf of the negro. We heartily wish her success, and trust that the movement commenced at Warrington will be extended to every town in the kingdom."[74] The reception of Remond, hailed as "the lady of great powers of speech," was remarkably positive, and England's progressive citizens applauded her initiatives, hoping that the antislavery movement would expand to cover "every town in the kingdom."

Remond's activism matured during the years she worked in England. She took possession and control of highly public, international, transatlantic, and transnational spheres in her role as a public speaker and as a founder and executive board member of leading London activist societies. As a pioneering, independent New Woman who developed and realized her potential, both in her private life and careers, she daringly trespassed the period's limiting racial and gender assumptions. In Europe she fully expressed her talent and reassessed her identity by assuming a significant role as an agent for racial and gender liberation, equality, and justice.

CHAPTER 4

Advocate for Racial and Gender Emancipation

SARAH REMOND'S INTENSE LECTURE TOUR STARTED ALMOST immediately upon her arrival in England, toward the end of January, with the first lecture scheduled in Liverpool on 21 January 1859.[1] The *Liverpool Mercury* and *Liverpool Daily Post* both reported on the event, which attracted such a large audience that members of the local elite complained about the lack of available seats. Many British newspapers as well as the American press, including William Lloyd Garrison's the *Liberator,* and Frederick Douglass's *Frederick Douglass' Paper*—the successor of his *North Star*—followed Remond's overseas success. Her reputation as a powerful speaker guaranteed overflowing audiences.

Remond's second talk, "Slave Life in America," was organized for Monday evening, 24 January 1859, and it took place at the local music hall. Similarly to the first speaking engagement, the second lecture generated such excitement that all the seats and standing room were quickly exhausted. The *Warrington Times* reported on 29 January that the music hall had never been so packed before. The newspaper praised Remond as "one of the best female lecturers" they had heard. The audience had been captivated by "her gentle and easy manner, combined with an animated and intelligent countenance."[2]

Newspapers underscored her conventional womanly attributes and ladylike behavior, thus negotiating Remond's position as a black woman speaking in public, a sensational novelty. As a consequence of such taming of her public persona, Remond was able to introduce such radical topics as the rape of black women into her speeches.

Remond gave a one-and-a-half hour talk during which she informed her enthusiastic listeners about corrupt American politics and the even more severe corruption of American churches, and she denounced discrimination of free blacks in northern cities like Boston where local transportation and hotels refused black men and women and where despotism crushed their intellect. She talked about the suffering of slave mothers and the pitiable condition of slave women unable to protect themselves from the licentiousness of slave owners. "What is slavery?" Remond rhetorically asked her receptive audience. In her reply she boldly introduced the subject of sexual exploitation, a shocking topic that generally was considered taboo and was avoided by other speakers. As Remond explained, "In the open market place women are exposed for sale—their persons not always covered. . . . They are exposed for sale, and subjected to the most shameful indignities. The more Anglo-Saxon blood that mingles with the blood of the slave, the more gold is poured out when the auctioneer has a woman for sale, because they are sold to be concubines for white Americans. They are not sold for plantation slaves."[3] Fearless of criticism or of shocking her audience, Remond addressed the sensitive topic of sexual abuse and left no doubts in the minds of the listeners about the nature of the treatment that a light-skinned slave woman might expect or how common it was in the American South to purchase women as concubines. She drew attention to the illegitimate racial mixing that stemmed from violence.

Remond informed her audience of black prejudice, how Americans treated black men and women as if they were criminals for no other reason than the color of their complexion. In her articulate speech, which demonstrated her rhetorical skills and education, she cited William Shakespeare's *The Merchant of Venice* so as to reinforce her message with illustrative literary examples. Furthermore, she drew on British-American antagonism by praising England for the noble action of abolishing slavery; she expressed her moral indignation by arguing against American despotism, winning further support from her listeners.[4] She, like other black orators, worded her speech so as to embarrass the United States in the eyes of what American nationalists perceived as an influential competitor. In this way, she joined other black lecturers who argued that slavery "should concern all moral men irrespective of their nationality."[5] The audience responded with enthusiastic cheering.

The success of her talk led to another speaking engagement scheduled for Monday evening, 31 January 1859. Another lecture followed immediately after, on 2 February at noon at the Red Lion Hotel where she addressed an audience chiefly of women. By then Remond was quite fatigued and unwell after the intense and powerful speaking engagements that had followed right after her long and tiring transatlantic crossing. On the fourth occasion, she spoke briefly about the 800,000 "mulattoes" living in the southern states, of mixed-race slaves who stood as evidence of the sexual exploitation of female slaves by white masters leading to legally prohibited racial mixing. "Sexual abuse of enslaved women," the literary historian P. Gabrielle Foreman affirms, "was neither visible to the law nor did it elicit public stigma for its perpetuators."[6] Therefore, Remond's talk, which brought attention to the topic when other sources (newspapers and other abolitionist speakers) preferred to ignore it, was a radical move toward raising awareness and triggering a change. Remond read excerpts from books, including a graphic description of the sale of a young slave, an educated and religious girl with high moral principles. By presenting the girl with highly admired attributes and virtues to which her Victorian audience could relate, Remond made her sale a more pronounced scandal to the white audience.

After the conclusion of the speech, a Mrs. Ashton of Warrington expressed her pride in acknowledging Remond as a sister. She then presented Remond with a watch that had the following inscription: "Presented to S. P. Remond by Englishwomen, her sisters, in Warrington, February 2nd, 1859."[7] Remond was quite surprised by the unexpected kindness the English women showed her and felt emotional when gratefully receiving the gift.[8]

In her reply, Remond said how she felt welcomed and accepted; she acknowledged the absence of color prejudice that permitted her entrance to an otherwise white sisterhood and allowed her to do so as a representative of her race: "I have been received here as a sister by white women for the first time in my life. I have been removed from the degradation which overhangs all persons of my complexion. . . . I have received a sympathy I never was offered before. I had therefore no need of this testimonial of sympathy, but I receive it as the representative of my race with pleasure. In this spirit I accept it, and I believe I shall be faithful to that race now and for ever."[9] Indeed, in several instances Remond expressed her pride in her ethnicity and roots, never a desire to renounce her race.

Remond forged ahead boldly speaking on behalf of her people. Her appearance in Warrington inspired the audience to collect one hundred dollars for the American Anti-Slavery Society and to prepare an address to the United States citizens, which was signed by 3,522 citizens of the town.[10] The *Warrington Standard* quoted Remond as saying that "for the first time in her life had she been removed from the pressure there always was upon people of colour in America; and every hour she had spent in England had been happiness to her, for she had felt none of that objection to her which existed in the United States because of her race."[11] Unlike others, who according to Paul Gilroy had a desire "to escape the restrictive bonds of ethnicity, national identification, and sometimes even 'race' itself," Remond experienced a rebirth in Europe as a black woman whose racial identity was fully accepted.[12]

In addition, despite the prejudice of which she had been a target, Remond considered herself American, as she explained in one of her lectures: "*Miss Remond* said she was not there to speak of America in disparaging terms, because she was herself an American born upon its soil, in the free State of Massachusetts."[13] Although she insisted on her American identity, she chose expatriation and what eventually became a permanent renunciation of the United States as her home. In Europe, the sense of freedom that greeted her enhanced her self-esteem, encouraged her to pursue her dreams, and created new hopes for the future progress of black Americans.

With great determination Remond continued speaking in front of receptive audiences. In March she was lecturing in Dublin, where in one of her talks she made references to *Uncle Tom's Cabin.* According to a Dublin paper, she personally knew Harriet Beecher Stowe:

> A crowded and influential meeting of the Dublin Ladies' Anti-slavery Association was held on Friday evening in the concert room of the Rotundo for the purpose of hearing delivered a lecture, or rather, as it proved, an able, eloquent, and comprehensive address, on the subject of the slave system in the American states by Miss S. P. Remond, a lady of colour, a native of Salem, Massachusetts, and a particular friend of Mrs. Beecher Stowe, the popular authoress of "Uncle Tom's Cabin." . . . She said she would not that evening enter on any descriptions of the revolting horrors, outrages and cruelties perpetrated every day under the abominable slave system; but she solemnly asserted that there were to be found throughout all the slave holding states numbers of characters, incidents and examples exactly similar to those portrayed in Mrs. Beecher Stowe's admirable book (hear, hear and cheers).[14]

However, at a later speech in January 1861, Remond argued that "Mrs Stowe's descriptions of slavery had only skimmed the surface of the evil; no pen had ever fully disclosed, and never could reveal the depths of that horrid system."[15] With their immense popularity, the antislavery novels and fugitive slave narratives circulating in Europe contributed to abolitionist propaganda. One of the most famous of them was, as expected, Stowe's story of Uncle Tom, published in 1852.

As a celebrated authoress, Stowe had toured in England first in 1853, when she stayed with Elisabeth Reid, who hosted Remond in 1860. Remond and Stowe may have met in England because Remond had written to Maria Weston Chapman from Warrington on 6 October 1859, asking for Stowe's address, "as I should like to see her," Remond wrote, "when she is in London."[16] It seems, then, that Remond knew Stowe but perhaps not well enough to contact her directly.

Remond seems to have been nearly as popular as Stowe. At the meeting in Dublin, as in many others, she was greeted with loud applause. Newspapers lengthily reported on her talks and the reception she received, carefully presenting her as a respectable woman: "Miss S. P. Redmond [*sic*], whose appearance at the table in the front of the platform was hailed with loud and repeated plaudits. Miss Redmond, whose appearance is remarkably feminine and graceful, coupled with a quiet, dignified manner, a well-toned voice and pleasing style of enunciation, proceeded to address the meeting."[17] Newspaper reports, in other words, underscored Remond's femininity, presenting her with attributes associated with the period's (white) ideal womanhood and thus disaggregating her from demeaning stereotypes created of black women. The scholar Carla Peterson argues that black women "sought to reject the dominant culture's vision of the black woman as grotesque and to ground their authority in middle-class respectability."[18] However, it was the Dublin paper that assured the readers of Remond's propriety, presenting her as graceful and dignified. Eager to appease the anxieties of many Victorians, who were unaccustomed to a black woman speaker, the newspaper neutralized Remond, whose presence in the lecture circuit was startling.

Black women who lectured publicly, as Peterson notes, were never entirely relieved "of the necessity of mediating the boundaries between masculine and feminine codes of behavior and in particular of negotiating the public exposure of the black female body."[19] Since Remond's presence on the platform distanced her from the dominant ideology of separate spheres that anchored women in domestic interiors and linked them with the home and family, newspapers and the general public were eager to domesticate her.[20] Presenting Remond as an embodiment of Victorian womanhood—feminine, graceful, quiet, and dignified—had a positive effect on British audiences, calming their anxieties concerning a female speaker who with her public appearances otherwise would have defied their conceptualization of proper womanhood. Ultimately, the presence of a black female lecturer on the platform intrigued many who came to hear the eloquent talks.

More conventional abolitionists were less welcoming toward a woman lecturer, especially one as bold as Remond. At a meeting in commemoration of the twenty-fifth anniversary of West India emancipation in London in August 1859, Remond was excluded from the platform because some of the organizers feared that "it might raise the much-vexed question of Woman's Rights." Lord Henry Peter Brougham, it seems, did not approve of women speaking at public meetings, and some "gentlewomen" disliked a woman "who earns her living."[21] Hence, similarly to conservative

Americans, the more conventionally thinking British resisted the advancement of progressive women. It was essential, then, to present Remond as reflecting traditional ideas constructed of women. Other British activists admired Remond for her courageous work as an abolitionist and they enjoyed her clever talks aimed at an intelligent and informed audience.

One of the Dublin antislavery leaders, Richard D. Webb, praised Remond as "really very clever—the most so of all the coloured people I ever met, except Douglass & [she] is a very much more sensible & thoroughgoing person than he." Webb, furthermore, identified her as the most powerful antislavery advocate after Wendell Phillips: "She has more common sense—& her devotion to the cause & its friends is thorough. We like her very much."[22] Another source recognized her as "one of the best female lecturers we have heard; her gentle and easy manner, combined with an animated and intelligent countenance, rivets the attention of her auditors." The article concluded that "this lady was a person of no ordinary character."[23] She had "a clear, musical voice," another article observed, "a distinct utterance, and—if it be not a needless remark of a lady—we may add she has at her command a great flow of language, for she speaks without any assistance from notes, and is never at a loss for words admirably calculated to express her sentiments."[24] In addition to appearing graceful, feminine, and devoted, Remond was recognized as intelligent, professional, and competent. She was hailed as an exceptional woman and hence she offered a new model of black womanhood.

Remond became close with the elite leaders in the racially tolerant British activist communities and made many friends among the British, both men and women, with whom she fought for the rights of the oppressed. She spoke powerfully to antislavery audiences and ladies' groups alike; she had speaking engagements at the Dublin Ladies' Anti-Slavery Society and the Edinburgh Ladies' Emancipation Society. Her talks appealed to all social classes; she and other black orators were lionized by the upper classes and well received by working-class audiences because "they symbolized successful resistance to oppression."[25] However, although England's poor wished to foreground similarities between their situation and that of slaves, black American speakers emphasized that slavery was the worst form of oppression, not comparable to the situation of the British working class. Likewise, Remond's impressive talks attracted many prominent people in Great Britain—lords, mayors, and members of Parliament—with whom she formed lasting friendships and worked together to realize social change.

In her talks, which contributed to such change, Remond boldly exposed the misery of slaves and revealed the cruel abuses of which they were victims. At the Dublin Ladies' Anti-slavery Association, she

> stood before that enlightened assemblage [as] the representative of four millions of men and women, robbed of every right, deprived of every privilege—a race of outraged and injured fellow-beings, whose wrongs should command the deepest sympathy. . . . She showed that over thirty millions of people, who ought to desire, not only to be free themselves, but that mankind should be free, were held in subjection by the influence of about one hundred and thirty-four thousand tyrants who uphold this vile system (hear, hear). . . . She quoted a thrilling passage from a recently-published work, describing the sale, by public auction, of a beautiful white woman, yet a slave—her accomplishments, nay, her very religious and Christian virtues, subserving the purpose of the auctioneer to enhance the price in dollars of this human chattel. Miss Remond, after drawing a fearful picture of the sufferings of helpless women in slavery, concluded her long and able address by a powerful appeal on behalf of a cause the noblest in which human energies could be engaged—the abolition of the hateful system by which man can buy and sell, enslave and degrade, his fellow-creatures. Miss Remond sat down amidst loud and enthusiastic applause.[26]

Remond's strategic introduction of the "white slave" relied on the premise that the "mulatta," as Foreman suggests, was "often seen as the most *affective* figure through which to move whites to recognize Black sentience and humanity."[27] In addition, the white slave in Remond's talk embraced Victorian values: pious religious virtues.

In her speech, Remond dwelt on the mission of Great Britain in overthrowing slavery, and demonstrated how the nation's aid would reflect "the spirit of true liberty."[28] After her speech the following evening, a local Irish gentleman who had long resided in the United States gave his testimony, confirming the truth of everything Remond had said. Hence, her talk was "authenticated" by a white man whose credibility and authority the audience accepted without hesitation or doubts.

Remond's success in England was immediate. In London she addressed several meetings before arriving in Manchester where she spoke with her American friend Samuel J. May at Manchester's Athenaeum on Wednesday evening, 14 September 1859. She spoke about the differences between the American North and South before introducing the topic of slavery. "The slaves are essentially *things,*" she said, "with no rights, political, social, domestic, or religious: the absolute victims of all but irresponsible power." Appealing to women for support, she reported that "women are the worst victims of the slave power." "Give us the power of your public opinion," she pleaded, "it has great weight in America. . . . Aid us thus until the shackles of the American slave melt like dew before the morning sun."[29] In her talk "Why Slavery Is Still Rampant," she asserted that "eight hundred thousand mulattoes, nine-tenths of whom are the children of white fathers" were constantly sold by their parents in the southern states.[30] Remond's choice to talk about white-looking female slaves and her rhetoric were conscious political acts. Her participation in discourses of equality and democracy meant that she directly contributed to social change. Her discursive talents, eloquence, presence on the platform, and capacity for persuasiveness were apparent in all her lectures, which were bold, powerful, and popular.

Remond contributed to the British antislavery crusade's goal to create the widest possible coalition against American slavery. During 1859 and 1860 she spoke to crowded audiences in Liverpool, Warrington, Manchester, Leeds, Bristol, and London, in addition to lecturing in Scotland and Ireland. In January 1860, the *Huddersfield Chronicle* reported that Remond, "a coloured lady from Boston, U.S.," had lectured in various cities with success, and her language "is said to be exceedingly impressive and delightful, and crowded meetings have welcomed her wherever she has stood up to advocate the interests of her oppressed people."[31] On Thursday, 24 January 1861, "Miss Remond, coloured lady from America," delivered a lecture on slavery in Birmingham, and she continued speaking in front of audiences through 1865.[32]

Remond's lectures, which covered topics ranging from abolitionism to moral reform, demonstrated her intelligence, testified to her education, and exposed the wide range of her concerns. She spoke of temperance for the first time at the first annual soirée of the Leeds Temperance Union, held on 26 December 1859, with more than a thousand people attending. The organizers had also hoped to engage Douglass for the event but failed. After tea, Remond addressed the audience, stating that she "took deep interest in this reform" and firmly believed that society was "just what woman made it."[33] Since financial collaboration was a significant form of the transatlantic antislavery movement, she was involved in fundraising efforts organized almost exclusively by women. She emphasized the role of women, arguing that they were the ones to pave the way, citing as an example the noble Florence Nightingale.[34] During her extended tour in Britain, Remond repeatedly returned to the topic of temperance and women's role in the movement: she delivered a lecture on "Total Abstinence" to the Total Abstinence Society in 1861, urging the importance and suitability of women for temperance reform activities.[35] With such arguments, she promoted gender empowerment, which often overlapped with her agenda on racial progress.

Remond repeatedly appealed to British women and underscored the importance of international collaboration. She predicted that the question of slavery, which was also economic and political, would culminate in a forceful crisis, perhaps leading to a war. In January 1861, when addressing an audience gathered in the Temperance Hall of Birmingham, according to local newspapers,

> [Remond] left the slave-mongers without a shred of right or reason on which to support their practices. She then gave a description of the state of society throughout America; showed how slavery was interwoven with the interests of every class; and pointed out the almost utter hopelessness of affecting the abolition of slavery by any home influence, other than by the fearful crisis that must come one day, if, indeed, it had not come already. . . . That the agitation would not decrease, that the matter would not be compromised, that the dislocation of the States would be completed she earnestly desired.[36]

Remond was a politically informed speaker with keen analytical skills and insight. She spoke of northern racism in terms of depriving free blacks of their social and political rights, of northerners' discrimination against blacks in education, housing, and transportation. She also talked against colonization, stating that "there is nothing the free colored people of the United States hate like colonization in the concrete. They are attached to their homes and their country; for America not Africa is their country."[37] With such statements she encouraged white Americans to accept an American black population who, Remond pointed out, belonged to the United States, who deserved equal treatment, and who had no intention of leaving. Her statements foregrounded powerful nineteenth-century tenets: family and patriotism.

In her lectures, Remond addressed women as wives and mothers, evoking empathetic reactions from them when talking about the degradation of black women in slavery. Her speeches rested on female solidarity, shared motherhood, and womanly empathy. She appealed to women when talking of Margaret Garner, a sexually abused escaped slave who chose to kill her daughter rather than have her return to slavery. Garner was a twenty-two-year-old Kentucky slave who was captured in Cincinnati in 1856.[38] The episode was discussed in contemporary newspapers that offered contradictory information of the events, however, because the incident was manipulated for political interests.

As Gilroy has noted, the reports of the episode involving Garner's escape and the killing of her daughter were "burdened with the conflicting political interests that framed its central strategy."[39] Abolitionists instrumentalized the sensational, touching, yet terrible case of Garner to enlist sympathies. They capitalized on a mother's supreme sacrifice, the killing of her child, which became a topic for newspaper reports, editorials, and pamphlets. The mother's misery became part of speeches delivered by Frederick Douglass, Theodore Parker, and Lucy Stone; the latter was an abolitionist and women's rights advocate who personally visited Garner in prison.[40] In their attempts to destroy slavery, abolitionists appropriated the slave mother's personal suffering; Garner's story served for moral critique of slavery. She was transformed into a political heroine and idealized as a woman who valued freedom more than life itself. Her story was presented as a tragedy; through a mother's desperate act to save her child, it evoked domesticity, a central tenet in nineteenth-century Anglo-American value system. Abolitionists and feminists, moreover, used for their own political agendas the sexual violation Garner's daughter would probably have been destined to face had her mother not acted to change the course of her destiny.[41] In addition, the historian Mark Reinhardt argues that, paradoxically, "slave suffering was, for a certain kind of consumer at least, a source of pleasure."[42] The dramatic events appealed to an audience whose entertainment consisted of melodrama and sentimental literature. Garner's tragic story triggered a particularly charged emotional response in the lecture halls.

In 1865, Remond, who capitalized on the audiences' craving for sensationalism, continued to attract attention despite the decline of British interest in racial activism. She collected money to assist slaves in their newly acquired freedom, as reported in the *Islington Gazette* of London on 16 June 1865: "Miss Remond, who has frequently delivered lectures in the metropolis on the slavery question, drew a touching picture of the present state of the coloured population in the Southern States, and earnestly appealed for contributions to the American Freedmen's Relief Association, in order to support her coloured brethren until agricultural operations shall once more be resumed. Miss Remond expressed great confidence in the future of the coloured race, and that they would properly appreciate and rightly use their newly-acquired freedom." After the Civil War, Remond continued to promote the cause of black freedom and progress. By then, however, British interest had waned, and her lectures were less popular than some years earlier. According to the newspaper, the meeting was only "tolerably well attended."[43]

In addition to her protest through lectures, Remond was involved in an incident concerning citizenship that captured the attention of journalists on both sides of the Atlantic. In November 1859, she applied for a visa that would allow her to travel to France with her sister Caroline Putnam, who spent much of her time in Europe after her husband had passed away in January 1859; Caroline's daughter Louisa Victoria had died in May 1858. The assistant secretary of the U.S. legation, Benjamin Moran, however, denied Remond's request on the grounds that she was "a person of color." He was convinced that Remond had obtained her passport—which was issued by the State Department on 10 September 1858, carrying the signature of Secretary of State Lewis Cass—through deception.[44]

In his journal, Moran recorded that on Tuesday, 22 November 1859, he had a visit from "two negresses, one of whom had a State Department Passport, which she asked me to visé." He refused to comply because he was convinced there was fraud involved; the passport described Remond without explicitly stating that she was African American. It merely described her as: "Age 32—Stature 5 feet ½ in—Forehead, high—Eyes—black—Nose straight—Mouth, full, chin, not prominent—Hair, dark, Complexion, dark—Face, thin. . . . Had she *sent* the document, I should have viséd it," Moran wrote. But since she came in person, he was able to recognize that Remond was "a dark mulatto with woolly hair." What he called a deception "practiced on the State Dep't.," he wrote in his journal, "was by calling her hair and complexion *dark*."[45] Interestingly, according to his reasoning, dark complexion did not automatically mean that the person in question was African American.

According to Moran, Remond had come to his office in person only to provoke the U.S. representative. As he wrote, she "evidently expected a refusal, and was so impudent" that he "had to order her out of the house." But Remond and her sister, who were experienced in challenging discrimination, were determined to insist on their rights to be considered American citizens. The following Monday a certain Mr. Fuller came to see Moran to ask "for a passport for Mrs. Caroline R. Putnam, aged 33, a native of Salem, Mass." Fuller "alleged that she could not come on account of illness." Moran, who realized that he had met the woman mentioned, asked if she "had African blood in her." The answer was positive, but Fuller "swore point plank that she was an American Citizen."[46]

By drawing attention to the incident, Remond raised important questions about the definition of citizenship and how the associated rights were distributed. As an African American she was excluded from officially having citizenship and hence, Moran was right in pointing out that it was impossible for her to have an American passport. And yet, Remond had assumed the duties and responsibilities expected of Americans, had paid taxes, and had contributed to the progress of her nation. Moreover, she had received a document that replaced a formal passport, which officially served to carry the function of it, testifying that she was American and should be allowed to travel freely. As Remond wished to demonstrate, nineteenth-century African American national belonging and the question of citizenship were controversial issues.

Remond insisted on having a visa issued, transforming the situation from an individual experience to a collective one. Newspapers wrote heated articles about the denial of her rights as an American citizen because of the color of her complexion. While British newspapers supported Remond in her demand that her rights be recognized, southern newspapers in the United States, such as the *New Orleans Daily Crescent,* were more critical, finding her behavior "not very lady-like." Her claim to be an American citizen, the newspaper observed, was "contrary to fact, the decision in the Dred Scott case having left no doubt upon that point." Claiming that Remond had tried to deceive the American representative in London, the New Orleans paper insisted that "free persons of color are not citizens of the United States."[47]

The British, instead, were scandalized by the discrimination. Remond publicized the incident through letters to the editors of the Edinburgh *Scottish Press,* London *Morning Star,* and London *Inquirer,* among others.[48] Many British newspapers reprinted the entire correspondence between Remond and Moran, while others such as the *Daily News* and the *New York Times* wrote of the episode. The "refusal to visé the passport of the negress" and the legation's "incivility" to Remond by "refusing to recognize negroes as citizens" fell "like a bomb-shell" on Moran. The legation received a letter from Remond to which Moran responded, only to learn that "Miss Sarah P. Remond" had replied "insolently, saying to Mr. D[allas] she did not expect such an answer from one whose salary she contributes to pay. This is vulgar ignorance," Moran wrote in his journal.[49]

A few months later, in January 1860, Moran was still involved in the matter. As he mused, "Miss Sarah P. Remond, the negress who has made herself so conspicuous of late about my refusal to visé her passport, has published a garbled and mutilated report of her correspondence on the subject with this Legation in the Daily News of to-day. A more flagrant attempt to get up sympathy on false pretences never was tried by anyone."[50] As is evident, he continued to accuse Remond of misrepresentation and refused to consider that his reaction might have been an indication of his own racism. The following morning nearly all the daily journals printed Remond's correspondence "in its garbled form."

The Bristol *Western Daily Press* ran an article entitled "Disabilities of American Persons of Colour" with the correspondence between Remond and Moran on 7 January 1860; "An American Lady of Colour in a Strange Position" appeared in the *Belfast Morning News* of Antrim, Northern Ireland, on 11 January 1860 (page 4) including the same correspondence, and again on 12 January 1860 on page 4. The news were also posted in the London *Morning Chronicle* (9 January 1860) and West Yorkshire *Leeds Intelligencer* (14 January 1860); yet another newspaper, the Buckinghamshire *Bucks Herald* published the letters ironically under the title "American Freedom" on Saturday, 14 January 1860, on page 7; and they appeared in the *Lancaster Gazette* on Saturday, 14 January 1860, under the heading "The Land of Liberty":

> A correspondence of a somewhat extraordinary character has just been made public. Miss Sarah P. Remond, a freeborn American lady, recently arrived in this country, furnished with a passport (dated 1858) from Secretary Cass, requiring, in the usual form, "all whom it may concern, to permit safely and freely to pass Sarah P. Remond, a citizen of the United States, and in case of need to give her all lawful aid and protection." Miss Remond, it appears, wished to proceed from London to Paris, a short time ago, and applied to Mr. Dallas, the American Minister, to have her pastport vised for France. She received the following reply:—
>
> Miss Sarah Remond,—I am directed by the minister to acknowledge the receipt of your note of the 12th instant, and to say in reply, he must, of course, be sorry if any of his countrywomen, irrespective of colour or extraction, should think him frivolously disposed to withhold from them facilities in his power to grant for travelling on the continent of Europe, but when the indispensable qualification for an American passport, that of "United States Citizenship," does not exist; when, indeed, it is manifestly an impossibility by law that it should exist, a just sense of his official obligations under instructions received from his government as long ago as the 8th July, 1856, and since then strictly conformed to, constrains him to say that the demand of Miss Sarah P. Remond cannot be complied with.—Respectfully your obedient servant,
>
> BENJ. MORAN, Assistant Sec. of Legation.

The letter was followed by Remond's reply, which argued:

> Miss Remond replies:—
>
> The purport of your communication is most extraordinary. You now lay down the rule that persons free-born in the United States, and who have been subjected all their lives to the taxation and other burdens imposed upon American citizens, are to be deprived of their rights as such, merely because their complexions happen to be dark, and that they are to be refused the aid of the ministers of their country, whose salaries they contribute to pay.[51]

The newspapers referred to Remond as a "lady" who had been furnished with a passport, testifying to her right to American citizenship. The British used such publicity once again to embarrass the United States. It is worth noting how in her own testimony of the incident, Remond's tone was forceful and relentless. It is evident how Moran could have deemed her reply impertinent, especially in light of prejudice and considering it was written by a black woman.

To further inflame the controversy, some newspapers, such as the *Bucks Herald,* poured more fuel on the fire by including the original document that had served as Remond's passport: "Passport.—I, the undesigned [*sic*] Secretary of State of the United States of America hereby request all whom it may concern to permit safely and freely to pass Sarah P. Remond, a citizen of the United States, and in case of need to give her all lawful aid and protection." It was dated "the 10th day of September, A.D. 1858, in the 83rd year of the Independence of these United States" and signed by Lewis Cass, Department of State.[52] It clearly stated that it was a passport whose function was to protect its holder, an American citizen.

The publicity Remond's case received made Moran afraid that the news would reach even the queen at Buckingham Palace. As he wrote on 25 February 1860: "On this subject of darkies, I am reminded that the Queen looked at me very scrutinisingly on Thursday, & I now suspect the Remond affair was dancing about in her mind, and that she wished to know what kind of person (if she thought of the matter at all) the Secretary was that refused that lady of color a visé."[53] As the *New York Times* concluded in "The Question of Passports," published on 25 January 1860,

> Once admitted to France, to which Miss REMOND wants to go, she will not need our protection or Gen. CASS' passport. She can enjoy, as can the meanest of her race, while walking the Boulevards, a sensation with which even full-grown white men on this side of the Atlantic are not very familiar—the consciousness that every hair of her head is under the protection of an efficient police, of upright courts and of a powerful army; and that, let but the smallest of her rights be invaded, she can put the whole machinery of the State in motion, if necessary, to secure her redress.

The passage contrasts the racist behavior of the American representative with the presumed protection people in France were guaranteed regardless of their race by social authorities. The newspaper, furthermore, announced that Remond had the right to protest should she meet with any action that could be considered in violation of her liberties. Still, toward the end of January 1860, the *New York Times* published articles that described the incident and brought attention to the ambiguous condition of free African Americans under prevailing national laws.[54] The articles also demanded a change in U.S. passport regulations, which would have meant a step forward in recognizing black residents as Americans and a move toward granting them full citizenship.

The confusion about Remond's status was a result of laws that positioned free blacks somewhere between aliens and citizens. The historian Leon F. Litwack explains that "the federal government and the individual states separately defined the legal status of ante-bellum free Negroes. Prior to the Fourteenth and Fifteenth amendments, each state determined their political and educational rights."[55] This meant that states could grant them citizenship, which, however, was not recognized on a federal level. Therefore, it was difficult for black Americans to obtain documents that would attest to their national citizenship. In the 1840s and 1850s, the U.S. State Department rejected many passport applications from blacks planning to travel to Britain to lecture and raise money for their antislavery cause. Some, however, such as William Wells Brown in 1849 and John Remond in 1854, were successful in obtaining a passport or its substitute, a certificate attesting that they were born in the United States, were free, and were under the protection of the government. Sarah Remond had received a similar document, which served as her passport, when she traveled to England in 1858.

It was not until Reconstruction that Congress granted some, though still limited, rights to all black Americans, most importantly in the Civil Rights Act of 1866. Two years later, the Fourteenth Amendment to the U.S. Constitution sought to clarify the issue once and for all: it declared that all people born in the United States were entitled to the full rights of citizenship without regard to race.[56] Before then, as Remond's case demonstrates, the conceptualization of national identity and rights of African Americans were ill-defined. Obviously, as history demonstrates, they continued to be so even after the Fourteenth Amendment and Reconstruction, which were unsuccessful attempts to eliminate racial discrimination in the United States.

Remond, however, was not alone in her insistence on the recognition of her rights to American citizenship. Douglass was another black American "in pursuit of the recognition of his and other African Americans' claim to U.S. citizenship, and by extension equality."[57] Decades later, W. E. B. Du Bois obtained fame for developing his influential concept of "double consciousness," that is, being black and American. He became well-known for his prophesy that the color line would be among the biggest problems of modern times.[58] Remond, however, was among the early protesters who raised the question of black rights to full American citizenship. According to the annual report of the American Anti-Slavery Society, Remond "subsequently obtained a passport from the British Foreign Secretary, who had not learned that a shade on the complexion is a forfeiture of human rights."[59]

Upon her return to England from France, Remond continued her pursuit of the same rights to which white women were entitled. She had made plans to continue her studies when she was in Warrington, as she wrote to Maria Chapman in October 1859: "On the 12th of this month I go to London, to attend the lectures at the Ladie's College. I shall on every occasion that I can still continue to lecture and do all I can for our cause."[60] In addition to her public speeches, Remond represented the cause in private circles. The *National Anti-Slavery Standard* reported that her heart was "quite set on continuing her present anti-slavery efforts amongst us, and accepting invitations to different towns which she had to decline until her College term had expired."[61] Remond had enrolled in Bedford College in London whose founder, Elisabeth Jesser Reid, was an English feminist, wealthy philanthropist, and ardent supporter of the antislavery cause. She was a relative of Mary Ann Estlin and a friend of Harriet Martineau, Harriet Beecher Stowe, and the influential Victorian suffragist, essayist, journalist, and social reformer Frances Power Cobbe.[62]

As the college records indicate, during the two years Remond studied there from October 1859 to June 1861, her courses covered such topics as ancient and modern history, English literature, French, Latin, elocution, vocal music, mathematics, and geography. In her first year she started a systematic course of study, covering between five and seven subjects that were necessary for obtaining a degree as stipulated by the Committee of Education. During her second year, however, she was attending classes only in modern history, English literature, and French. She probably lacked proper preparation and time for continuing to study Latin, mathematics, and music, all courses she took for just one term. A handwritten note in the college register states that "these classes were found to be quite unsuitable owing to the peculiar circumstances & age of the student."[63] For the second academic year, then, Remond studied subjects that interested and were useful to her in providing a cultural background, rather than choosing topics geared toward obtaining any particular degree. During her time at the college, Remond lived in Reid's house on 6 Grenville Street, known as "The Home." Reid had turned it into a boardinghouse for students attending lectures at Bedford College.

Many of the professors who taught at Bedford also held positions at the University College London, which, similarly to Bedford, was nonsectarian. Reid herself was a fervent abolitionist, as her correspondence testifies, and she was closely connected with American antislavery activism. She read the *Liberator* and worked as a London agent for antislavery bazaars in America. She also followed the situation in Italy, exchanged letters with Giuseppe Mazzini, and was invited to see Giuseppe Garibaldi.[64] Moreover, Reid believed that women should be entitled to scientific education, and in

1859, when Dr. Elizabeth Blackwell was in England, Reid contemplated the founding of a hospital and a college for female physicians and female patients.[65] In a similar vein, many early students at her college campaigned for women's suffrage, educational rights, and women's property rights. Among them was Remond, who stayed in touch with Reid after her graduation, as noted in a letter to Reid from a former student, Florence Kelly, dated 16 August 1864: "Of course I remember Miss Remond," Kelly wrote from South Africa, "please give her my very best love when you see her. I am so glad she is comfortably situated."[66] The extended stay in England provided Remond with opportunities to obtain education and connect with other women who shared some of her same goals and ambitions.

While in London studying, Remond continued publicly voicing her convictions concerning black liberation and lecturing on behalf of her race even after her graduation. In an address in London in 1862 before the International Congress of Charities, Correction and Philanthropy, she pledged for the support of the people of Great Britain to maintain "their position as the friend of the oppressed negro."[67] In her talk, she delineated the history of slavery in the United States and concluded her speech with a statement about the lack of opportunity and the potential she saw as still dormant in members of "this deeply injured race":

> The real capacities of the negro race have never been thoroughly tested; and until they are placed in a position to be influenced by the civilizing influences which surround freemen, it is really unjust to apply to them the same test, or to expect them to attain the same standard of excellence, as if a fair opportunity had been given to develop their faculties. With all the demoralizing influences by which they are surrounded, they still retain far more of that which is humanizing than their masters. No such acts of cruelty have ever emanated from the victims of slavery in the Southern states as have been again and again practiced by their masters.[68]

Remond emphasized the injustice of existing laws, which hindered African Americans from obtaining education and realizing their potential. She underscored her view that equality of the races could only be accomplished if both whites and blacks were given the same rights and opportunities for study.

Remond's studies at an institution of higher education in London and contacts with British activists pursuing the goals of gender and racial emancipation enhanced her self-conception and increased her responsibilities and visibility within organized movements. She formed friendships and alliances with prominent leaders. In 1859, when she was "an inmate" with the Crafts near London, Lord Brougham came to visit her: "Of the thousands of white ladies who annually cross the Atlantic to see the 'lions' of the old world, very few indeed on their return can boast of having had such an interview with such a man," wrote the *London Anti-Slavery Adverts* (subsequently quoted in the *Liberator*). During part of her stay in Bristol, she was the guest of an eminent philanthropist, Mary Carpenter and stayed with Cobbe, who originally came from Dublin.[69]

Cobbe worked ceaselessly for workhouse reform and to improve women's legal status and opportunities for higher education. She was well-connected with women activists and reformers across the Atlantic but also associated with Americans living in Italy. She often visited Florence where she became friends with the poet Elizabeth Barrett Browning, the English novelist Isa Blagden, the famous orator Theodore Parker, and she even met Stowe there.[70] In Rome she befriended the American sculptress Harriet Hosmer and actress Charlotte Cushman, who both supported abolitionism and the Italian Risorgimento. Hosmer, Cushman, and Cobbe were all representatives of the progressive and radical New Woman figure that gained force starting from the mid-nineteenth century. Through Cobbe, Remond connected with Italy, which already was familiar to her through such literary works as Barrett Browning's "Casa Guidi Windows," which discussed Italy's Risorgimento.

Remond met Cobbe again when she was in Dublin attending the National Association for the Promotion of Social Science (NAPSS) meeting of early feminist activists in August 1861. One of the recurring subjects at NAPSS conferences was the after-care of workhouse girls.[71] Among the papers that were presented at the Dublin meeting, according to a *New York Times* report, was that of "Miss SARAH REMOND," who "read a paper on 'American Slavery, and its influence on Great Britain.' "[72] In addition, the issues discussed at the conference included women's education and medical reform, topics that would become increasingly important in the collective feminist discourse but also to Remond personally.

In London, Remond became further involved in racial and gender liberation, first as a member of the London Emancipation Committee, then by becoming an active member in the executive committee of the Ladies' London Emancipation Society, formally organized at the home of Peter Alfred and Clementia (Mentia) Taylor in March 1863. The home of the radical and liberal Peter Taylor, who was a member of Parliament and treasurer of the London Emancipation Committee, was a central meeting place for many London abolitionists. It also welcomed women reformers because the equally radical Clementia was actively involved in the women's suffrage movement. Remond, who was boarding with the Taylors at their Aubrey House from December 1861 until October 1864, was involved in establishing the first two emancipation groups. Remond informed William Lloyd Garrison in a letter written from London dated 22 October 1864, that she was residing with "a dear friend, Mrs. P. A. Taylor," who was the honorary secretary of the Ladies' London Emancipation Society and "the wife of P. A. Taylor, Esq., M. P., the member for Leicester, whose voice, in and out of Parliament, has been heard in behalf of the American slave, and whose testimony is recorded against a Southern Confederacy based upon chattel slavery."[73] Hence, she joined some of the most powerful and highly influential London activists.

The London Emancipation Committee, in which Remond and the fugitive slaves William and Ellen Craft were actively involved in until August 1859, concluded its activities in February 1860, by which time the membership had become male-dominated. In 1863, women abolitionists and women's rights advocates formed the new Ladies' London Emancipation Society with female leadership. As Clare Midgley has convincingly argued, in addition to "drawing on anti-slavery for its ideological approach, the developing feminist movement made use of the networks of female abolitionists in creating its own network and leadership."[74] Remond, who together with Clementia Taylor was involved in founding the society, contacted the activist Esther Sturge about the "Female Emancipation Society" in April 1863, asking her to aid it.[75] The founders argued that slavery was an issue especially concerning women. Many of the society's members were leading figures in reform movements and in campaigns advancing women's higher education and suffrage. In addition to Taylor and Remond, members included Cobbe, Martineau, and Mary Estlin, a nationalist activist who worked in Bristol promoting the Garrisonians and had participated in founding the Garrisonian Manchester Anti-Slavery League.[76] Estlin's husband was a familiar name to those who read the *Liberator.* The newly formed organization, whose activities included preparing pamphlets that the feminist publisher Emily Faithful printed, soon had over two hundred members.[77]

Remond, who was a committee member and pamphleteer, compiled one of the many tracts the society published on slavery, *Negroes and Anglo-Africans as Freedmen and Soldiers,* which appeared in January 1864. The pamphlet provided testimonies of black freedmen and soldiers and included Remond's introduction and concluding words. The last page positioned "Miss Remond" among the association's Executive Committee members next to "Miss Cobbe," "Miss Estlin," "Mrs. Manning," "Mrs. H. Martineau," and "Mrs. Taylor."[78] Listing the radical activists as "Miss" and "Mrs." served to underline their Victorian propriety, respectability, and social status, and render the women less controversial. The society brought together women from England, Ireland, and, in the person of Remond, the United States.

Remond also functioned as a contact person between British and American activists. In July 1864, she contacted Garrison on behalf of a "lady" who, she wrote, "desires me to ask you if you have any biographical notice of yourself."[79] In the same letter she enclosed a note to Estlin and sent Charles Roundell's mailing address to Garrison, who had asked for it. As a central figure in international reform movements, Remond passed on information and connected activists transatlanticly staying in close contact with American abolitionists while working with British protagonists. At the time, Remond was living in Hampstead.

Remond's responsibilities within the organizations demonstrate the trust and respect that British women activists placed on her. As a committee member, she was involved in various aspects of the society's organizational tasks, compiling pamphlets, and taking part in decision-making.

The society's leadership and membership consisted almost exclusively of women, with Mazzini as the only active male member.

Mazzini, who personally knew the London ladies, assiduously corresponded with them and exchanged ideas not only about revolution and emancipation but also on cultural topics. For instance, he expressed his opinion and dissatisfaction with Cobbe's book on Italy (*Italics: Brief Notes on Politics, People, and Places in Italy, in 1864*), which came out in 1864. According to him, it was "a usual hastily superficially made book, not a deed, a moral duty performed," which he would have expected from somebody like Cobbe, who "loves Italy and her future."[80] Among other radical female activists who were friends of Mazzini's and recipients of his many letters were Caroline Stansfeld as well as her sisters Emilie Venturi and Matilda Biggs. They all worked closely together with Clementia Taylor and Remond supporting women's suffrage and abolitionism and raising funds for the unification of Italy.

In January 1865, Remond was in Bristol and in February had not yet returned to the Taylors, according to Mazzini's letter written in London and addressed to Biggs: "Things here are going on much as usual," he wrote. "We have had an evening at William's: some sisters of Bessie, ourselves, the Blinds, the Oswalds, Hungarians, Mr. Gillman, Shaen, the Taylors, and their new shadow. The black one has temporarily disappeared, and now they have a white one."[81] The black "shadow" must have referred to Remond. Mazzini noted her absence and deemed it worth mentioning.

In addition to shouldering responsibilities as a leading figure dedicated to eradicating unequal power structures, Remond continued her studies in London, graduating as a nurse. According to Mazzini, she should then have devoted her time to helping former slaves in her native United States: "Miss Remond is in Bristol," he wrote in January 1865. "Had she not better being now in the midst of the emancipated negroes, nursing the wounded or educating the others? The problem now lies with themselves; and the agitation ought to turn to a different channel."[82] Mazzini considered Remond's mission to be in the United States where the emancipated slaves were in great need of assistance. However, Remond, unlike the Crafts and Douglass, remained in Europe pursuing her personal goals though she continued to speak out against American racial discrimination. In February Remond still had not returned to the Taylors but had stayed on in Bristol. Soon, however, she reappeared in London, and toward the end of the summer 1866 was on her way to Italy. Her plan was to continue her studies.

During her years in England, Remond had developed her abilities to propagate her convictions through the written and spoken word. In her leading role in international emancipation movements she had worked closely with her white British colleagues, participating in discussions, meetings, and various events that often were hosted at the Aubrey House in London. The issues and concerns debated at the Taylors's home were many and varied, as testified by Cobbe, who in her autobiographical *Life of Frances Power Cobbe* (1894) reported an instance (which took place years before the publication of her book) when Mary Carpenter of Bristol, in charge of Reformatory and Ragged School and author of *Juvenile Delinquents*, during a pause in the conversation remarked:

> "It is a thousand pities that everybody will not join and give the whole of their minds to the great cause of the age, because, if they would, we should carry it undoubtedly." "What *is* the great cause of the age?" we simultaneously exclaimed. "Parliamentary Reform?" said our host, Mr. Peter Taylor; "The Abolition of Slavery?" said Miss Remond, a Negress, Mrs. Taylor's companion; "Teetotalism?" said another; "Woman's Suffrage?" said another; "The conversion of the world to Theism?" said I. In the midst of the clamour, Miss Carpenter looked serenely round, "Why! the Industrial Schools Bill *of course!*" Nobody enjoyed the joke, when we all began to laugh, more than the reformer herself.[83]

The passage clearly attests to how varied the activist women's interests were and how they fought to bring about change in various societal concerns.

In addition to lectures and remonstrations, Remond published a protest letter in the *London Daily News* as a response to the attacks by the London press against blacks after a Jamaican insurrection. She also joined the Freedman's Aid Association with Ellen Craft after the Civil War.[84] Remond, then, fearlessly defended people of her race and raised awareness for the cause of black emancipation. Her fervent desire was to break racial prejudice, as she wrote in 1865: "No matter what a colored man may do—whether it is a crime committed, or some slight impropriety, it is exaggerated, and noticed in the most insulting manner. . . . Our cup of bitterness is more than full."[85] She was bold and courageous in her attacks against injustice, and with her actions she influenced the nineteenth-century sociopolitical landscape.

Remond's appeals for racial justice continued in Britain even after Abraham Lincoln's 1863 Emancipation Proclamation, which declared slaves free in areas under Confederate rule. She remained in Europe after the end of the war and the ratification of the Thirteenth Amendment, which made slavery illegal throughout the United States. Subsequently, though, as is well known, the U.S. federal government failed to enforce the newly granted rights or to protect the nation's black population against discrimination and violence. Scholars have observed that Andrew Johnson, the vice president who succeeded Lincoln in 1865, was a former slaveholder and particularly Negrophobic; black codes and the Ku Klux Klan followed the end of slavery and the government failed to ensure the safety and liberty of African Americans.[86] However, since the political and legal stipulations secured black freedom, at least in intent, Remond moved on to realizing her personal dreams. She continued her studies first at the London University College, graduating as a nurse, before she moved to Florence, Italy, the cradle of art and the hub of intellectual cosmopolitanism, where she furthered her educational goals and promoted social change.

From Florence, Remond continued to follow Reconstruction in the United States and the attitudes of Englishmen toward newly emancipated slaves. She participated in the debates by voicing her opinions publicly through the British press. The *London Daily News* published her letter to the editor, dated 22 September 1866, written in Florence on 19 September, in which she pondered the reasons for continued discrimination and the reasons why "neither freedmen nor their friends find any longer suitable protection" in the United States. She concluded that the "Southerners and their Northern allies are determined that the black race shall not be recognized, shall not receive justice."[87] She continued her address by accusing Thomas Carlyle, "the literary leader of public opinion," for insulting black people and influencing others to join "negro haters" on both sides of the Atlantic. Carlyle had publicized his anti-black opinions, his conviction of the existence of a racial hierarchy, and his belief in the inferiority of blacks.[88] Remond's response to such discriminatory views was a powerful denunciation of white British and Americans' failure to accept a race whose complexion happened to be "of a darker hue."[89]

In addition to publishing her opinions in British newspapers, Remond occasionally returned to England. She was one of the distinguished people to receive an invitation to attend a breakfast celebration organized in honor of Garrison on Saturday, 6 July 1867. There were between three and four hundred notables present, and in addition to Remond, the invited guests included representatives of British nobility such as the Duke and Duchess of Argyll and Lady M. Stanhope, Member of Parliament Peter Taylor, and numerous other dignitaries. The event commemorated "one of the greatest of great triumphs of freedom," the liberation of slaves.[90] An article written in celebration of the event appeared in the *Manchester Times* on the same day and covered almost an entire page. In addition to the public breakfast, Remond met Garrison privately in London on 26 July 1867. As Garrison wrote to his wife, "Sarah P. Remond has called to see us since we came back. She thinks of going to Florence in September. She is looking finely."[91] Hence, Remond had decided to return to Florence to continue her studies.

Newspapers and American activists' own writings reveal that during their stay in the Old World, Remond and other African Americans who were raised to believe in their inferiority, could demonstrate that they were equals with cultured Europeans. The facility with which Remond connected with members of high society became manifest not only in England but also in her new adopted home, Florence, known as the capital of cosmopolitan refinement par excellence. Before permanently moving to "Firenze La Bella," Remond was introduced to Italian realities by Cobbe but also by Mazzini, who dedicated his life to achieving his goal of "Italia Unita."

CHAPTER 5

Abolitionists for Italian Risorgimento

IN THE NINETEENTH CENTURY, PEOPLE, IDEAS, AND information circulated across oceans, among nations, and among activist groups that were established and operating in various parts of the world. People of different nationalities fought to "redeem words like democracy."[1] Since such recovery of democracy and freedom was an international phenomenon, it is important to place the various reform movements and independence struggles within a larger historical context of despotism, racism, and discrimination, and to situate them in the history of transatlantic collaboration that can be connected with the civil and human rights movements that were shaping the transatlantic world. Such collective resistance to oppression became manifest in the transatlantic collaboration webs and networks whose members campaigned for social, racial, political, and moral justice. Sarah Remond was one of the many progressive women to collaborate with activists and revolutionaries who were representing various nationalities and ethnic origins.

By the time Remond started to support Italy's struggle to become one nation, Americans had already raised the question of unification in their private and public commentaries. As early as the late 1820s, James

Fenimore Cooper was convinced of the future unification of the peninsula. He had no doubts that "Sooner or later, Italy will inevitably become a single State."[2] Such comments from foreigners contributed to the advancement of the idea of one nation among Italians themselves. Henry Wadsworth Longfellow, whose life and entire career were closely linked to Italy, considered the unity of Italy "a sacred cause, which has, and always has had, my most sincere and fervent sympathy."[3] Others, such as the American artist Horatio Greenough, actively participated in the political events that were transforming Italy into a unified political entity. Many Americans visiting Italy during the Risorgimento met with Italian revolutionaries. Giuseppe Mazzini's personal friends included Margaret Fuller, who had introduced the sculptor William Wetmore Story to the Italian patriot in 1849.[4] Fuller's dispatches to American newspapers were fundamental in keeping American interest in Italy's struggles alive, and Americans on both sides of the Atlantic followed the events with keen concern and contributed to the nation's birth with dynamic involvement.

According to the historian Emma Detti, it was Fuller who initiated the manifestation of sympathy and support for Italian national independence and constitutional freedom that was advertised in the New York *Tribune* on 27 November 1847. It included an appeal, which was signed by seven hundred Americans, among them some of the most influential New Yorkers, and an event organized to support Italy. At the end of it, an Italian exile in New York, Professor Felice Foresti from Columbia College, a fervent supporter of Mazzini, delivered a speech in which he expressed his gratitude for the sympathy demonstrated toward his country. Fuller was quite disappointed that Italian papers practically ignored this American demonstration of support, and commented on it in a letter to her friend Costanza Arconati, who responded that the indifference was due to Europe's failure to do justice to the United States, a country that Europeans still continued to look down upon.[5] And yet, in addition to many Europeans and expatriate American residents in Italy, enlightened intellectuals, particularly in the United States, perceived the Risorgimento as part of a more universal struggle for the liberation of all of humanity from all forms of despotism.

Abolitionists in the United States and Great Britain participated in revolutionary struggles fought in various European countries under despotic regime. In particular, during the decades between the 1840s and 1860s, the transatlantic world was united in a fight against oppression that manifested itself in discourses on slavery, reform, and national unification, that is, in various forms of social and political protest. It is important to bear in mind, however, that the views of more radical thinkers differed from the official positions of many nations and even from the opinions of other radicals within the same movements. Consequently, although Mazzini for one supported abolitionism, not all Mazzinians agreed with him on the question of slavery.

Several of the few black American orators touring in Britain were among those who sustained that oppression had to be fought in all its forms. According to R. J. M. Blackett, "Blacks came to see their struggle as part of the wider resistance to all forms of oppression."[6] Charles Remond was one of them; he expressed his conviction in the following words: while oppression "existed in the world, it must mar the sacred cause of freedom elsewhere."[7] America's slavery, thus, was linked with European revolutions and discussed overseas nearly as much as in the United States. National struggles transformed into transnational activism when abolitionists, social reformers, and revolutionaries perceived similarities between the various movements. Such parallelism was promoted in newspapers and magazines that published articles and letters in which activists and journalists articulated their opinions and agendas on such comparisons. Although censorship was instigated in many countries, information traveled efficiently, as did activists who built networks of coalitions that crossed national borders.

Men and women who joined forces transatlanticly to reach common goals of freedom, peace, and self-sovereignty often organized their activities on gender-specific lines. For instance, the Boston Female Anti-Slavery Society, founded in 1832, supported the efforts of the New England Anti-Slavery Society. In the United States, England, and Ireland, in such cities as Philadelphia, London, and Cork, both the more general and the specific women's organizations combined efforts in campaigns dedicated to promoting abolition of slavery. For example, Cork's activists had formed the Cork Anti-Slavery Society and a parallel women's organization, the

Cork Ladies Anti-Slavery Society. In these organizations, men and women shared goals but had separate power and leadership structures.

In their fight against despotism, men and women assumed different strategies for implementing their political programs. Men tended to be more directly involved in politics and in recruiting supporters publicly; they were engaged in writing petitions and participated in political action. In their gender-specific activities, the support women provided often included making and donating garments or organizing fund-raising bazaars. In other words, they were involved in activities that were commonly considered more pertinent to women and their domestic spheres. However, as the historian Karen Sánchez-Eppler argues, "in their work against slavery these female societies transformed conventional womanly activities into tools of political persuasion."[8] Moreover, the activities in which Remond was involved were quite similar to those carried out by men. In addition, women's charity bazaars and other philanthropic activities had an inherent political intent that enlarged the extent of women's influence.

In England, both the charity and commercial bazaars became popular around the same time in the 1820s. Women organized bazaars to support a variety of causes: to benefit hospitals, schools, missions, and various other causes. Usually they were advertised in local and national newspapers, attracting large numbers of supporters. Women were quite successful in collecting large amounts for various causes, often related to reform movements that were directly related to women. Women excelled in their activities; they were enthusiastic and they had the ability to turn men's auxiliaries into profitable activities.[9]

In addition to their abolitionist and women's suffrage agendas, members of the Ladies' London Emancipation Society that Remond was involved in founding assisted political groups in Europe with such fund-raising efforts as bazaars and with delivering, distributing, and publishing pamphlets and letters. Their activities included public talks, writing appeals, and recruiting supporters, both men and women. Many intelligent and cultured women who felt frustrated with their daily realities directed their time, energy, and attention to activism, including aiding Mazzini, whose fervent desire was to see Italy achieve unification and autonomy.

Mazzini, who was born in 1805 as the son of a Genoan physician, dedicated his life to his ambitious goal of liberating Italy from foreign despotism and the pope's authority. Before joining the Carbonari, a secret society whose goal was to overthrow despotism, Mazzini had worked as a lawyer and advocate for the poor. As a member of the Carbonari, he was charged with conspiracy but released due to lack of evidence. Nonetheless, he fled in fear of further attacks, first remaining for an extended exile in France, where he established himself in Marseille and started a society called "Young Italy" (*Giovine Italia*) in 1831. Many young Italians joined the newly formed secret society, which was dedicated to unifying the various states of the Italian peninsula into one democratic republic.

The historian Meg McGavran Murray argues that Johann Gottfried Herder, who has been called "the father of the idea of national unity, or nationalism," in particular cultural nationalism, inspired both Mazzini and the Polish revolutionary leader and poet Adam Mickiewicz. Herder's message was to encourage Germans to develop their own, particularly German nationalist culture, and he theorized that "individuals need to belong to an identifiable group with its own outlook, traditions, and historical memories."[10] His message promoted the idea of one nation, one national character. In a similar way, Mazzini's plan was to create national unity, but he differed from Herder on his vision of freedom, which embraced people beyond national borders: his ambition was to establish a democratic republic but he also wanted to obtain political and social equality and justice for all the oppressed peoples of Europe. As Mazzini stated in his 1833 declaration, the Young Italy society promoted revolution "in the name of the people, for the people, and by the people," a statement that was echoed in Abraham Lincoln's Gettysburg Address. Indeed, Mazzini's message traveled far, and historians have argued that Lincoln received copies of Mazzini's writings, some of them from the economist Carlo Cattaneo.[11]

Mazzini's crusades and exiles were discussed in newspapers in England and the United States, where people were divided between his supporters and those who did not share his goals or his vision of how to achieve them. Despite the differing views, Europeans and Americans followed his activities closely. Mazzini, who was a sought-after revolutionary, had to remain secretive about his chosen abodes but it is known that from France he traveled toward England, passing through Switzerland, with the intention of establishing himself in London where he continued his activities for the liberation of Italy.[12]

Already in the 1830s, Britain was known for welcoming revolutionaries of different nationalities. It attracted large numbers of European exiles from Poland, Italy, Russia, Scandinavia, Holland, and many other countries that were struggling to realize a democratic nation. Some of the exiles in Britain included Lajos Kossuth, Alexandre Ledru-Rollin, Karl Marx, Giuseppe Garibaldi, and Mazzini, among others. Black abolitionists often met European political refugees such as the Hungarian Emerick Szabad, who attended a farewell soirée organized in Edinburgh in honor of a former slave, Jim Pembroke, known as James William Charles Pennington. Pennington was an educator and orator who toured in England, Germany, and the West Indies. In 1849, he attended the Paris Peace Congress as a delegate. Similarly, William Wells Brown and the black nationalist Martin Delany met the political ideologist Victor Hugo, who was known for his campaign against the death penalty and his support of American abolitionists.[13]

Remond, like these other black Americans, met revolutionaries who had escaped to Britain. Her meeting with Neapolitan exiles took place in Dublin in May 1859:

> Miss *Sarah Remond* was of the social party that met them at the house of a friend on the evening of their arrival. I have seen fairer faces; but I have never seen one brighter, more intelligent, or better "lit up," than was hers that whole evening. The exiles were deeply interested on being informed that she was here as the representative of a down-trodden race in a land of liberty, and their advocate before the British people. The Duca di Cabellino begged to be presented to her, and desired that she should be informed how, as one who had himself suffered from cruel oppression, he entirely sympathized with her and her noble mission. Several of the exiles handed her their cards, and the Baron Poerio gave her some lines with the autograph.[14]

The exiles had been in Cork and were on their way to London. They claimed to be familiar with the name of Harriet Beecher Stowe and to regard her as a sister.[15]

When Giuseppe, or Joseph Mazzini as the British called him, arrived in London, Britain's attitude toward exiles was welcoming and supportive. Britain's decision to abolish slavery in its own territories, which included the West Indies, further contributed to the image of Britain as a haven for political refugees. Moreover, foreigners tended to consider Britain as the "moral arbiter of the western world."[16] The British were especially eager to support causes that would embarrass the United States. The rivalry and jealousies between the two nations fueled British fervor to participate in international campaigns and express their solidarity against American actions and demonstrations of injustice. Antislavery activists condemned the refusal of white Americans to grant passports to African Americans and criticized their insistence on excluding blacks from obtaining the rights to American citizenship. The British encouraged the outside world to condemn a nation that sustained racial discrimination and maintained a system of slavery; as they pointed out, Americans not only kept it active but regarded it as legal. The black American antislavery lecturers capitalized on such rivalry, stirring international animosity by presenting America as a nation devoid of moral values.[17] As Charles Remond observed, a nation that boasted of freedom and equality yet held three million people in slavery was nothing more than "an asp in a basket of flowers."[18] Similarly, Mazzini's aim was to put political and diplomatic pressure on the foreign leaders who at the time controlled various Italian states.

Mazzini, who sacrificed his personal freedom for the liberty of Italy, was one of the most important Italian patriots. He lived a good part of his life in exile, away from his native country and family. Repeatedly he chose England as the destination of his enforced emigration. In London he became a close friend of the Taylors, who subsequently welcomed Remond at their home. Working from England, Mazzini pursued the revolutionary ideas that were simultaneously taking shape in Milan, Venice, and Rome.

Since the early 1840s, Mazzini had been working in various ways to gain sympathy and awaken British interest in the national and political rights of Italy. He influenced a relatively large community of liberal and radical activists, who admired him and donated their time, energies, and funds to support his cause. At the time of his early exile, he was living in London's Bloomsbury district, at 47 Devonshire Street, Queen's Square.[19]

With Mazzini Remond participated in practical efforts to assist in the mission to dramatically change Italy. The relationships Mazzini established with many radical reform advocates, including Remond, went beyond mere participation in social and political campaigns. He formed affectionate friendships with many, among them Remond, Fuller, and the Taylors. With Remond in particular, he must have shared a sense of belonging and acceptance, a feeling of having found a home among the English. They both had emigrated from their native countries and chosen England as their temporary homes. They both were dedicated to helping those who had remained behind, suffering under tyranny.

Mazzini, whose vision of freedom bridged nations, races, and classes, was greatly admired and respected by London radicals, including many belonging to the working class. In 1846, he became the source of inspiration in the formation of the People's International League. It was established by British supporters of democracy and its principles were inspired by Mazzini, whose reputation by then was well established in Britain. The People's International League was the first English association that declared an interest in foreign affairs. Its object was to spread the principles of national freedom and progress, and its goal was to secure the right of every nation to self-government and the preservation of its own nationality. The group also aimed to further such pacific and idealistic goals as establishing an understanding among the peoples of all countries.[20]

Thus, Mazzini's ambitions went beyond the (proposed or perceived) national borders of Italy. In letters to his English friends he discussed his plans to support the oppressed in obtaining freedom and addressed current topics and political events. He followed political events in other countries through private contacts and newspaper reports. He was interested in the protests and revolutionary ideas that emerged in various European countries, at times linked to the black protests propagated especially in Britain and the United States. The political turmoil throughout the Euro-Atlantic world reached a climax in the 1860s when the United States became involved in its Civil War: Italians obtained their independence in 1861, the

Polish uprising took place in 1863, national unification of Germany ensued between 1866 and 1870, Austria conceded self-government to Hungary in 1866, and in 1871 a republic replaced the French Empire. Moreover, bourgeois democracy was considered nearly as revolutionary as any country's striving for independence.[21] The political debates in Italy, Germany, Hungary, and Poland revolved around slavery, democracy, independence, and national unity. In addition, with the *Communist Manifesto,* Karl Marx and Friedrich Engels were promoting the revolution of the proletariat so as to transform the working class into the ruling class. Similarly to other radical thinkers with cosmopolitan vision, Mazzini, who was against all despotic states, perceived democracy as a universal governance system, ideal for the future and one that should be adopted in all European countries.[22]

Mazzini became friends with influential European and American intellectuals and followed their publications, just as they followed his writings and ideas. Other leading figures who promoted radical social change included, among others, John Stuart Mill, with whom Mazzini agreed on the importance of national education. The question of education was a topic addressed also in Sarah and Charles Remond's discourses; it was a fundamental concern for African Americans, who saw it as an opportunity for social ascent, essential for political participation, and, ultimately, a significant factor leading to greater self-esteem and respect. In other words, education served to prove the falseness of the binary white-black positioning of such concepts as racial supremacy and inferiority.

Race, class, and gender, equal rights and education, then, were concepts and concerns that overlapped in activist discourse. The same principles that reigned among activists in the United States—the conviction that the socially, financially, and politically more privileged should help the less fortunate—was the guiding rule with Mazzini and the British who were involved in reform movements. In Mazzini's view, rights and responsibilities were linked together, and the socially marginalized should demonstrate their capabilities and capacity to exercise equal rights; they should prove this to themselves as much as to others.

Mazzini expressed this idea in a letter to his British friend and supporter Matilda Biggs, somewhat ambiguously arguing against her views regarding mixed associations and societies, which, nonetheless, were exclusively dedicated to and mainly controlled by women: "I am not entirely agreeing with your view about exclusively feminine Societies; mixing them up and thinking that by that something has been achieved is merely substituting an illusion to reality," Mazzini wrote. "When a whole element, a class, wants emancipation," he continued, "the first thing is Self-assertion: to prove that you *are* equal, not only claiming rights, but proving that you are capable of exercising them. . . . Emancipation is nothing but capability ascertained; and to have it ascertained, you must be alone and conspicuous. If they [Italian working-class societies] would have begun by merging in Masters' Societies, they would have perennially undergone their influence, and never educated themselves to a consciousness of their own rights and strength."[23] Mazzini supported women's emancipation movements and encouraged women activists to take control of their societies so they could demonstrate their capabilities and power.

Remond was one of the women activists who corresponded to Mazzini's ideals: she shouldered the responsibility of independently concretizing her potential, revealing her talent, and assuming control in order to realize her goals and ambitions. With her actions Remond demonstrated women's capacities and capabilities but she also validated demands for black power. As Mazzini pointed out, women working alone would make their efforts and success more conspicuous.

The tension Mazzini felt struggling to promote his ideals was visible in his countenance, as testified by Elizabeth Barrett Browning, who met him in London in July 1852. "Mazzini came to see us the other day," Barrett Browning wrote to a Miss Mitford, "with that pale spiritual face of his, and those intense eyes full of melancholy illusions. I was thinking, while he sate there, on what Italian turf he would lie at last with a bullet in his heart, or perhaps with a knife in his back, for to one of those ends it will surely come. Mrs. Carlyle came with him. She is a great favorite of mine: full of thought, and feeling, and character, it seems to me."[24] Mazzini was a revolutionary whose life was constantly in danger. And yet, such women as Remond or Barrett Browning never thought of their own reputation or safety but befriended and supported him. Barrett Browning wrote about Mazzini again in a letter written at Casa Guidi, dated 17 March 1853: "I am much relieved by hearing that Mazzini is gone from Italy, whatever Lord Malmesbury may say of it. Every day I expected to be told that he was taken at Milan and shot."[25]

In November 1854, Mazzini, who had to change his place of exile repeatedly, returned to England, which to him had been his "second country; the spot out of Italy where I love the best and am loved the best."[26] He lived under a false name, kept his London address a secret, and never left his residence during the day for fear of being discovered.[27] It was true that he had many influential friends who were loyally supporting him in England, including James and Caroline Stansfeld, Matilda Biggs, and Peter and Clementia Taylor, but he feared for arrest, which would paralyze his progress and deprive him of his liberty. His network of collaborators formed the social circles Remond subsequently joined, and included the English revolutionary Jessie White Mario, who was married to the Italian federalist Alberto Mario and who supported Mazzini's republicanism by lecturing in Great Britain and the United States.

However, Jessie Mario and her husband had a bigger part in the revolution than merely promoting it through speeches. Barrett Browning informed her sister-in-law, Sarianna, in a letter of 11 May 1861, posted from Rome that "Jessie Mario and her husband have been taken up at Ferrara. They were *only* going to begin the war with Austria on their own account."[28] Since Jessie Mario received instructions directly from Mazzini, who sent directives through Peter Taylor not only to her but even to Garibaldi, it is possible that the idea of starting "a war with Austria" (which surely was an exaggeration) had been Mazzini's. Remond connected with these radicals and revolutionaries who were active in London upon her arrival in Europe. Barrett Browning remarked in the same letter that Mazzini was "a man without conscience." However, his conscience, similarly to that of Remond, went beyond the well-being of individual or personal safety as he fervently worked to rid Italy of despotism.

During the American Civil War years, when Italy was completing its unification, a dialogue existed between American and Italian political forces. The Italian ruling class, together with politicians, sympathized with the

Confederacy.[29] Moreover, both Italian radicals and moderates were appalled that "the land of freedom," as the United States defined itself, kept a large number of its population in slavery.[30] Americans, instead, frequently perceived foreign revolutions as "a reenactment of their own," whereas Italians considered the ideological roots of their insurrection to be European, not transatlantic, embedded in the patriotic struggles of their past.[31] Garibaldi, who Americans perceived as a symbol of the values expounded in the Declaration of Independence, was nearly as popular in the United States as in Italy. The *New York Times* suggested that the achievements of Garibaldi "carried Americans back to the days of their own struggle for independence, and revived in the person of the patriotic general, their own heroic Washington."[32] The Italian revolutionary received attention in the press, appeared in American poems, and, thanks to his fame and support, successfully collected funds, as much as $100,000 in 1859, to cover the expenses of his campaigns. His success was such that Americans wished to introduce him into their own army's ranks. Therefore, George Perkins Marsh, who had been appointed the U.S. minister plenipotentiary in Turin in 1861 and subsequently became Remond's friend, approached Garibaldi with an offer to take command of a Federal Army Corps in July 1861. Americans needed competent generals, and Garibaldi had both experience and popularity. However, the conditions Garibaldi set for accepting the command—the immediate abolition of slavery and his appointment as commander-in-chief—obviously were refused.[33]

The news "about Garibaldi being offered the command of the American army" circulated among Americans in Europe and was mentioned in a letter the American art collector James Jackson Jarves wrote to the Greek author Madame Margherita Mignaty from Paris on 29 September 1861.[34] Americans followed Garibaldi, Mazzini, and the Risorgimento movement in the United States where articles discussing Italian political events appeared in newspapers and magazines.

Remond, who contributed to the Italian movement and came to know Mazzini in 1861 through Peter and Clementia Taylor, may also have met Garibaldi during his brief visit to the Taylors on 14 April 1864. It was Garibaldi's second visit to England, where people idolized him and received him with great enthusiasm.[35] While living with the Taylors, Remond had an invaluable opportunity to meet influential international leaders and to broaden the extent of her political agenda. Through the London Emancipation Society, Remond gained access to international political communities and activities linking the efforts of British and Italians who were promoting the Italian cause. She gained a transatlantic perspective through her efforts to contribute first to the liberation of oppressed slaves and women, then to enlarge the scope of her activism to Italian struggles for freedom and independence. Remond personally met and befriended Mazzini, and she may well have made the acquaintance of Garibaldi with whom she seems to have connected again in Italy.

Already before meeting either man, Remond had drawn parallels between abolitionists working for the liberation of American slaves and Italian revolutionaries. A reference to Garibaldi appeared in one of her early speeches delivered in England on Thursday, 24 January 1861. A report of the event with a summary of the main points of her talk appeared the following day in the *Birmingham Daily Post:*

> Last evening Miss Remond, a coloured lady from America, delivered a lecture on the above subject [American slavery] before a numerous audience assembled in the Temperance Hall, Upper Temple Street. His Worship the Mayor presided, and Mr. Recorder Hill occupied a seat on the platform. Claiming for the Negro, at the outset, the full rights given by God to those beings, whom he had made "a little lower than the angels," the lecturer demanded the authority by which America held four millions of her brethren in bondage; . . . Adverting to the cases of Anderson and John Brown, she expressed her firm adherence to the moral suasion principle, but at the same time claimed for them an equal right with a Washington or a Garibaldi to fight for the freedom of their race. She afterwards spoke of the present crisis in America, and said the events of the last six months had only revealed the hideous state of things that had existed there for the last thirty years—that had grown with the country's growth and strengthened with its strength. . . . The lecture, eloquent and powerful as it was, drew forth loud applause.[36]

The speech indicates that the name of Garibaldi was equally well known as that of George Washington. By juxtaposing the two men, Remond drew a parallel between two revolutions, one that was directly related to the

British and American antagonism. Remond, thus, delivered a powerful, fierce speech that disgraced the United States because of the question of slavery.

Remond appealed to the British audience for a condemnation of the United States, where, she argued, slavery had an impact on every class of society. She referred to the unavoidability of a war when calling attention to the "fearful crisis" she expected would erupt over the question of slavery. Remond vowed to save her "brethren," calling for her audience's support, sympathy, and moral aid. Although Remond supported moral suasion, considering it the correct strategy to achieve the emancipation of slaves, she at the same time promoted more aggressive action by claiming that American slaves had the same right "to fight for the freedom of their race" as such revolutionaries as Garibaldi had to claim freedom for his nation. In other words, she encouraged radical action that would lead to the liberation of the oppressed, and by mentioning Garibaldi, she underscored the similarities between abolitionism and European movements against despotism.

The speaker who followed Remond, a Mr. Recorder Hill, concluded that Remond's talk had

> stirred one's inmost soul to listen to the words of the gifted lady who had just sat down, and to recollect, amongst other matters, that the race which had produced that exalted mind speaking through those eloquent lips, was looked down upon as inferior—as so much inferior that there was a sect of so-called philosophers who doubted whether the negro race, or those who had one drop of negro blood in their veins, were men and women. He had heard the negro race treated with contempt by minds for which his own had felt a contempt approaching to loathing, and if those persons were there he could with triumph refer them to the lady who had that night taught them a lesson in humanity.[37]

This speaker presented Remond as living proof of the erroneousness of dominant racial theories that tried to convince others of black inferiority. Remond, "the lady" who "had that night taught them a lesson in humanity," had assumed a socially superior role as the one to teach her audience and to demonstrate the capabilities of black women. In England, Remond gained admiration and popularity for her talks, and became a shining example of confidence as she continued to work on behalf of the less fortunate, of those who were held in bondage.

Like other black abolitionists, Remond drew parallels between black Americans and Italians. In Manchester, where she spoke against colonialization, she explained that black Americans were attached to their homes and their country, "and they have no more idea of leaving it than the oppressed Italian people have of leaving Italy."[38] She constructed a strong link, presenting both black Americans and Italians as patriots who valued their nation and home, with core values that centered around the family.

As his letters reveal, Mazzini shared common goals with Remond, whom he personally liked and admired. He expressed his fondness for Remond and the Taylors in a letter addressed to Clementia Taylor on 31 December 1863: "One word of deep earnest affection on this day to both you and Peter, who have been, are and will be amongst my best friends in England." He ended the letter, similarly to many others, with "Love to Miss Taylor and to Miss Remond."[39] Mazzini relied on Remond and British women activists for their support. To Taylor and Remond he sent booklets, most probably on the situation of Italy, to be sold and distributed to others.[40] He recognized the importance of the contribution women were making to advance radical social change, and at one point he dreamed of a female nucleus of the Unity of Garibaldi Society that would have included Clementia Taylor, among others.[41] Since Remond was extremely closely associated with Taylor, it is highly probable that Mazzini would have included her among the London women in charge of the society.

With British women activists Mazzini organized a bazaar in London to raise funds for the Italian cause. The women of London involved in the fundraiser sold "English produces in Italy" and Garibaldi's photographs in England.[42] By the beginning of 1863, the London ladies had formed a committee to realize another event geared to collect funds: Mazzini's Bazaar for the "Rome and Venice Liberation Fund," whose purpose was to assist émigrés from Venetia and help the press in its propaganda against Napoleon and the Pope. Mazzini stated that the profits from the bazaar would be used to promote the emancipation of Rome and Venice.[43] When considering various venues for the fundraising event, Mazzini rejected Biggs's suggestion to hold it at the Aubrey House, the Taylors's residence, because in his view, it was "a comet in the London system excentrical [*sic*]."[44] It was a great privilege for Remond to belong to the central "comet" of London activism.

Instead of using such a pivotal location, Taylor and her activist friend Kate Crawfurd went in search of rooms they could hire for the event, which was scheduled to take place on 25 April 1863. Organizing such events required months of preparation, from locating an ideal venue to advertising, preparing and selling entrance tickets, and distributing stalls where vendors could sell products to benefit a common cause. Mazzini expressed his gratitude for Taylor's and Remond's efforts: "Give my cordial thanks to Miss Remond for her active cooperation in our Bazaar. I rejoice at the doings of your Negro Emancipation Society."[45] Mazzini clearly was grateful and appreciative for Remond's contribution.

In addition to helping organize the bazaar, Remond impressed Mazzini with her understanding of the political situation in Europe. Mazzini specifically mentioned her in a letter whose purpose was to ask his friends to encourage the Polish to take action: "Peter, you [Clementia Taylor], Miss R[emond], somebody ought to state to him the *true* fact that active European sympathies have abated since their movement has visibly fallen in the hands of Bonaparte and of the Moderate Party."[46] It is no surprise that Mazzini held a high opinion of Remond, who continuously demonstrated her capabilities and potential for future development.

Remond not only assisted Mazzini but became his friend. In June 1864, Mazzini made plans to take her to the opera in London. Since he had succeeded in putting aside some money to spend on gifts for his friends, he decided to take an opera box and invite Remond, together with Emilie Ashurst Venturi, to go with him: "Either on Thursday or Saturday, we shall go to the *Africaine*," he wrote to Venturi. "If you will not go, on account of the face," Mazzini continued,

> I shall regret it: although in a cab to Th[urloe] Sq[uare] and from there in a carriage to the Opera, you do not run any risk. But if you will refuse on account of other to me unintelligible reasons, I shall grieve and feel displeased. Shall I be doomed to go with Miss Remond alone? I usually put aside from any money I

receive a mine a fraction for presents to friends I love. . . . If I chose to spend it in an Opera Box, why on earth would you object?[47]

Mazzini was set on going, and concluded the letter by stating that "I shall have a box, no matter how."[48] Mazzini, then, valued culture and appreciated music. Because he was determined to have a box at the opera, it is highly probable that the Italian revolutionary and black American female abolitionist went to the opera together. Mazzini's letter indicates that the two shared an interest in music, and that he was looking forward to their evening together; he clearly seemed pleased to share his opera box with Remond. His comment about being "doomed to go with Miss Remond alone" most probably was meant to persuade Venturi to change her mind and join them.

In addition to attending public entertainments with Remond, Mazzini never failed to mention her in his letters. Whenever he wrote to Clementia Taylor, he sent his "kindest friendly regards to Miss Remond" and often inquired about her.[49] Their friendship was such that while in Birmingham, he had "an unexpected call from Mrs. Malleson and Miss Remond."[50] It was a surprise visit, which demonstrates the confidence regarding the reciprocal nature of the relationship between Remond and Mazzini.

Elizabeth Malleson, who accompanied Remond, was related to Peter Taylor. She was the wife of Frank Malleson, whose brother, William T. Malleson, married Taylor's sister and became the chairman of the Social Purity Alliance for which his wife also worked. The society was established in 1873 to promote temperance, legal reform, and high moral principles.[51] Elizabeth Malleson was actively involved in promoting women's rights and defending prostitutes, whom she and other London women perceived as victims of social adversity. She was a member of the Ladies' London Emancipation Society and of the Society Promoting the Employment of Women.[52] In this way, through her friendship with Malleson, Remond further enlarged her views on philanthropic work, which now encompassed women who were prostitutes or victims of "white slavery." Malleson subsequently became involved in the Ladies National Association and the Westminster Committee for the Repeal of the Contagious Diseases Acts, which were engaged in a political campaign led and conducted by women against the Contagious Diseases

Act, which gave police officers the authority to arrest prostitutes if, after a forced medical examination, they were found to be infected by venereal disease. Others who were active in the mixed-gendered National Association or its Ladies National Association branch included several London radicals, many of them Mazzinians and friends of abolitionists. Among them was Emilie Venturi.[53]

In addition to her personal contact with Mazzini, Remond's name appears in a letter from February 1866, published in the Italian newspaper *Dovere* on 2 June of the same year. She is listed among the prominent British who were supporting the Italian cause and raising funds. The letter was addressed to the "Commissione della Società del Progresso" (Commission of the Society for Progress) of Faenza, which promoted support for Mazzini and remonstrations against his condemnation and exile. Mazzini's English friends joined the protest thus demonstrating their backing of Mazzini and Italy.[54]

The letter included 387 signatures of supporters of emancipation, liberty, and democracy, and the renowned British specifically mentioned by name included the director of *Macmillan Magazine,* David Masson; the novelist George Meredith; Peter and Clementia Taylor; Emilie Venturi, who also translated Mazzini's works into English; Matilda Biggs, who authored a story narrating the situation of African Americans before their emancipation; and an "illustrious American Miss Remond" ("un'egregia Americana Miss Remond").[55] The article and original letter highlighted the presence of Remond's signature among the other dignitaries by mentioning her separately and defining her as "egregia"—illustrious, eminent. She seems to have been the only American mentioned by name. The letter makes no reference to her race or the color of her complexion but simply defines Remond as an American, which would indicate that she was considered an equal to the notorious British mentioned by name and would suggest that she was highly admired.

In March 1867, after Remond had permanently moved to Italy but still occasionally visited England, Mazzini sent his "Love to Miss Remond" at the end of a letter to Clementia Taylor, suggesting that Remond had possibly returned to London for a visit after starting her studies in Florence in the autumn of 1866. She did indeed return to England in 1867 but it was later in the year, in July, when she appeared as one of the prominent guests invited to a public breakfast celebration organized in honor of William Lloyd Garrison. In the letter mentioned above, Mazzini responded to Taylor's appeal to assist black Americans. Unfortunately, his response was negative because, as Mazzini explained, he already had more causes to fight than he could handle: "I saw your appeal; bless you. I wish I could do something for it. But I have more than I can, in trying the enfranchisement of the *whites;* . . . Besides," he wrote, "you want nothing but women."[56] Although his agenda was full and he was working for more causes than his time and health allowed, Mazzini managed to establish schools for the instruction of poor Italians in London.[57] He continued to regard education as important and to support the poor, especially when they came from his beloved Italy.

Although he refused Clementia Taylor's appeal, Mazzini supported women and African Americans in their struggle for emancipation. When he heard of Lincoln's death, he wrote to Taylor expressing his sorrow: "Yes, I mourned for Lincoln and much more for his wife and all those who loved him. As for him, he died with the consciousness that the cause to which he had devoted himself was triumphant; and the tought [*sic*] must have soothed his last hours."[58] According to Susan Castillo, "Abraham Lincoln's central preoccupation, even more and above the issue of slavery, was to preserve the unity of the American nation."[59] Moreover, as the historian John Hope Franklin has noted, Lincoln was among those who "saw the differences between the two races as quite real and insurmountable," whereas Mazzini was a supporter of black emancipation and equality, perhaps even more so than Lincoln.[60] With Lincoln, Mazzini, however, shared the same altruistic dedication to a cause that embraced the ideals of freedom and national unity. Mazzini's words echo his feelings concerning the satisfaction he himself had obtained for having altruistically fought for the oppressed. His sensibilities allowed Mazzini to understand the grief Lincoln's wife experienced in losing a husband, and he thus displayed his transatlantic empathy. At the same time, he conveyed his own sadness for the loss of a leader who, like Mazzini himself, had dedicated his life to concretizing his political goals.

Throughout his involvement in changing history, Mazzini was forced to live in exile and constant fear that his correspondence would be censored unless the letters arrived at an unsuspected address, and yet he remained relentless in his determination to create a better future for Italians. The British newspapers monitored his activities during his expatriations in France and Switzerland, and continued to follow Mazzini after the unification of Italy. They reported on the various proposals put forth by Italians to grant him amnesty so that he could return to his native country. The British wrote petitions on his behalf, publicizing them in newspapers, so as to encourage those who had known and admired Mazzini to sign their names in support of the appeals drafted by British gentlemen. For instance, the *Dundee Advertiser* opined that the "life and labours of Mazzini have proved a source of inspiration not only to Italians, but to many of the leading thinkers in our own country, who have been led by his teaching and example to take wider and nobler views of human life, and of the destiny which lies before the race."[61] Remond can be included among the leading thinkers promoting noble ideals for humanity. Mazzini inspired many and, like Remond, fearlessly propagated a cause he firmly believed in.

Remond's projections of freedom followed a similar line of thinking as Mazzini's. At a Bolton meeting she addressed the controversial topic of colonization, illustrating her point by comparing black Americans to Italians. The aim of her talk was to correct the false impression "that free blacks wished to return to Africa to civilize the natives and raise cotton. The idea was as ludicrous, she told her audience, as thinking that the Pilgrims wished to return to England to civilize the natives."[62] She would explain to her Manchester audience a few days later that "there is nothing the free colored people of the United States hate like colonization in the concrete" because they were attached to their country, America, not Africa. They had every intention of remaining in America, similarly to Italians who wished to live peacefully and independently in Italy.[63] In her illuminating speeches, Remond further argued that any oppression, including slavery, should concern everyone, irrespective of their nationalities.

Remond, who excelled in all her endeavors, was an intellectual race leader who articulated future possibilities for African American racial pride and self-esteem. Her message of empowerment bore similarities to the one Mazzini was delivering to his countrymen. Moreover, both abolitionists and exiles were looking to generate international disapproval of the subjugation of their fellow citizens, thus using foreign opinion as a weapon in their battle for freedom.[64]

The British who were fighting to eradicate slavery to some extent instrumentalized abolitionism to serve their own needs. The fervent support of American antislavery lecturers who were touring in Great Britain served as an attack on the former colony. In this way, the British added nationalist propaganda to the political abolitionist agenda. In the United States, instead, two separate dimensions existed in the evolvement of racial groups: their evolution occurred as internal development and through responding to international power struggles.[65] The nation that had at its core the controversial question of slavery, thus, remained for decades under both internal and external pressures.

Newspaper articles, political dispatches, and even poems served to press Americans on the question of slavery but also to support Italy. The historian Paola Gemme suggests that American poets who generally were "connected with the abolitionist movement, lamented the Italians' enslavement to Austria and celebrated their emancipation from foreign imperialism."[66] The writings referring to Italy's unification included Henry Theodore Tuckerman's "A Word for Italy," which appeared in the *Democratic Review* in September 1845, making it one of the early works addressing Italy. Quite frequently American writers dedicated their articles specifically to a particular leader or martyr or perhaps to persons they presented as heroes sacrificing their lives for democracy and freedom. Such articles included "Silvio Pellico, The Italian Martyr," which appeared in the *Christian Examiner* in July 1854, and "Giuseppe Garibaldi," which came out in the *North American Review* in January 1861.[67] Garibaldi, as mentioned earlier, was also brought up in Remond's speeches, which were printed in American and European newspapers. According to the historian Eugenio F. Biagini, to such poets as William Cullen Bryant, John G. Whittier, and Henry T. Tuckerman, Garibaldi "symbolized the values of the Declaration of Independence." They perceived him as upholding Protestant ideas because of his dislike of the pope and the pope's political power.[68] Other poems on the same themes included Tuckerman's "The Siege of Rome," which appeared in 1864; and William Ross Wallace's "The Triumph of Italian Freedom" (1860).[69]

Others, such as William Dean Howells, who assumed the responsibilities of American consul in Venice during the Civil War, were interested in the works of contemporary nationalist writers including Giacomo Leopardi, Alessandro Manzoni, Ugo Foscolo, and Silvio Pellico. Longfellow, instead, had a collection of the patriotic poet Francesco Dall'Ongaro's works, which ranged from historical to political publications to dramatic and lyrical writings. Dall'Ongaro promoted his nationalist beliefs in his works, celebrating republicanism and freedom in his poems.

Longfellow, who had always been drawn to Italian art and letters, starting with Dante Alighieri whose *Divina Commedia* he translated, met the Italian nationalist poet Dall'Ongaro in Florence during Longfellow's visit there in 1868. Remond, who at the time permanently resided in Florence, was invited to one of the musical soirées also attended by Longfellow at Dall'Ongaro's. The patriotic poet had fervently supported Italian unification and liberation from Austrian rule, and gradually he assumed a more radical stance toward the unification movement, consequently forming personal ties with Garibaldi and Mazzini. After his travels across Europe, Dall'Ongaro established himself in Florence in 1859. As Anne Longfellow Pierce, who accompanied Longfellow to Italy in the 1860s, explained in her journal, "Signor Ongaro was a particular friend and compatriot of Garibaldi's—was exiled with him—after ten years came back to Florence and was made Prof. in the University under the change of administration—a poet of rank & a literary man."[70] During their stay in Florence in 1868, Longfellow and his family met with Dall'Ongaro several times, and they were also introduced to his friends, among them Remond.[71]

Hence, American descriptions of the Italian Revolution were not merely informative but also artistic or poetic, and they included personal encounters, even consolidated friendships, with leading patriots. Moreover, American interpretations contributed to nationalistic ideology and to the discussions of national identity and definitions of nation-state. More importantly, equating Italy's aspiration for independence with American slaves' desire for freedom was a powerful linkage used to justify black emancipation. It gained strength when Italian ambitions for independence were presented as paralleling America's own revolution. Remond's pamphlets, speeches, and protest letters, which circulated transatlanticly through American and European newspapers, belonged to the radical and influential body of texts—poems, letters, essays, travel writing, and newspaper articles—that raised awareness of injustice and demanded the extension of citizenship to include the racially marginalized. Moreover, in the works and through friendships of poets and writers, American support for Italian independence struggles became an individual, not only a collective quest. Americans who visited Italy formed friendships with Italian patriots and voiced their personal views, both privately and publicly. With Mazzini, Remond shared ideals and took action to achieve transnational ambitions concerning racial and national liberty.

The Italian Risorgimento was used to reinvent American national identity through comparing it with revolutionary Italy. "Like black slaves in the American republic, Italians had been subjected to brutal despotism for centuries, and knowing how they conducted themselves upon obtaining freedom could be used to speculate about how bondsmen would react to manumission," Gemme argues.[72] Italian political events served to voice controversial views concerning the suitability of domestic marginalized groups, such as African Americans, to participate in U.S. democracy, their fitness to be invested with the power of republican citizenship. The aspirations of Americans who supported other nations in their attempts to achieve independence and to obtain democratic governments obviously reflected and advanced American national ideals. Abolitionists capitalized on American support of European revolutions to advance their own domestic causes.[73]

The United States, Biagini notes, "was the first government to recognize the Kingdom of Italy in April 1860 (even before the official proclamation of the new state)."[74] Italy, with the aid and contribution of its revolutionary thinkers, poets, and artists, realized its long-cherished ambition of uniting the peninsula into one nation. Remond arrived there in 1866, at a time when Florence was the new political and administrative center of the unified country. In this new capital of Italy she connected with the local society and had many and varied opportunities to meet with numerous prominent Anglo-Americans visiting or residing there.

Many of these foreigners had followed or personally taken part in the Risorgimento movement.

For many foreigners, Italy was a site of emotional and political turmoil but also of self-fulfillment. Both Rome and Florence were popular choices among American expatriates, providing environments in which Americans could concretize their potential as artists, writers, and passionate women. For instance, during the years of the revolution in the early 1850s, the sculptor Harriet Hosmer established herself in Rome, where she shared her home with another woman artist, Emma Stebbins. From her residence, Hosmer followed the political turmoil in Rome, informing her friends and relatives in the United States of the developments that led to Rome's liberation under the French occupation. During her stay in Florence in 1859–60, Mary Somerville, a Scottish mathematician and scientist interested in the physical sciences and chemistry, met Hosmer and her English art teacher, John Gibson, as they were passing through the city on their way to Switzerland. Gibson, Somerville wrote, looked upon Hosmer as a daughter; he was proud of her work, just as Somerville herself was. She expressed her "admiration for Miss Hosmer, who has proved by her works that our sex possesses both genius and originality in the highest branches of art."[75] Hosmer, like Remond and the African American artist Edmonia Lewis, was demonstrating what women were able to achieve when given the opportunity to freely express themselves. Hosmer, who lived in England and Italy, may well have met Remond either in Rome or in Florence.

In Florence, Somerville also met Frances Power Cobbe, a friend of Remond's, "the cleverest and most agreeable woman."[76] Together with Cobbe, Somerville took part in a protest against some "barbarous vivisections" by a German professor of physiology.[77] Both women were activists in protecting animal rights.

When Cobbe was in Rome, she stayed with the women artists who were gathered around the famous American actress Charlotte Cushman, who had chosen Rome as her home, in a similar way to other professional women. Many of the women in Cushman's entourage were abolitionists who also keenly followed and reported on the Risorgimento in Rome in their letters to friends.

Like Rome, Florence became the adopted home of artists such as Horatio Greenough and Hiram Powers, among many others. Several visiting Americans contacted Powers, who assisted them with logistics and introduced them to resident Anglo-Americans and his Florentine friends. The Longfellow family met with Powers and the artists Thomas Ball and John Adams Jackson during their visit to Florence in 1868. Anne Longfellow Pierce described Powers in her journal when they met in 1868: "Powers has lived thirty one yrs. in Florence, without once going home to America, but is still a true hearted patriotic countryman."[78] Likewise, Remond would stay in Italy for approximately thirty years without going back to the United States.

In October 1860, the *New York Times* reported from Florence that in addition to Powers, Ball, Joel Hart, and his nephew Robert Hart, "among the other American artists at present in the neighborhood of Florence, may be named Mr. HOTCHKISS, Mr. GOULD, Mr. WAUGH, Mr. VEDDER, and Mr. FORD."[79] Since the American social circles in Rome and Florence were small and expatriates were well connected with each other, it is highly probable, again, that many of these artists knew and befriended Remond. They were busily executing orders they received from their native America, and visiting Americans often came to their studios to look at American artworks. In the 1860s, however, the number of commissions from the United States declined, as did the number of American visitors in the artists' studios, due to the Civil War, which discouraged foreign travel. Therefore, the articles that appeared in the *New York Times* promoting the works of American sculptors in Florence and Rome served the important function to keep art collectors informed and commissions flowing in.

Another article appeared in March 1864 that advertised the achievements of several other artists in Rome and Florence, where Remond may have met them (Powers, Hart, Jackson, and L. G. Mead Jr. in Florence; in Rome, Story, Chauncey Bradley Ives, Hosmer, Stebbins, Margaret Foley, and William James Stillman, who served as the U.S. consul from 1861 to 1865).[80] Moreover, around the time that Florence was the unified Italy's capital and became Remond's permanent residence, several prominent American writers arrived there either for brief visits or longer stays. They included Mark Twain (Samuel Clemens) in 1867, Longfellow in 1868, Henry James in 1869, and Charles Eliot Norton (1869). Numerous others came after, including Frederick Douglass and William Dean Howells. Other Americans and British, such as the travel writer Janet Ross and her niece Lina Duff Gordon, both known for their guidebooks of Tuscany, lived most of their lives in Italy where they befriended British and American visitors, among them Twain and Virginia Woolf.

The sculptress Lewis was among the many who connected with the Anglo-American expatriate circles upon her arrival in Italy. In 1865, she traveled from Paris to Florence, where Marsh introduced her into the society of Italians and expatriate Anglo-Americans. Soon after, Marsh welcomed Remond, her sister Caroline Putnam, and her nephew Edmund and his wife, Gertie, to Florence, and, therefore, it is highly probable that he similarly introduced all of them to his friends and acquaintances, who included Italian revolutionaries, authors, and poets as well as American artists and writers. Lewis, for instance, met with other artists, including Powers, Ball, and the painter Elizabeth Adams, who at the time were working in Florence. Powers and Ball helped Lewis get started with her new career as a professional artist by assisting her with finding a studio, material, and tools.[81] Subsequently, Lewis moved from Florence to Rome, where she started working on commissions she received from the United States and England.

Lewis's choice to establish herself in Italy may have influenced Remond's decision to exchange her home in England for one in Italy. British papers, which Remond surely followed, indicate that in March 1866, "Miss Edmonia Lewis, a lady of colour, has taken a studio in Rome, and works as a sculptress in one of the rooms formerly occupied by the great master Canova."[82] A week later, the same announcement appeared in the *Sussex Advertiser*, which makes it highly probable that Remond saw the notice before finalizing her plans to move to Italy. Newspapers followed the success of Lewis, observing a year later that "In the studio once occupied by Canova, I found Miss Edmonia Lewis, who I presume is the only colored sculptress in the world—a lady perhaps twenty-three years of age, with African and Indian blood in her veins. . . . Her genius is of no ordinary kind. There are but few girls, or men either, who can fight so brave a battle at such an age, against such odds."[83] Similarly to Lewis, Remond had courage, perseverance, and genius that were "of no ordinary kind." She possessed talent, was ready to continue her brave battle toward success, and hence became perhaps the only African American female doctor at the time, when two years later she completed her medical studies in Florence, then the capital of Italy, which she personally had helped become a nation.

CHAPTER 6

Firenze "La Bella"

SIMILARLY TO AMERICAN ARTISTS, WRITERS, AND COMMON tourists who repeatedly equated travel with self-improvement, Sarah Remond embarked on her geographical and metaphorical journey toward the Old Continent, traveling for acculturation and enlarged personal and professional opportunities; she, like white Americans, journeyed toward self-realization. In the nineteenth century, Mary Suzanne Schriber observes, "Americans undertook travel to better themselves culturally and intellectually."[1] Their quest for culture contributed to the conceptualization of an enhanced idea of national identity as it was reflected against the foreign background. According to William W. Stowe, "Early American travelers such as Thomas Jefferson and John Adams were eager to define themselves in transnational terms as ex-Europeans with a special relation to European culture, whereas their successors in midcentury—Fuller, Greeley, and Twain, for example—were more concerned with asserting a uniquely American identity."[2] In 1866, when Remond moved to Florence, she joined other Americans who were in Italy asserting their Americanness, defining their nation, national identity, and culture, often through antagonistic comparisons with the foreign Old World. Remond's presence in Florence, then, signifies black inclusion in national discourses in a transatlantic context.

Remond and Edmonia Lewis were among the few nineteenth-century black career women who chose Italy as their residence. Soon after she had established herself in Florence, Remond was joined by her sister Caroline, who had visited her regularly, together with her son Edmund, after Caroline's husband, Joseph Putnam, had passed away in January 1859. Living alone with her son (her only daughter, Louisa Victoria, had died in May 1858 when she was only nine months old[3]), Caroline Putnam decided to spend more of her time in Europe where Edmund studied medicine in Vienna starting from 1865, a year before Remond enrolled in medical school in Florence. While studying medicine, Edmund also wrote articles that appeared in the *New York Herald Tribune, Independent,* and *National Anti-Slavery Standard.*

After his graduation, Edmund practiced his profession in London. It was in England where he met his future wife, Gertrude Agnes "Gertie" Elliston. They married in Cheltenham, St. Mary, Gloucestershire, on 24 May 1868.[4] Although they chose Rome as their permanent residence, Edmund and Gertie frequently visited England, where Gertie's father lived in Bournemouth. Since Caroline's only son had decided to establish himself in Europe, and her sister Sarah was also permanently living in Italy, Caroline and another sister, Maritcha, joined them, moving to Europe where they resided both in Italy and England.[5] Remond's and her sisters' examples demonstrate that nineteenth-century black women traveled; as they did so, they challenged "cultural anxiety about free black citizenship."[6] By the time the Remond sisters had established themselves in Rome and Florence, Italy had already been well stabilized on white American Grand Tour itineraries and had frequently become the chosen home of white expatriate Americans.

The first American visitors to choose Italian cities such as Florence for their temporary or permanent residence arrived in the 1820s. They were mainly artists and writers who used Europe, as William W. Stowe suggests, "as a stage for independent self-definition, for establishing personal relations with culture and society that did not necessarily fit the conventional patterns prescribed by hometown and family standards."[7] The contrast Italy formed to the reality Americans experienced in their native country was dramatic. For Henry Wadsworth Longfellow, Europe served to provide an education that led to a lifelong career and international fame. At the time of his first visit, Longfellow was a student of foreign languages and cultures, preparing himself to take on the responsibilities of a professorship in modern languages at Bowdoin College. Another author to arrive in Italy around the same time, in 1828, was James Fenimore Cooper, who had already obtained fame among both American and European readers for his novel *The Last of the Mohicans* (1826). He traveled to Europe in search of material and a publisher for his subsequent novels. Both Longfellow and Cooper were among the first Americans to write about their foreign travels and use their writings to build careers. Moreover, travel was fundamental for them and for those who followed in the process of identity construction, both individual and collective.[8]

These American intellectuals of the early decades of the nineteenth century were fluent in foreign languages and were thus able to communicate with members of Florentine high society in French, Italian, and, when necessary, Spanish. Following the polyglot Longfellow and Cooper came Margaret Fuller, who knew Italian, which enabled her to discuss politics with Italian revolutionaries. Those who arrived after them, especially in the post–Civil War decades, were equally eager to connect with the local society but often failed in their attempts because of the language barrier. The novelists Henry James and Constance Fenimore Woolson are examples of American Grand Tourists who knew rudimentary Italian but somehow failed to fully immerse themselves in local life. Others, like Mark Twain, had children who were multilingual, equally at ease speaking English, French, Italian, or German, whereas Twain himself relied on his dictionary and sign language when talking with his servants. Therefore, it was quite exceptional to find African American women, such as Remond and Lewis, who mastered Italian to the extent of being able to conduct their studies, professions, and social lives in the language of their adoptive country. Consequently, for them, entering the local society, where international cosmopolitan intellectuals exchanged ideas in French and Italian, was not problematic. Moreover, in Italy, where racial difference was not used as a distinguishing attribute to implement or justify segregation, the intellectual salons welcomed black Americans on equal terms, exactly as they did white Anglo-American expatriates.

The cosmopolitanism of the Old World in such countries as Italy embraced difference, national and racial, and welcomed representatives of ethnic diversity, treating all with equal respect. Cosmopolitanism, which is a concept with multiple, often contested meanings, stands as a term that dates back to the fourth century BC. Scholars have used it in its more general application as referring to a "citizen of the world." Indeed, "cosmos" translates into "world" and a "polites" indicates a citizen of a "polis," or city.[9] More recently, the definition of cosmopolitanism has been disputed within various fields of study but scholars have repeatedly associated it with globalization and multiculturalism, albeit with dissimilar, even unrelated meanings and connotations. According to the scholar Kwame Anthony Appiah, for example, among the concept's main characteristics are respect and acceptance of diversity that form the foundation for enlightened international cosmopolitan dialogue.[10] Both Appiah and the scholar Gillian Brock underscore the importance of equal respect in the concept of cosmopolitanism, "no matter what" a person's "citizenship status or other affiliations happen to be."[11] The respectful consideration of each individual despite difference, Brock affirms, stands for the commitment to moral equality. Cosmopolitans, she argues, "are committed to the ideal that each *person* is entitled to equal respect."[12] Moreover, scholars consider self-determination and political autonomy as key issues in generating tolerance.

Old World cosmopolitanism, which Florence in particular epitomized, corresponded to such prerequisites. In Florence, pluralism was accepted and diversity valued in various intellectual salons where people from different societies, historical backgrounds, and with dissimilar religious values and beliefs gathered together to exchange ideas about politics, arts, and literature. However, the recognized and approved differences were limited to certain characteristics that excluded others. Intellectuality, culture, and class—all prerequisites pertaining to Remond—were common denominators of the international participants in the polyglot cosmopolitan circles that welcomed, and united, representatives of various nationalities and societies.

The cosmopolitan society, best exemplified in Florence, furnished "a variety, brilliancy, and piquancy not readily to be found in other cities," opined the American art collector James Jackson Jarves.[13] American authors repeatedly linked intellectualism with nobility, thus using intellectual capital as an indicator of class distinction. This, of course, reasserted the social hierarchy of American society in which the elite was distinguished from other social classes and where the cultured assumed the role of social leaders.[14] As the historian T. J. Jackson Lears puts it, "they [members of the elite] were the moral and intellectual leaders of the American WASP bourgeoisie, who joined their British counterparts in shaping a transatlantic Victorian culture and who helped (sometimes unwittingly) to maintain dominant norms and values."[15] Such assumptions, however, excluded educated and cultured black intellectuals, who in Italy could join the society's thinkers and trendsetters. Such women as Remond were entitled to participate in social events and enjoy cultured entertainments without having to confront racial segregation.

Already in her native America Remond had expressed interest in literature and theater, but she had been denied access to integrated schools and had been forced to accept inferior seats at segregated sections reserved for black theatergoers. Florence, instead, offered entertainments at venues that were desegregated. In addition to theater, among the chief attractions in Florence was the opera. At the city's two opera houses, Tuscans listened to the music of Mozart, Rossini, Verdi, and Donizetti, whose repertoires were popular after Italy had become a kingdom and Florence its capital. The Pergola, the main opera house, had been established in 1656 and occasionally presented foreign performers, such as the American dancer Augusta Maywood, who appeared in ballets introduced between opera acts or the Swedish opera singer Jenny Lind (known as the Swedish Nightingale), who astonished audiences during her European tour in 1871.[16] Hence, not only the audiences but also some of the performers came from the United States and other foreign countries. The polyglot nobility, together with expatriates and foreign visitors, enjoyed theater and ballet performances, attended the opera and concerts, both public and private, and mingled at cosmopolitan receptions before, during, and after Italy's unification. Since

Remond had studied vocal music and most probably had attended the opera with Giuseppe Mazzini in London, it is highly probable that she participated in the cultural entertainments Florence offered to its temporary and permanent residents.

When Remond arrived in Florence it was the most important city of unified Italy. The preparations for transferring the capital from Turin to Florence started in 1864: on 11 December, Florence was proclaimed capital of the Kingdom of Italy, a status it officially held from 1865 to 1870. The head of the nation, Victor Emmanuel II, established himself at the Pitti Palace, which had been built around mid-fifteenth century, whereas some ministries found headquarters for their activities at Palazzo Vecchio.[17] The city went through major urban developments as soon as it was proclaimed the capital. In 1865, the architect Giuseppe Poggi, who was born in Florence in 1811, suggested that the medieval walls that encircled the city should be torn down to give way to large boulevards. After the demolition of the walls, he designed the broad Viale dei Colli that led to Piazzale Michelangelo, which also was his design. In addition, the city center was enlarged and new neighborhoods built including one around Piazza d'Azeglio, and one large piazzale was constructed by the entrance to the Cascine Park. In addition, such bridges as Ponte alle Grazie and alla Carraia were widened to better allow carriages to cross over the Arno River. In this way, the city went through a transformation; as a consequence, prices increased.[18]

Another change was caused by the presence of the nation's political and administrative leaders in Florence. Foreign diplomats, among them the American representative George (Giorgio) Perkins Marsh, moved from Turin to Florence, where they took part in an active political and social life. The American embassy found premises on Via de' Serragli 13, and foreign representatives from Austria, Brazil, France, Greece, Mexico, Russia, Sweden, Turkey, and others established embassies that were all centrally located.[19] Senators, ministers, and dignitaries made the capital a vibrant center of social and political change. The government brought up for discussion important questions, one of them the reinstatement of the death penalty, which Grand Duke Pietro Leopold had abolished in 1786, making Tuscany the first European state to eliminate capital punishment. Since the death penalty was implemented in other parts of the kingdom, the government tried to reintroduce it in the capital region but without success.[20] Thus, during the years when the governing bodies of Italy were stationed in Florence, Tuscany continued to be considered one of the most enlightened regions of Italy, and Florence its refined center.

Florence had a cultured social life that consisted of numerous meeting places that included several cafés such as Caffè Michelangelo on Via Larga (now Via Cavour) where the Tuscan Macchiaioli painters (Silvestro Lega, Giovanni Fattori, and Telemaco Signorini) met until its closing in 1867. Caffè Doney, Pasticceria Giacosa, Gambrinus, which was known for not allowing women to enter, Caffè la Rosa, located next to the Baptistery, and a Viennese brewery in Piazza Signoria all made the city lively. Florence also boasted of its intellectual salons, which included those of the banker Emanuele Fenzi, Countess Eufrosina Gamba, and Maria Rattazzi in Piazza Santo Spirito. Emilia Peruzzi Toscanelli and Ubaldino Peruzzi, who was the mayor of Florence, hosted one of the important Florentine salons where the habitual guests consisted of members of the nobility and members of the educated international elite.[21] The Peruzzis entertained the period's most prominent artists and scientists, who were Italian, German, Swiss, American, among other nationalities.[22] Subsequently, Countess Edith Peruzzi (who was the daughter of the American sculptor William Wetmore Story, married to Simone Peruzzi dei Medici in 1876) would organize her gatherings that were attended by such Americans as Henry James.

Moreover, Florence was generally considered an ideal place for artists and writers, as testified by James Jackson Jarves, who described it as "a paradise for exiles in pursuit of artistic ease or literary quiet."[23] Throughout the nineteenth century, the city's attractions included museums and art galleries, palaces and churches, music and performances. Indeed, in his travel book *Italian Sights and Papal Principles* Jarves opined that "there is something in the very name of Florence that suggests refinement and pleasurable emotions."[24] Therefore, many artists, writers, and art collectors who came from abroad decided to stay there indefinitely. Jarves was one; another was Remond.

Remond and Jarves met in Florence. Jarves, who came from Boston, was the leading American art critic of the time. He also functioned as the American vice consul in Florence between 1880 and 1882 and was one of the most noteworthy American collectors of the nineteenth century. With the help of the Greek painter Giorgio Mignaty, Jarves first started collecting Italian art for himself, then for other Americans. Following the advice, suggestions, and instructions of Mignaty, who permanently resided in Florence, Jarves toured all over Italy purchasing objects that ranged from paintings and drawings to textile and glass; he collected Primitives, Venetian glass, Renaissance fabrics, laces, and costumes, and assembled an impressive collection of drawings by Michelangelo, Raphael, Rembrandt, Titian, and others. His aim was to sell the art to newly formed museums in the United States. He was also a prolific author who published several books on Italian life and art. His most famous works include *Old Masters of Italy* (1861), *Art Thoughts: The Experiences and Observations of an American Amateur in Europe* (1869), and *Italian Rambles: Studies of Life and Manners in New and Old Italy* (1883). He was one of the American collectors determined to "bring culture home."[25] Through Jarves, Remond connected with the world of art collecting and cultural expertise.

Unfortunately, a certain James W. Stillman, who attacked Jarves's ambition and fervent desire to educate Americans in art, claimed that artists in the United States owed nothing to European artists and with such arguments pushed Jarves to financial ruin. Many of his collections were sold at auctions rather than acquired directly by museums in New York and Boston, and they sold at prices lower than if the negotiations had directly been carried out between the collector and an interested purchaser. The artworks Jarves had collected in Europe in general, and in Italy in particular, were divided between various museums and galleries: his collection of drawings, which was mainly made by Count Maggiori of Fermo, ended up at the Yale University Art Gallery; his glass collection found a home at the Metropolitan Museum of Art; and the textiles from his collection were placed at Wellesley College.[26]

In Italy, Jarves became friends with poets Robert and Elizabeth Barrett Browning, the novelist Isa Blagden (whose manuscript he forwarded to the United States), the historian Pasquale Villari, and the art collector Seymour Kirkup, who appeared in Nathaniel Hawthorne's novel *The Marble Faun*

(1860). Villari, who was an internationally famous Italian historian, professor of history in Pisa and Florence, and senator of the Kingdom of Italy, had been forced to leave his native Naples for political reasons. He became especially well known after the publication of his book on the life of Savonarola (1861). Before his success as a historian, he had been earning his living by teaching Italian to English ladies while working on his first historical publications in Florence.[27] Villari, who was well-connected in Florentine society, made the acquaintance of several American intellectuals residing in the city, among them Jarves, who then became a friend of Remond's.

Jarves joined the social circles of Florentines but also connected with the American communities in Florence and Rome. During a visit to Rome in 1855, Jarves attended a party organized by Charlotte Cushman and her partner, Matilda Hayes, at their "beautifully furnished home."[28] Cushman was perhaps the most celebrated actress of her time and a central figure in the Anglo-American art circles in Rome, where she had an entourage of protégées, a group of American women artists, who included Harriet Hosmer and Emma Stebbins. It was the "strange sisterhood" Henry James referred to in his biography of Story.[29] In 1868, when traveling to Rome with Jarves, Remond connected with Anne Whitney, another American sculptor residing there at the time. Remond attended a gathering organized at Whitney's home, which provided an opportunity to meet other members of the Anglo-American colony established in the city. Many of the women lived in same-gender households free from social constraints and financial dependence on men, realizing their potential and using their talent to address contemporary controversies in the statues they chiseled in white Italian marble.

Charmaine A. Nelson points out that "the energetic pursuit of professional recognition, unchaperoned social mobility, rigorous physical activity, independent maintenance of living environment, financial independence, and the overwhelming rejection of heterosexual marriage and open lesbianism that these women lived were simply not possible to the same degree in mid-nineteenth-century America."[30] Italians, indeed, tended to be relatively tolerant toward foreigners whose behavior deviated from the norm. Moreover, Italy had a centuries-long history of the presence of homosexual communities that included women. In addition, in a foreign country such as Italy, American women living in same-gender couples were excluded from the social parameters of their own country but also from the norms of their adoptive home. Hence, nineteenth-century American women in Rome were able to live in relative freedom, detached from the pressures of heteronormative society.[31]

Together with Hayes, Cushman entertained Americans passing through Rome in her centrally located residence at 38 Via Gregoriana. Mazzini mentions in his letters of a meeting with her when she was on her way to England to stay with Emilie Venturi, who subsequently was planning to join Cushman in Rome.[32] Such connections demonstrate that once British or American visitors were introduced into the Anglo-American social circles, the intermingling guaranteed that eventually practically all of them became connected with each other. For instance, the Brownings, whose neighbor in Casa Guidi was the authoress Anna Jameson, were friends with Jarves and Blagden but also knew well the American composer Frances Boott, who was Blagden's neighbor. The Brownings also befriended Margaret Fuller, who passed the last night with them before sailing to her destiny with her husband and son.[33] The ship sank before reaching the American shore.

The Brownings also met Harriet Beecher Stowe, whom Remond seems to have met in London; as Barrett Browning wrote to a friend, E. Fanny Haworth in 1861:

> When she [Stowe] came to us in Florence some years ago, I did not think I should like her, nor did Robert, but we were both of us surprised and charmed with her simplicity and earnestness. At Rome last year she brought her inner nature more in contact with mine, and I, who had looked for what one usually finds in women, was startled into much admiration and sympathy by finding in her a largeness and fearlessness of thought which, coming out of a clerical and puritan *cul-de-sac,* and combined with the most devout and reverent emotions, really is fine. So you think that since "Uncle Tom" she has turned infidel, because of her interest in Spiritualism.[34]

In the 1850s and 1860s, spiritualism was much in vogue among Anglo-Americans in Florence. Jarves shared an interest in spiritualism with Barrett Browning and Hawthorne's wife, Sophia, who also was a believer. Others interested in spiritualism and mesmerism included Story, Kirkup, and the

American sculptor Hiram Powers. Members of Florentine society were divided over spiritualism between believers and those who remained skeptical. In Jarves's letters to Margherita Albana Mignaty, the wife of Giorgio Mignaty, he expressed his views about spiritualism, which was a common interest for many who attended Mignaty's receptions.

The beautiful Greek Margherita Mignaty was one of the hostesses of the multinational salons for which Florence was famous. She was born in 1827 in Corfu, and it was in Rome where she met the painter Giorgio Mignaty, originally from Cefalonia, who soon married her. After touring in several European cities, Mignaty chose to remain in Florence, where her hospitality and intelligence attracted intellectuals and politicians who eagerly joined her social circle.[35] With her dark eyes and cultured personality, she charmed everyone. Her intellectuality and passionate patriotism for Italy impressed such literary figures as the French Edouard Schuré, the Italians Francesco Dall'Ongaro and Villari, who attended her receptions together with the English Trollopes, Brownings, and Blagden, and such Americans as Jarves and Longfellow, who both were abolitionists and supporters of racial equality. Among other frequent visitors at the Mignaty residence was Giorgina Crawford Saffi, who was an English Mazzinian living in Florence, while another close friend of Mignaty's was Mazzini himself. Dall'Ongaro, who knew Mazzini personally, had remained in contact with him while living in Brussels and Paris before establishing himself in Florence in the summer of 1859. Dall'Ongaro, who was nominated professor of Italian literature at the University in Florence under the change of administration in 1861, also held his own intellectual salon attended by young Italian writers such as Giovanni Verga and Carlo Lorenzini (known as Collodi, the author of *Pinocchio*). In 1866, when Remond established herself in Florence, Giuseppe Garibaldi, another friend of Mignaty's, was in the city promoting the idea of Rome as the future capital of Italy.

During 1859 and 1866, Mignaty, who was a writer and journalist, passionately supported the concluding phases of Italian unification by publishing articles about the political turmoil in such English newspapers as the radical *Daily News,* whose first director was Charles Dickens. She also wrote articles on Lord Byron and Percy Shelley; one on Dante entitled "Dante and His Times," which appeared in *Rivista di Firenze;* and on women in society, which appeared in French. She also wrote books, in French and English, on a variety of topics, including on such illustrious figures as *Dante* (1865), *Wagner* (1873), and *Correggio* (1881). In addition, Mignaty started writing a historical treatise during the years that her friend Villari held a professorship of modern history in Florence. She published her study, *The Sketches of the Historical Past of Italy: From the Fall of the Roman Empire to the Earliest Revival of Letters and Arts,* in 1876.[36] She was a well-known and respected personality among Anglo-Americans residing and visiting Florence. Remond entered such an intellectually and culturally vibrant environment when she moved to Italy. Likewise, Caroline Putnam and her son, Edmund, became close friends of Madame Mignaty, who introduced them to her circle of friends.

Sophia Hawthorne provides a description of Mignaty, whom she met at a reception Blagden had organized at her Villa Brichieri on 11 September 1858. She encountered a Greek gentleman and lady at the party, Sophia wrote. The latter was "a queenly woman, with glorious eyes and brow, and shining black hair, curling, from a coronet of braids, down her cheeks, like flexible paragon (a brilliant black pietra dura). Her husband was also very handsome—having the same eyes, like deepest night, with stars in the abysses. Oriental eyes they must be, for the likes are not to be found in the Occident."[37] On 16 September, Mignaty, together with her daughter Astasia and Villari, came to visit the Hawthornes on Bellosguardo where they were renting a castle that appeared in Hawthorne's *The Marble Faun* as Donatello's Castello di Montebeni. In the garden of the castle, which in reality belonged to the family Montauto, the party sat in the moonlight looking over Florence "in a kind of poetic dream," as Hawthorne reflected.[38]

Next to the Hawthorne's residence was the villa where James started writing his novella *The Aspern Papers* when residing there as a guest of Woolson in 1887. The fourteen-room Villa Brichieri was a local gathering place; at various times when Blagden resided there she counted among her guests Cushman, the American journalist Kate Field, Jessie White Mario, Dall'Ongaro, Villari, and Frances Cobbe, whose guest Remond had been in Bristol in 1859. In February 1860, when Cobbe arrived in Florence, she stayed as Blagden's guest at the Bellosguardo villa. Cobbe may well have provided Remond with letters of introduction to expatriate and Florentine residents who included many other famous artists and writers such as Elizabeth Boott Duveneck and Francesca Alexander.

Barrett Browning, who met Cobbe in 1860, wrote to her sister-in-law that Cobbe expressed hardly any interest in the Italian movement as she was concerned about the poor in England.[39] The letter to Sarianna Browning was dated June 1860:

> A distinguished woman has been here lately—a Miss Cobbe (a fellow-worker with Miss Carpenter)—who, having overworked herself, was forced by her physician to come here for three months and rest, under dire penalties. She went to Isa Blagden's, and returned to England and her work just now. She is very acute, and so perfectly without Continental prejudices, that she didn't pretend to much interest even in our Italian movement, having her heart in England and with the poor. But she was much struck, not merely with the order of foreign institutions, but with their superior tenderness and sympathy. The account she gave of the English workhouses and hospitals was very sad, very cruel, corresponding, in fact, to what I have heard from other quarters.[40]

Cobbe, who was originally from Ireland, had first met Remond in Bristol where Cobbe resided and dedicated her time to reform work. After her stay in Florence, Remond met Cobbe again in Dublin in the summer of 1861. Cobbe was, indeed, concerned for the English poor, who were the beneficiaries of her philanthropic activities.

During her stay in Florence in April 1860, Cobbe witnessed the arrival of Victor Emmanuel into the city; somewhat later in the spring she also met Theodore Parker, who was already nearing his death.[41] The Brownings had met Parker in the winter of 1859 in Rome, where they had tête-à-têtes with him. According to Barrett Browning, he had been writing "a little Christmas book for the young just now, to prove how they should keep Christmas without a Christ."[42] Already that winter in Rome, before traveling to Florence, Parker had been extremely ill. He passed away in early May and was buried in the Protestant Cemetery of Florence. Cobbe had seen him only three hours earlier, "lying calmly, while life was ebbing away unconsciously to himself. He left written directions for his funeral," Cobbe wrote to Frank Newman, "limiting to five persons the attending him to the grave, of whom I am one."[43] While in Florence, Cobbe, like so many other visitors, met with other foreign and American celebrities passing through the city. On 19 May 1860, Cobbe wrote that Stowe had drank tea with her and Blagden on the terrace of their Bellosguardo villa. Unfortunately, Stowe had arrived too late to see Parker before he died.[44]

While residing in Florence, Cobbe started writing for British papers: she became a correspondent for the *Daily News,* while some of her other reports appeared in *Fraser's Magazine* in which she published twenty-eight articles between 1861 and 1870. These articles mainly dealt with social reform, whereas *Cornhill* published a series of correspondence and poems from Florence.[45] In December 1861, however, Cobbe became more involved in the political events that were changing Italy: she became an active political journalist, reporting on the turmoil from Rome in articles that appeared in the *Daily News.* As the scholar Sally Mitchell notes, Cobbe's reports included "eyewitness accounts of demonstrations, reports of rumors that the government was buying up lead to make bullets, and secondhand stories about arrests and troop movements."[46] She kept her readers informed about the national striving for liberty and justice while she simultaneously enjoyed the cultural riches and social life of Italy. Cobbe was a member of the Anglo-Florentine colony and well-connected to the intellectual cosmopolitan circles that included Mignaty. As suggested earlier, it is possible that she, in addition to Mazzini, introduced Remond into Florentine society when the latter decided to move to Florence.

Several members of the Florentine Anglo-American social circles, including Cobbe, shared a friendship with Mignaty, who also knew such American writers as Charles Eliot Norton. In a letter that he wrote in response to one received from Mignaty, he thanked the Greek authoress for a book she had sent him, which most probably was the *Sketches of the Historical Past of Italy,* written by Mignaty herself. Unfortunately, Norton had been "occupied with many cares" and had been unable to find time to read the book, but the "few pages that I have read have interested me much, & have shown me that I have much to expect from the remainder. I look forward to the quieter days of later summer," he continued, "for the pleasure of renewing through your words some of the most delightful memories and associations connected with Italy."[47] Mignaty's decision to become a historian at a time when it was an uncommon career choice for women testifies to her progressive views. She, like Remond, moved beyond patriarchal heteronormative society's limitations, offering new alternatives for women. Resembling women travelers in general, the expatriates Mignaty and Remond were among those who "worked both to deflect negative responses to their unorthodox behavior" and to revise "cultural ideas about what women could do."[48] Remond, and especially her nephew Edmund and his wife, Gertie, became close friends of Mignaty during their Florentine residencies.

Remond was one of the few fortunate African American women able to travel to Europe and remain there, while others, such as Charlotte Forten, merely fantasized about visiting the Old World, where her desire would have been to see places and artworks she had read about in travel books. For the few black Americans who found the courage and means to travel, reinventing themselves in the context of the transatlantic world was even more significant than for white Americans. Charmaine A. Nelson argues that "while for many bourgeois whites, travel was a means to reinforce or elevate social and cultural status, for blacks, enslaved or free, it often symbolized a search for racial equality and demarcated rapid and dramatic shifts in identification."[49] Travel for such prominent race leaders as Remond, however, whose social and cultural background was not inferior to white Americans, became also a means to realize her potential and explore new avenues for self-fulfillment. Forten, instead, never realized her dream of a European tour but instead remained in the prejudiced Pennsylvania, where she participated in reform movements that were mainly under white leadership. Remond, in contrast, not only visited Europe but made it her home.

In the late 1860s, when Remond chose to move from England to Italy, Florence had approximately 120,000 inhabitants and could boast of eighty-seven churches and as many as twelve theaters. At the time of Remond's residence, three British physicians, whom she may have met in London when studying to become a nurse, had established themselves in the city: one was a Dr. Wilson, physician to the British legation, member of the

Colleges of Physicians and Surgeons of London, and a licentiate in midwifery in London, formerly physician to a London hospital. He lived on 33 Via di Santo Spirito, close to where Remond found lodgings. Another one was a Dr. Duffy, fellow of the College of Surgeons in Ireland, and the third was Dr. R. Fraser, licentiate of the College of Surgeons of Edinburgh.[50] Dr. Duffy and later Dr. Baldwin, another English-speaking doctor established in Florence, were most frequently consulted by American expatriates, including Twain, James, and Woolson (who all became Baldwin's personal friends). Dr. Duffy befriended the official American representative, George Perkins Marsh, as well as Longfellow.

Other notable Americans visiting or living in the Italian capital during the time it was Remond's residence included Powers, who had established himself in the city in 1837. In 1867, Twain arrived for a brief visit during his European tour, which he narrated in his literary success *The Innocents Abroad* (1869); Thomas Ball was working in Italy on his historical compositions and portrait busts, including a statue of *Lincoln the Emancipator* in which he himself posed as the slave. In addition, Frances Boott lived on Bellosguardo hill with his daughter Elizabeth and remained in the city for decades, and finally, the sculptor Larkin Goldsmith Mead, the brother-in-law of William Dean Howells, established himself in Florence in 1866 after his marriage to a Venetian lady. While residing in Italy, Mead worked on a statue of Lincoln for the president's home city, Springfield, Illinois, and a piece known as the *Soldiers' Monument* for Vermont.

Other visitors included James, who was in Florence on his first Italian journey in 1869 and would return repeatedly in the following years; Longfellow, whose second visit to Italy, this time with his family, took place in 1868; and in the same year, according to Levina Buoncuore Urbino, "Dr. Appleton, of Boston, a resident of Florence for the last fifteen years (to whose politeness and attentions we are much indebted)." It seems that Appleton also knew Remond well. In Buoncuore Urbino's testimony, Dr. Appleton "considers Florence in a very progressive state."[51] Its progressiveness was detectable in politics, culture, and its intellectual society. In summary, Florence attracted American visitors in increasing numbers, and many of them returned repeatedly to the Renaissance capital, sometimes alone, at other times together with their families. It can be assumed that many of them met or became friends with Remond and the Putnams who for several decades resided in Florence.

At the time of Remond's arrival, Marsh was the American diplomatic representative in Italy, appointed by President Lincoln in 1861. Marsh was the first American minister to the unified Kingdom of Italy.[52] When he moved from Turin to the new capital, he established himself in the Villa Forini on Via Aretina, where he stayed even after his government duties were over. He was fluent in several languages, interested in history and philology, and knew Garibaldi, Jessie White Mario, and Ubaldino Peruzzi, the Florentine mayor. Marsh's friends included Powers, Mignaty, and Trollope, and he knew Horatio Greenough, Dr. Duffy, Dr. Gould, and many other important foreigners residing in Florence and Rome. At various times, Marsh entertained Americans at his home with dinners and receptions that were attended by Powers, the poet William Cullen Bryant (in 1866), travel writer Bayard Taylor (in 1867 and 1868), and Norton (in 1869). Taylor was among those who not only befriended Marsh but also Garibaldi and Madame Jessie Mario.[53]

In 1865, Marsh commented that Florence had become a "mighty poor residence": housing was expensive, food prices had increased, and the overall financial situation was quite desperate.[54] During the following years, the city accumulated debt, which led to a financial crisis in the 1870s, after the capital had been transferred to Rome. A decade later, however, the situation had improved and the number of American visitors in Italy once again increased, now including the more ignorant tourists and young girls who resembled James's fictional American character Daisy Miller. These uncultured girls were quite the opposite of such energetic, determined, educated, cultivated, and independent women as Remond.

Remond demonstrated her independence, agency, and determination through choosing where to travel as well as when and for what purpose. She made a conscious choice to move to Florence where her ambitious goal was to study medicine, an audacious aspiration for any nineteenth-century woman but even more so for a black woman. The choice of her residence and career had a fundamental impact on the conceptualization of her identity: she was first and foremost a woman, African American, and a doctor, a cultured cosmopolite, and an activist who had dedicated her life to empowering others. Her independence, courage, and progressive success characterized her choices and actions.

Remond, who often traveled alone, made no exception when changing her residence from England to Italy. On 14 August 1866, she was in Lucerne, Switzerland, heading for Florence, as Mazzini informed his friend Caroline Stansfeld. Since Mazzini was in Switzerland in exile, he was anxious not to be recognized and hence was afraid of meeting Remond, who supposedly was spending that week in the same Swiss town where Mazzini was hiding. Mazzini's fear of running into Remond was clear in a letter he wrote in August 1866: "I have been trembling at the probability of meeting here in the streets, Miss Remond, who is to be at Luzern this very week; but I did not see her. From Luzern to Florence she is to travel alone, and with her ignorance of the languages I wonder how she will manage. And in Florence? What will she do if there is no war? It will be very difficult for her to get an employment in our hospitals in peace time."[55] Mazzini seemed concerned about Remond's limited possibilities in finding work once in Florence. He expressed his doubts regarding the possibilities of employment available to Remond, by then a professional nurse, because the wars had been waged and the wounded cured. His patronizing attitude comes across in his comment about her ignorance of languages, an attitude that overlooked the fact that Remond had recently studied French and Latin at a prestigious college during her extensive stay in London. Remond had also traveled practically alone not only while touring Continental Europe but also on her initial transatlantic crossing from the United States to England. Mazzini was concerned about her but at the same time ignored, or possibly was unaware of, Remond's education and independence.

It seems that right from the start Remond planned to continue her studies rather than look for employment. A letter to the *National Anti-Slavery Standard,* written in 1866, states that from Switzerland Remond traveled to Italy: "I arrive at 'Firenze La Bella'. With some interest, I look around to all that I can," she wrote. "I am soon on my way to a hotel which had been highly recommended to me, and very soon I am in a most comfortable room."

That room was in a respectable pension, Casa Jandelli, located at 1 Piazza dei Soderini (now Piazza Nazario Sauro), right by the Arno River. Remond further explained that "I am not here [in Florence] for pleasure, but for study."[56] Indeed, on 29 August, she was established in the Italian capital, where she signed up for a one-month membership at the Vieusseux newsroom and circulating library, which was centrally located in the Palazzo Buondelmonti in Piazza Santa Trinita.

The Gabinetto of Jean Pierre (or Giovan Pietro) Vieusseux, with its section of foreign-language journals and books, epitomized the nineteenth-century polyglot cosmopolitanism of the city. It boasted an extensive collection of books and newspapers in Italian, English, and other foreign languages. Vieusseux himself was a distinguished man of letters and an editor of a liberal journal, *Antologia Italiana,* and he was known for his hospitality to foreign visitors. Scholars have acknowledged Vieusseux as the intellectual who opened a dialogue between Tuscans and foreigners. His publications, including *Antologia,* circulated widely, and his reading room became a central venue for intercultural and international networking.[57] As a member of Gabinetto Vieusseux, Remond had an opportunity to meet local people and foreigners, including Anglo-American expatriates. Moreover, the library was an ideal place for study. Located close to Remond's pension, it was an apt place for consulting books and other publications in preparation for her entrance examination to medical school.

The direction Remond's studies took may in part have been influenced by Forten's decision to become a nurse in the United States where she entered one of the hospitals to help the wounded soldiers of the all-black 54th Massachusetts Regiment in July 1863. Her task was to sew up bullet holes and bayonet cuts.[58] In addition, as mentioned earlier, Remond's nephew Edmund studied medicine in Vienna and then practiced as a doctor in London. Remond herself had first enrolled at the London University College's department of midwifery, which was associated with the All Saints University College Hospital ("Tutti Santi spedale del Collegio dell'università") and was used as a training ground for the All Saints nurses. The department was run by nuns who had a reputation of being efficient and dedicated. In addition, they were known for offering a high-quality education as well as special knowledge and experience in nursing. At the time of Remond's enrollment, many of the nuns working in the hospital were representatives of higher social classes than their predecessors. Remond, who received her education at the college and her training at the hospital, worked in the department of surgery. She was dedicated to her work, competent, and energetic, and she showed unwavering attention and kindness to the ailing who were assigned under her care, as testified by the recommendation letters her supervisors wrote on her behalf to support her application to the Santa Maria Nuova school in Florence.[59]

The Santa Maria Nuova hospital school had a long history of training doctors. At the time Remond became a student there, it was one of the most prestigious medical schools of Europe. As Jarves explained in his book on *Italian Sights,* Santa Maria Nuova was "one of the finest and best organized [hospitals] in Europe."[60] It was founded in 1287 by Folco Portinari, the father of Dante's Beatrice. Between the eighteenth and nineteenth centuries, the Medical College of Florence (il Collegio Medico di Firenze) was the institution to grant the official licenses that were required to practice medicine or surgery in Tuscany. As the archival documents demonstrate, the first woman to obtain a license to officially work as a surgeon was Maria Petroncini, who received her permit in September 1788. She was the wife of Francesco Ferretti from Anghiari, a surgeon who became her first instructor. He practiced medicine in Bagnocavallo, close to Ravenna, where Petroncini was originally from.

During the 1780s, after training under Ferretti, Maria Petroncini received her formal education at the Santa Maria Nuova and degli Innocenti Hospitals under the supervision of two excellent surgeons, Angelo Nannoni and his son Lorenzo, who had been certified in France as well as Italy. Petroncini's only publication, *Memoria per servire alla fisica educazione dei bambini* (1789), proposed her progressive views on how to take care of infants as patients. She suggested new ideas concerning their treatment and placed particular emphasis on hygiene. She may well have been influenced by the work done on obstetrics by one of her supervisors, Lorenzo Nannoni, whose publications she must have read and whose work she perhaps continued. At the conclusion of her studies, Petroncini insisted that she be allowed to take the examination that would officially recognize her as a surgeon in exactly the same way as her male colleagues. Petroncini, who was twenty-nine years old when she graduated from the Medical College of Florence as the first female surgeon, soon after moved to Ferrara. She passed away in 1791 but her daughter Zaffira continued her profession, following her parents' career path. Exactly like her mother, Zaffira received her initial training from her father, whereas her formal training in surgery took place in Bologna where she received her license in 1810. She became a famous and sought-after surgeon who was called to operate in such capitals as Milan and Paris.[61]

Thus, the hospital school Remond enrolled in had a significant history in training women doctors. In 1867, it had room for approximately two thousand patients, and the professors who taught at the school were all renowned in their field. The famous Murray guidebook from 1867 informed that "the wards are large, better adapted to a hot than cold climate. . . . Besides the wards for general diseases, it contains one for midwifery cases, others or incurables, and two *Camere Nobili* for male and female patients paying 2 pauls a day. It is the great school of Practical Medicine of Florence, and has produced some of the most eminent physicians and anatomists of Italy."[62] The hospital school had a chemistry laboratory, anatomy amphitheater or auditorium, and an exhibition of the famous Girolamo Segato's fossilized body parts.[63] The late professor Segato, who had discovered a process for petrifying animal substances, had established an anatomical history museum adjacent to the hospital. The students who entered the medical school had the advantage of studying anatomy at the museum located next door to where the human bodies and body parts were exhibited.[64] Subsequently, perhaps, Remond was among the Italian students who studied the anatomical museum's collections.

Remond's training and experience as a nurse in London formed the basis for her medical studies in Italy. When applying to the school, she wrote a letter in which she formally requested to be admitted as a student in the clinic of obstetrics. In the letter, dated 30 October 1866 and written in Italian, she informed the admissions office that she was a resident in London but was planning to spend the winter in Florence. The two reference letters that accompanied Remond's official request to the school both came from London and were translated into Italian. One of them was from Sister Rosmonda from the All Saints University College and the other was signed by M. Berkeley Hill, one of the head surgeons of the University College. Both letters testify to Remond's seriousness in taking care of her duties at the London University College. Moreover, Dr. Hill's letter also provides his evaluation of the high quality of education that Remond had obtained under the supervision of the nuns.[65]

As a reply to the formal request of admission, "Remond, Sarah, negra d'America" was granted permission to audit the classes during the academic year 1866–67.[66] Remond joined a number of other women, all Italian, who were admitted to study in the department of obstetrics at the Spedale di Santa Maria Nuova. Hence, Remond, who as an African American woman in the United States had been excluded from participating in academic culture, was able to enroll in the medical school of Florence as a student and was treated as an equal with all the other women who started their studies there at the same time.

During the academic year of 1866–67 Remond audited classes. She also traveled during this period. In March 1867, she was staying at the Taylors, as suggested by a letter Mazzini wrote to Clementia Taylor, which he ended by sending his "Love to Miss Remond."[67] She again spoke on the British lecture circuit where one of the speaking events scheduled during this time had as many as three hundred men and women in attendance. In the audience were William and Ellen Craft, who also were in London. In May 1867, Remond was traveling on the continent where she spent some time with her sister in Paris.

During her visit to France, Remond met William Lloyd Garrison, who on 31 May 1867 wrote to his wife of their several attempts to see each other:

> Sarah Remond called to see me the other day, but, to my regret, I was absent. Fanny, however, was at home, and learned from her that she had been residing in Florence for some months past. We reciprocated her visit last evening, but were told she had just gone out. A short distance from the house we met Mrs. Putnam and her son, and were warmly greeted by them. I am to see Sarah to-morrow forenoon. She does not fancy Paris, Mrs. Putnam said, and will return to London next week.[68]

Remond, then, seemed to prefer the cities of England and Italy to the French capital. On 6 July of the same year, she participated in a public breakfast organized in honor of Garrison in London.[69] Subsequently, Remond returned to Florence where she took up her studies, no longer auditing classes but fully participating in theoretical and practical instruction with other students, all of them Italian, all of them women.

To be able to continue her studies and officially enter the medical school as a student, Remond had to take the entrance examination, which she did immediately after her year of auditing classes. It can be assumed that, like other nineteenth-century Americans, her knowledge of Latin was useful in learning to master Italian, which she needed to pass the examination. In addition to the theoretical part, the admissions test also included a practical assessment. She passed with top marks, "benissimo," and so could officially start her medical studies at the school. Out of the nineteen candidates taking the test, six obtained the highest grade ("benissimo"), while seven apparently failed. Remond, who signed the register as "Sara Parker Remond," was asking to study at the obstetric clinic; she became one of eighteen women who were registered in obstetrics classes that year. This may indicate that others, possibly from the previous years, joined the new arrivals in attending the courses that started at the end of November and continued through June.[70] In the formal request letter in which Remond asked to be allowed to continue her studies, dated 13 November 1867, she gave her address as 8 Via Santo Spirito, which was around the corner from Casa Iandelli's, her previous residence. In her letter, she explained that she had already taken classes at the school for a year and desired to have a career in obstetrics.[71]

The school register shows that Remond, whose first name now was Italianized to Sara, participated in practical study and clinical service together with other students. In groups of four they took turns in twenty-four-hour shifts to assist pregnant women, those who were expected to give birth, and those who had just delivered babies. The students had to write reports of the patients who recovered at the department where the students practiced under the supervision of one of the medical assistants, without any help from the midwives.[72]

During her second and final year of attending classes and obtaining practical training, Remond was joined by Caroline Putnam and her son, Edmund. In October 1867, they visited the Vieusseux lending library, signing their names in the register on 18 October. Likewise, Powers had renewed his annual membership in May of the same year, Princess Strozzi paid for a three-month library entrance in November, and Bayard Taylor signed the register on 7 December. Once again, the city's local and foreign elite mingled at the Vieusseux, where the Putnams were also members. In the meantime, Remond was finishing her final year at the medical school.

In a letter dated 2 July 1868, "Remond Sara di America (Stati Uniti)," who had completed her studies and practical work, requested to be admitted to the final examinations scheduled to take place in July 1868 (despite, as the documents indicated, her absence of two months the previous year).[73] In a reply dated 29 July 1868, the school authorities gave her permission, and so, in summer 1868, "Remond, Sarah Parker, daughter of John, native of Salem, United States" ("Remond Sarah Parker figlia di John nativa di Salem Stati Uniti"), took the practical and habilitation exams, which were evaluated together with her studies.[74]

A newspaper article published in 1868 confirmed that Remond had studied at Santa Maria Nuova for the past two years, and, "after a regular course of study and also of hospital practice, she has recently passed the necessary examinations, and received a diploma for professional medical practice."[75] In a letter written in 1868, Anne Whitney also mentioned that Remond, who was present at Whitney's home on Easter Sunday, was "now a physician in Florence." She exuded success and style as she appeared with "her handsome dark person set off by a broad gold chain wound round and round her head and a white shawl," Whitney wrote to her sister.[76] Remond, then, was a pioneer in her role as a transatlantic abolitionist, progressive women's right's advocate, and professional woman entering the field of medicine, commonly accessible only to men. After her graduation, Remond remained in Florence where, it seems, she started her medical career.

CHAPTER 7

Transatlantic Cosmopolitan in Italy

THROUGHOUT HER LIFE SARAH REMOND REMAINED ENGAGED in a strongly intertwined dialogue between gender and race. She provided a model of empowered womanhood and professionalism to contemporary black (and white) women. In Florence, Remond's work prospects as a doctor were good, even though she was black and a woman; she also joined the circles of Florentine high society as reported in *Harper's Bazaar* on 28 August 1869: "Another woman, colored at that, has tussled herself through the little oppositions of common life in Italy, and by study and the requisite demands of the proper scientific people, been admitted as a practitioner of midwifery in Florence; and her name is Sarah Remond, maiden. She has good professional prospects. Her merit has won her friends in England and on the Continent, and she goes among the best people in Florence, notwithstanding her cuticle is tinted."[1]

A similar notice appeared in the newspaper of Elizabeth Cady Stanton and Susan B. Anthony, the *Revolution,* which identified Remond as "a highly gifted colored lady" who had been "travelling and residing abroad for a number of years." It further stated that she had successfully formed friendships with the most prominent people of Florence:

> She has availed herself meanwhile of the opportunity to study medicine and midwifery, and has lately been admitted a regular practitioner in Florence, Italy. It is said her great merits have won her friends on the continent of Europe, as they did in England. On going to Italy, she had excellent letters of introduction from Mazzini, among others. With this satisfactory passport, Dr. Appleton went with her to call on Garibaldi; and though many others were waiting for an interview, they were instantly admitted. *Miss Remond* is said to be not only well received everywhere in Florence, but she has friends among the very best people there.[2]

With letters of introduction from Giuseppe Mazzini, one of the century's most noteworthy Italian figures, Remond had entered Florentine society, as confirmed by a notice published in the *Christian Recorder* on 7 August 1869: "Miss *Sarah Remond,* a gifted colored lady, who studied medicine with Dr. Appleton—the friend and physician of Theodore Parker, during the latter portion of his life at Rome and Florence, has been regularly admitted as a practitioner of midwifery in Florence, where she is now residing, with excellent prospects of employment and success."[3] The rest was a verbatim repetition of the announcement that had previously appeared in the *Revolution.* The information was again replicated on 7 October 1869 in the *Revolution,* which claimed that she had "studied medicine under Dr. Appleton in Boston," and reported that "she had excellent letters of introduction from Mazzini and others. Dr. Appleton went with her to call on Garibaldi."[4] Despite this article, it is unlikely that she had studied medicine in Boston before moving to Europe and had probably met Appleton in Italy where she, perhaps, studied under his supervision.

After her graduation, Remond assumed her new function as a certified doctor. In the 1860s, obstetricians could work in Florence either as independent professionals or they could be hired by the city. Those working as city employees were in charge of a specific neighborhood where they were responsible for assisting poor and lower-class women through labor. The majority, however, worked as specialists who assisted women of all social classes during pregnancy and childbirth.[5] It is highly probable that Remond worked as an independent obstetrician. She knew Italian and was well-connected with foreigners and local Florentines alike.

In Florence, Remond became friends with James Jackson Jarves, who had arrived in Florence in 1851. Remond may first have met his wife, who had joined the lending library where Remond paid her one-month membership in August 1866. The Jarveses remained in Florence for forty years, first residing in Piazza Indipendenza, then in Palazzo Guadagni in Piazza Santo Spirito, which was close to where Remond's residence had been in 1867. It is with Jarves that Remond supposedly traveled to Rome in 1868 when she attended the artist Anne Whitney's Easter reception.[6] Perhaps it had been Jarves who introduced her to Dr. Appleton in Rome.

Both Mr. and Mrs. Jarves became close friends with Remond and her relatives, and they were involved in introducing Remond and the Putnams to others. As the letters Edmund and Gertie Putnam wrote to Margherita Mignaty indicate, Mrs. Jarves was vacationing in Viareggio when the Putnams were there in June 1871. Through her, the Putnam couple met other vacationers who were resting at the seashore. Moreover, since Jarves was a close friend of Mignaty, the recipient of the Putnam letters, it is very likely that he was instrumental in introducing the Putnams and Remond to Mignaty herself. Although none of the Mignaty letters discuss Remond per se, they do mention her. Gertie Putnam, who in her letters addressed Mignaty as "Mammy," reveals that Caroline Putnam was also in Mignaty's circle of intimate friends. It is highly probable that Remond, as a permanent resident in Florence, participated in Mignaty's intellectual, cosmopolitan *conversazioni* on a regular basis.

The relationships Remond formed in Italy with local representatives of high society, then, would reflect what the scholar Tania Friedel has indicated as relevant to cosmopolitanism that opens the possibility for intercultural affiliations.[7] In its ideal form of expression, a cosmopolitan is expected to acknowledge and respect difference, and thus embrace a pacific cohabitation of people representing different nations, ethnicities, religions, genders, and races. The cosmopolitanism Remond connected with was intercultural but also multiracial and, obviously, multinational. Moreover, Kwame Anthony Appiah argues that respect of diversity and acceptance of hybridity lead to the building of communities where enlightened men and women from across the world can engage in dialogue. To quote Appiah: "Cosmopolitans think that there are many values worth living by and that you cannot live by all of them. So we hope and expect that different people and different societies will embody different values."[8] Remond was one who demonstrated how to live by different values in different societies. The cosmopolitan commitment in its ideal form, as experienced by Remond, is to tolerance and pluralism. Hence, the attachment to and respect of pluralism should be examined and understood in connection to but also separate from countries, nations, and states.

According to Gillian Brock, the concept of world citizenship can be placed in contrast to patriotism, because "the worldly citizen has attachments to entities within the country, rather than to the country itself; and she experiences the country not as a component of her identity, but as one country among many."[9] Remond, for one, formed her sense of belonging within the tolerant Florentine circles where national barriers were blurred in the international gatherings of cosmopolites, or world travelers. Her attachment, if anything, was racially defined through her commitment to fellow African Americans rather than patriotically linked to her white compatriots. As she became immersed in the life of her adopted countries, she considered herself an American but a representative of her race. Remond was a true cosmopolitan, a "worldly citizen," one who had "strong attachments to particular localities and ways of life, without identifying those localities and ways of life with any particular country."[10] Remond's familiarity with and adjustment first in British society and subsequently to the life of Florence demonstrates her capacity to assimilate into different nations and localities where she felt attached to the way of life and people without, however, completely identifying with them.

Moreover, as Brock continues, a worldly citizen "has broad knowledge of other values dear to other ways of life and can more honestly reflect on possibilities, given this enhanced knowledge."[11] The definition, again, is applicable to Remond, who lived in various countries and had a vast knowledge of different values and lifestyles that ranged from those of American society's white and African American customs to upper- and lower-class British mores, to the ways and worldviews of Italian society. Her concern in promoting African American self-knowledge and a reassessment of black identity qualifies her for yet another definition of a cosmopolitan citizen: "Cosmopolitans can and *should* promote collective agency and collective self-determination on the sub-world state level," Brock suggests.[12] Remond's cosmopolitan feat for racial justice was a form of progressive political action that reached beyond national borders. The intellectual society of Florence had achieved "the cosmopolitan's invitation," in the words of the scholar Michael Blake, "to think seriously across borders, and to examine the implications of moral egalitarianism internationally," egalitarianism that blurred racial and national borders.[13]

In Florence, the concept of cosmopolitanism changed Remond's perspective on social inclusion and exclusion, while her identity became increasingly hybrid, reflecting diaspora identities. Her identity was in flux rather than fixed, and changed in relation to the community she became part of at various moments of her Grand Tour experience. Remond reconciled her transatlantic cosmopolitanism into a single, complex expression that embraced the concept of "double consciousness," the African American experience of twoness stemming from being simultaneously inside and outside their nation and culture.

Double consciousness, a term that was coined by the black American intellectual W. E. B. Du Bois, consists of the reconciliation of twoness, of being American and being black.[14] As Du Bois himself expressed it: "One ever feels his two-ness,—an American, a Negro; two souls, two thoughts, two unreconciled strivings; two warring ideals in one dark body."[15] In the Old World cosmopolitanism experienced by Remond, the twoness was embraced in the hybrid nature of cosmopolitanism; she truly was a citizen of the world who assumed an identity position that refuted her belonging to any specific nation. At various times, she belonged to the United States, England, or Italy, while in the cosmopolitan societies she was deracialized, her racial and ethnic origins stripped of meaning. At the same time, however, she strongly held on to a specific identity position: throughout her European residencies, she remained anchored in her identity conceptualized as an African American woman.

Remond, the black transatlantic cosmopolitan, may already have belonged to the intellectual society of Florence during the period of her studies, and unquestionably was a participant in social events after her graduation, as testified by Henry Wadsworth Longfellow, who returned to Florence with his family in 1868. He had an active social life that included a visit to the studio of Hiram Powers, who met the poet and his family "in his long white apron and funny little cap."[16] Longfellow also attended a reception at Edward Perkins's villa on Bellosguardo, and on Sunday 13 December, he and his family met Dr. Duffy with his "fine looking wife" of uncommon beauty.[17]

The Longfellows also met Remond, who by then had become acquainted with Francesco Dall'Ongaro. As Anne Longfellow Pierce wrote in her journal: "H.W.L. Alice, and Edith!, went to a musical party at Prof. Dell'Ongaro's. . . . The music was long, and I was late to bed—a youthful genius played most wonderfully on the piano to them—Rendano—destined they think to make a name in the musical world. And they also met a 'Lady of / color': from Salem, Mass. Very intelligent and agreeable, studying medicine in Florence, and H.W.L. met hosts of gentlemen."[18] It is highly probable, then, that Remond knew many of the same people with whom Longfellow was connected during his stay in Florence.

In the evenings the Longfellow family attended receptions, dinners, and musical parties or went to the opera. Music, which represented cosmopolitanism, was an epitome of secular reconciliation of cultures and races. The Italian opera, which enjoyed transnational and global fame, represented an expression of local ethnicity. The Longfellows, like others who were fond of music around the same time, saw Gioachino Rossini's opera *Cinderella* and remained to watch the ballet that followed. Longfellow Pierce remarked in her journal how the opera tickets were "truly wonderful in size and thickness, as large as this page and thick as the corner of a book."[19] Longfellow, together with such illustrious Florentines as Ubaldino Peruzzi and professor Pasquale Villari, belonged to the social circles of Mignaty.

In particular during the years that Florence was the capital of Italy, Mignaty's salon on Via Cavour (previously called Via Larga) was attended by eminent Florentines and foreigners. Longfellow, who corresponded with Mignaty when he was not in Italy, remembered her exactly the way she had been, sitting in her drawing room with the light falling on her face, as he explained in a letter he wrote to thank her for the copy of her book *Historical Past of Italy*, which she had sent him in 1877: "Full well do I remember my pleasant evening visit to you in the Via Cavour. I can see the room now, and the very place where you sat, and the lamp-light falling on your face."[20] The American poet praised Mignaty for her achievement in successfully writing a historical book with the liveliness of real life: "Your book is excellent. I have been reading it with the greatest interest and pleasure. Wherever one opens its pages he is sure to come upon something that at once enchains the attention. You have written history, but have known how to give it all the charm of romance."[21] Charm, romance, history, revolution, and culture were among the features that had always rendered Florence so appealing to foreign visitors.

Intellectuality and culture were the valued expectations set for those who wished to engage themselves in refined cosmopolitan activities. The conversations among the attendees of the Mignaty salon were not racially charged nor were the participants separated on the basis of their nationality. Therefore, the American participants included Remond and the Putnams, whose social connections extended from Florence to Rome and Paris, and included the fashionable society that was vacationing in the resort area of Viareggio.

After his marriage in the spring of 1868, Edmund Putnam traveled with his wife between England and the continent, and in the summer, the Putnam couple joined others who were enjoying their vacations in Viareggio, a fashionable Tuscan seashore resort. Before then, Edmund had traveled with his mother and Remond, his "aunt Sarah," for example, to France. Subsequently, his mother, who occasionally returned to the United States, visited the young Putnam couple in England and spent time with them in Italy, mainly in Florence and Rome but also in San Remo. Gertie's letters bear testimony to the pastimes they enjoyed during their vacations by the sea. On 17 June 1871, Gertie wrote from Viareggio to Mignaty informing her of their daily routine. Gertie, as she explained, had just had her first bath:

> Last Sunday the weather changed to agreeable, & on Monday I took my first bath[.]
>
> I have had five & they agree with me perfectly, when I have been capering a few minutes in the sea I race out on to the sands & lie down flat while two women cover me all over with hot sand then I rush back again float, swim, & then get out for good, dress myself & sit in the sun until dinner time (2 oclk)

After suffering from neuralgia, resting by the sea made her feel stronger, but Gertie was less pleased to realize that she was "very much tanned & every day my skin becomes coarser," as she complained to Mignaty.[22]

Edmund Putnam gave a more detailed description of their days at the beach where they enjoyed the sand baths, or *sabbiature* as they were called in Italian: "The way they have here of taking baths, is rather droll," he wrote to Mignaty.

> You rush into the sea, take a few plunges, then run out upon the beach, and fall flat upon the hot sand. The bathing man then covers you with sand and you remain thus motionless, for five or six minutes, when you jump up and dash again into the water. This is repeated two or three times, and then the bath is finished. This system of taking sea baths is highly recommended, for it seems that the sand, heated by the rays of the sun, does one a great deal of good, and certainly, if making one very red and coarse looking is a sign of the improvement, Gertie and I must be *very much* better, for we are both of us fiery red from head to foot.[23]

The sun and the sand treatments were good for Gertie's back and made her feel "jolly," she wrote.[24] These treatments were very much in vogue until well into the twentieth century when doctors realized that covering bodies in damp sand was not as beneficial for health as they had thought. However, in the nineteenth century the *sabbiature* were still quite popular and considered an effective alternative to thermal baths.

During their vacation in Viareggio, Mrs. Jarves kept the Putnam couple company, and they met with a Marquis de Péon, a friend of Mignaty's who was delighted to make the acquaintance of Gertie and her husband. Their other friends included Elizabeth Seeley, with whom the Putnams visited Pisa, where Seeley's sister Ann was buried; they were also planning a trip to Lucerne together. Overall, the Putnams' social life in Viareggio was active with English, American, Italian, and French friends with whom they visited the nearby towns or went sailing. Other vacationers, as Edmund explained, watched them admiringly as they sailed along the coast: "When all were seated, M. de Lucca, who is a very handsome young man, stepped into the boat, and giving the order to start, the sailors bent to the oars, and we glided out from the pier, to the admiration of all the loungers assembled on the promenade."[25] In other words, their vacation was one of leisure and luxury, or, as Edmund put it, of "lazy tranquility." They woke up early and spent most of their day on the beach, while evenings they read before joining others on an evening stroll on the promenade.

The Putnam couple formed a daily routine of vacationing, as Edmund explained:

> In the morning we rise at 6, take a walk on the beach, and then come into breakfast at 8. After breakfast, we repair again to the beach, where we sit down or lie upon the sand, {protected from the sun's rays by little straw hats} and remain there, hardly without stirring until noon, when we take our baths. That finished, we resume our seats upon the sand until dinner. We dine at 2 p.m. and then remain in the house reading until 6, when we make "grande toilette," for the evening promenade. We walk with our friends on the pier or the beach 'till half past 8, when we return home and at nine we are in bed. Voilà notre ordre de jour! Is it not shockingly lazy?[26]

The letter testifies that they were reveling in their vacation, which included sailing, reading, and socializing with others. Similarly to other Americans who enjoyed the Italian *dolce-far-niente,* or the sweetness of doing nothing, Putnam reveals his sense of embarrassment, perhaps guilt, about his thorough enjoyment of such unproductive leisure. T. J. Jackson Lears argues that relaxation was recommended for hardworking Americans as a prevention and cure for neurasthenia toward the end of the nineteenth century, when doctors encouraged rest and advised Americans to learn relaxation from southern cultures.[27] Until then, (white) Americans focused on the productivity and capitalist pursuit that their consumer culture promoted.

The vacation in Viareggio may have been an attempt to cure Gertie, who admitted to having suffered from neuralgia, or neurasthenia, which was a common "disease" of Victorians who valued respectability and whose "sexual and social propriety seemed to stifle every genuine impulse and emotion."[28] What contemporary physicians would diagnose as psychological disturbances, nineteenth-century doctors would identify as disorders "originating from some sort of disturbance in the functioning of the nervous system" with such symptoms as melancholy, anxiety, and fatigue. Consequently, doctors would recommend rest, "a change of scene, and exercise as a cure for nervous problems" that belonged to the nineteenth-century gendered culture of illnesses.[29] The late-Victorian civilization, with its emotional repression, inhibition, and restraints, caused nervousness, especially among those living in metropolitan areas.[30] The social pressures and frustrations of black Victorians must have exceeded white anxieties. In addition to health, some minor problems kept the Putnams from fully enjoying their vacation: in her letter to Mignaty, Gertie expressed her concern about their cat, who had eaten two young ducklings of their friend Sabina.[31]

With his letter to Mignaty, Edmund Putnam enclosed a pamphlet in Italian titled *Appello a tutte le donne del Mondo* ("Appeal to Womanhood throughout the World") which was originally written in Boston in September 1870 by Julia Ward Howe. It was an appeal to all women in the world asking for their contribution to securing peace. Putnam had received a request to forward a copy to Mignaty since, he wrote, "your name is very well known to the ladies who have the matter in hand." They had asked Mignaty to use her influence to promote the pamphlet among the women of Italy.[32] Similarly to Remond, then, Mignaty promoted women's emancipation and sustained racial equality.

In the years they were in Italy, the Putnams spent much of their time in Florence visiting with Mignaty and staying with Remond, but they also traveled to Viareggio and Pisa, and to La Spezia, Milan, Como, and Lucerne, where they waited for the arrival of Gertie's father. During their absence from Florence, Mignaty stayed in touch with Gertie's "aunt Sarah."[33]

In addition to staying connected with Florentine residents, Remond received visitors from abroad. In 1871, Lucy Chase, an abolitionist, colleague, and friend of Charlotte Forten, visited Remond at her home, which she shared with her sister Caroline. Chase mentioned that writers and German opera stars were also among those who visited the Remonds at their Florentine home.[34] In October of that year, the Vieusseux register carried the signature of Edmund Putnam, who signed for the library and newspapers for six months, indicating that at the time he was living in Villa Sanna outside the Roman Gate. Powers, Villari, and other famous expatriates signed the register around the same time, and since they were all participants in the Anglo-American circles, it is highly likely that Remond, her sister, and her nephew received many of them as well at their home.

It seems that Remond remained in Italy without ever traveling back to the United States, whereas her sister made quite a few transatlantic voyages. In June 1872, Caroline Putnam and her young artist friend Christine Keadie "Kitty" Sargent were first visiting Edmund and Gertie in London before heading to the United States. Sargent, with whom Caroline traveled and lived, was the daughter of an abolitionist, Unitarian minister of Boston, John Turner Sargent, related to the painter John Singer Sargent and Supreme Court Justice Joseph Story. John Turner Sargent was a supporter of women's rights and the Underground Railroad, and his friends included Harriet Martineau, Theodore Parker, William Lloyd Garrison, Wendell Phillips, and Charles Sumner. His daughter Christine lived in Europe for approximately thirty years. "The 15th June [1872]," Gertie wrote, "we two left Papa at Bournemouth & came to London to receive Mrs. Putnam & Miss Sargent, well, dear, they only staid a week with us & then went to America; & we were alone again in the warm weather of the summer months."[35] The two women had the time and means to travel not only in Europe but also on long and costly transatlantic crossings.

Gertie and Edmund, who were at the time staying with friends at Woodford Lodge in Blackhead, England, were unable to return to Bournemouth because Gertie's father's house was already full since his two sons with their families were staying with him. "The lady of the house," a Mrs. Legge, was unwell, so Gertie had taken up "nursing her & acting little mother for her children & making night shirts & dinner napkins with a sewing machine, the use of which I pretty well understand now," Gertie wrote. "Taking care of this friend & being useful makes me very happy," she continued. "My Papa told me," Gertie further explained, "that I should always have a home at Bournemouth & seemed very sorry when I came to London & wept when we parted & yet he filled his house & has never said a word about my return to his house [.] Is it not strange, dearest?"[36] To Mignaty she confessed that she suspected her father was not particularly fond of Edmund, whose health suffered so that, according to Gertie, he was unable to work.

Consequently, the Putnams faced financial difficulties and had hoped to stay in England with Gertie's father:

> Between *you & me, nobody else* I think he [Gertie's father] does not like Edmund & is not happy to have him with him in the house; *we shall see.* They did *not* get on *too well* together; I am *very sorry* about it. Where we shall go or how live this coming winter I do not know[.] My Papa never makes me a present of any money now so we are often perplexed about it.
>
> Do not say a word of this *to any living creature not a soul.* I suppose we shall be allright some day & better off.[37]

It was unfortunate that the relationship between Gertie's father and her husband was strained because it caused some anxiety to Gertie.

At the time Gertie wrote the letter above, she was reading a book that "aunt Sarah" also had a copy of entitled *Meditations on Death and Eternity* by Heinrich Zschokke, published in London in 1863. The following week, the Putnam couple headed for London to wait for the arrival of Caroline Putnam and her friend from the United States: "Mrs. Putnam & Miss Sargent are now crossing the Atlantic & we go to London next week take lodgings & prepare to receive them on the 26th or so[.] when the[y] leave us they go direct to Florence for the winter & they *will see you,* darling, & that is what I most of all envy them, 'seeing my Mammy.' I expect the good dears will be very fatigued & I shall care very tenderly for them."[38] The two women would, indeed, continue their journey from London to Florence where they expected to see Mignaty.

Putnam and Sargent were then back in Florence again when Elizabeth Buffum Chace, an American suffragist and abolitionist originally from Providence, Rhode Island, visited Remond and her sister during Buffum Chace's tour of Italy in 1873. Buffum Chace's father, Arnold Buffum, had been involved in founding the New England Anti-Slavery Society in 1832 together with Garrison. It was one of the first organizations to insist on immediate emancipation of slaves. In the 1830s, Buffum had toured in New England and abroad, enlisting sympathizers to support the cause of black emancipation. His daughter, Elizabeth, had always been dedicated to promoting racial and gender justice and was not only a supporter of abolition and against segregation but was instrumental in helping slaves escape to Canada on the so-called Underground Railroad. She was the president of the Rhode Island Woman Suffrage Association for more than twenty years, and after the Civil War, she became a prison-reform advocate. Frederick Douglass, to whom she was like a sister, as well as William Wells Brown, Frances Ellen Watkins Harper, Sojourner Truth, and Lucy Stone, among many others, were often seen at her home.

During the Italian part of her European tour, Buffum Chace stopped in Rome where she visited the sculptor Edmonia Lewis, and upon her arrival in Florence, she first toured the museums, the Uffizi Gallery and Pitti Palace. On her second day in the city, she went to see the grave of Parker, who was buried at the Protestant Cemetery on what to her seemed "consecrated ground." On one of the following days, after a visit to Pisa, she wished to rest, but in the afternoon, she went, "by invitation, to take tea with Mrs. Putnam, Sarah Remond and Miss Sargent. We had a fine visit," she wrote. She was quite fascinated with Remond, whom she praised as an energetic, determined, and socially prominent woman, an admirable representative of her country: "Sarah Remond is a remarkable woman and by indomitable energy and perseverance is winning a fine position in Florence as a physician, and also socially; although she says Americans have used their influence to prevent her, by bringing their hateful prejudices over here. If one tenth of the American women who travel in Europe were as noble and elegant as she is, we shouldn't have to blush for our countrywomen as often as we do."[39]

As Buffum Chace's comments testify, she thought very highly of Remond, who was excelling in her chosen career. Buffum Chace also testified to the bigotry Americans were guilty of even in the more liberal Europe, far away from the racially charged and segregated United States. Remond had, then, encountered Americans who viewed her race unfavorably and approached her with hostility, perhaps because their prejudice was mingled with envy of a black woman's achievements in the refined society of Florence. Had it not been for the prejudiced Americans in Italy who brought their racism across the Atlantic, Remond would fully have accomplished her freedom from racial discrimination.

Between 1874 and 1877, Remond lived in a fashionable Florentine neighborhood, close to the Arno River, not far from the church of Ognissanti. Her home was located on Via Garibaldi, which was a new upper- and middle-class neighborhood of charming buildings designed by the architect Luigi Buonamici and constructed in 1865.[40] The Putnams lived at the same address, according to the lending library's register: on 2 February 1874, Caroline Putnam, who paid a three-month membership at the Vieusseux library, indicated her residence as 5 Via Garibaldi, the same address that in the 1880s became the home of the prolific writer Violet Paget (Vernon Lee). Edmund Putnam had paid his three-month membership fee a few weeks before, also giving his address as 5 Via Garibaldi.[41] His name appears in the Vieusseux register right after that of James and before that of Jessie White Mario, Ariana Curtis, and Caroline Putnam. Putnam and Sargent, still living on 5 Via Garibaldi, paid the library and reading room membership for three months again on 6 June 1875. Remond herself paid a one-month membership in May 1877. By then she was married and signed the library register accordingly as "Madame Remond Pintor," also indicating her address as 5 Via Garibaldi. She lived on the third and top floor of the building, whereas the Putnams and Sargent had their living quarters on the second floor.

Remond's cross-racial contacts became more intimate, and supposedly attained a physical and sexual dimension, when, on 25 April 1877, she ceased working as an obstetrician and married an Italian office worker, Lazzaro Pintor, who originally was from Cagliari, Sardinia.[42] The wedding certificate indicates that "Sara P. Remond" was a housewife ("atta a casa") at the time of her marriage. She was fifty years old, approaching her fifty-first birthday, while her spouse was forty-four. The impressive full name of her husband, who was born on 11 February 1833 to parents Vincenzo Pintor, a doctor in law, and Chiara Piccaluga, was Lazzaro Tommaso Efisio Bernardo Pintor. Both his godfathers were lawyers.[43] Lazzaro Pintor, in other words, came from an educated, upper-class family. Once again, Remond defied conventionality through her interracial marriage to a man who was younger than she. Moreover, she refuted the racist and sexist stereotypes of black women as sexually promiscuous and women as domestic caretakers and child-bearers by choosing education and career first, then marrying late in life. She balanced her role as a public speaker and professional career woman with a more conventional idea of female respectability, renouncing her vocational ambitions at the moment of her matrimony.

The two witnesses at the wedding ceremony were Eugenio Alessandri, an office worker, and a Scottish priest, Giovanni (John) McDougall. Reverend McDougall had opened the Scottish Church, which was housed in the Casa Schneiderf on the Lung'Arno. According to the anonymously published guidebook *Firenze in tasca* (1867), the exact address of the Scottish Church was 11 Lung'Arno Guicciardini, located next to the Swiss Church.[44] McDougall, according to the influential Murray guidebook, was "a Free Kirk minister, officiating twice every Sunday" at the Scottish Church; he was formerly of Brighton.[45]

The witness Alessandri, instead, was born in Florence on 8 December 1847. The year of Remond's marriage with Pintor, Alessandri himself married Emma Solmigli on 2 June 1877. Alessandri worked as vice director of a post office in Siena, and after his retirement in 1892, moved to Florence. His wife was the daughter of Elisa Schoberlechner, born in Florence in 1848. The soprano Sofia Schoberlechner and her husband, the composer Franz Schoberlechner, who moved to Florence in the 1830s, may well have been her relatives, perhaps Elisa's parents. That would explain why some sources suggest that Remond befriended German opera singers and musicians.

Approximately one year after her marriage, Remond was in Rome at a reception where two English women, Anne and Matilda Lucas, met her and the Putnams. The reception was an intercultural gathering of the English, American, Italian, and German residents of Rome. Commonly the Roman receptions, Matilda Lucas explained, were informal; they started at around nine and finished at about eleven at night. Alternatively they took place in the afternoon, from four to six. Instead of a heavy meal, visitors had tea, coffee, sponge cakes, and wine.[46]

Matilda Lucas's observations of the African American guests reveal the racist attitudes of the Roman Anglo-American colony:

> *March 17, 1878.* Tell Madgie that the P—s were there with their black aunt. She was a bride, having just married an Italian, and wore her bridal dress of grey silk. It must have been very trying for Mrs. P—. People came up to question her. One Italian said, "*Chi è quell'Africana?*" It appears that she is very clever, and a female doctor. She was taken up a good deal in London by different people who were interested in negroes. I think she lived with the Peter Taylors. She has giv-

> en lectures. I went to sit on the sofa with her, to the amusement of Franz, who cannot rise above her appearance. Dr. Baedtke was much impressed to think that anyone has had the courage to marry her, and said, "In that I should have been a coward."[47]

Lucas's hateful comments reflect the attitudes of the prejudiced Anglo-Americans Buffum Chace had referred to in 1873, and reveal that in Lucas's view, the prominent people in London had socialized with Remond only because they were interested in "negroes" in general, not because Remond was a talented and cultured individual whose company they cherished. The passage also reveals that Americans were not the only ones to express racist views. A Dr. Baedtke, who was a close friend of the Lucas sisters, was a German who had established himself in Rome.

The sisters themselves made rude and prejudiced comments about others as well, people no less famous than the king of Italy, whom they several times saw driving in the Cascine Park of Florence. The sisters found him "dreadfully ugly."[48] They did, however, find positive qualities in Remond, who appeared to be "very clever," and recognized that she was a female doctor and public lecturer. Such acknowledgments can be interpreted as expressions of admiration that were supported by Matilda Lucas's gesture to publicly defy race discrimination by choosing to sit next to Remond.

The Lucas sisters met the Putnams and Remond again in Rome one month later. This time the reception, it seems, was organized by the Putnams:

> *Rome, April 28, 1878.* For Tuesday we had three invitations, only two of which we accepted. First we spent an hour with Mrs. Westmacott, and then went on to the P—s'. The music was first-rate, chiefly from professionals—Sgambati, Tosti, Pinelli—all well-known names here. The black aunt was there, elegantly dressed in lavender silk. She was a foil to Miss Vertunni, one of the prettiest girls in Rome. She is the daughter of the artist, and about fifteen or sixteen. . . . We enjoyed the P—s' party. We were introduced to Mrs. Lynn Linton, the authoress of "Joshua Davidson" and "Patricia Kemball." She was very agreeable.[49]

Through music, which denoted the superiority of upper-class cosmopolites in Italy, Remond and her family members displaced racial categories and inverted racialized social hierarchies. The music denoted the black Americans' place in the collective, socially constructed idea of Italian cosmopolitan identity. Music was socially relevant and often could function as a class divider.

The selection of music at this particular event demonstrated the black hostesses' sensibilities and knowledge of contemporary artistic expression. The performers mentioned in the passage were among the most celebrated musicians of their time. Giovanni Sgambati was Franz Liszt's pupil, an Italian composer and pianist who launched the Italian composer and singer Paolo Tosti toward fame. Liszt himself was Lewis's friend, as testified by the future temperance leader Frances E. Willard in 1870. Similarly, Ettore Pinelli was a key figure in the nineteenth-century Roman musical scene. All three performed, often together, at the salons of Roman high bourgeoisie and aristocracy.[50] Hence, the choice of music and performers testify to the sophistication of the host and hostesses of the event. At the same time, it reveals that they could afford to engage the most talked-about musicians to play at their receptions.

The cultured guests who attended the party further indicate that Remond and the Putnams had secured social prominence. Among the other guests Lucas mentioned was Lynn Linton, an English novelist and journalist; in public she was antifeminist but privately she was leading an independent life. Her most successful works were *The True History of Joshua Davidson* (1872) and *Patiricia Kemball* (1874). Lucas made no special reference to the Putnams but mentioned the "black aunt" as if she were a curiosity. Once again, however, Remond appeared as a fashionable nineteenth-century lady: in her silk dress of delicate hues, of gray and lavender silk, she looked elegant and classy. Clothes, the scholar Mary McAleer Balkun suggests, were useful in creating social identities and conveying a particular message about the person who wore them. Women, Balkun continues, had the "ability to use clothing to reinvent the self," a process which was "also a concern for social critics at the turn of the century."[51] Remond's elegant silk dresses confirmed rather than created her social identity and testified to the recognition of her black cultivated self. Her stylish dress, in addition, testified to her taste and fashion-consciousness, and indicated that she was financially prosperous, which would imply that she had obtained success in her career.

Therefore, it is quite surprising to learn that two years after her marriage, in 1879, the English abolitionist William Robson reported that "Miss Remond is living in great poverty in Rome, her profession of medicine having been a failure."[52] It is possible, however, that Remond lost her investments in the financial crisis that hit Florence after it ceased to be the capital of Italy. By the time the dignitaries had left the city on 1 July 1871 to establish themselves in Rome, Florence had incurred massive debts due to expenses caused by urban developments and accumulated during the years as the capital. Rome now refused to reimburse Florence. An economic crisis followed in 1876, with businesses and banks going bankrupt, leading individuals into economic ruin.[53] That may be the reason why Remond moved to Rome to live closer to her family.

In the 1880s, the Putnams were established rather permanently in Rome, where Caroline Putnam, Maritcha Remond, Sarah Remond Pintor, and Kitty Sargent joined them. Edmund Putnam had taken up writing articles for various journals, as noted in a letter written from Munich, dated 30 May 1880, following an earlier visit to Turin. He had been "ordered by telegram" to describe the Passion Play in Oberammergau in Bavaria for "one of the journals to which I am accredited," he wrote.[54] The letter further attests that he and his family continued to fight against discrimination, of which they were targets in the American circles of Rome. They were excluded from official entertainments organized by the American consul and his wife in the new capital of Italy.

Putnam accused the recipient of the letter, the American consul, a Mr. Schuyler, of racism and of rendering public a private matter between them concerning his earlier protests against discrimination:

> I found also that besides making our correspondence public & handing it about among your American friends, you, as an excuse for not inviting me to the official reception which you gave immediately after the incident above referred to, brought forward my letter to you, stigmatizing it as "*scurrilous*," & adding expressions insulting to myself & to my family, which I will not soil this paper by repeating. Now this is certainly not conduct becoming a gentleman, or the posi-

> tion which you hold in Rome as an official representative of the American government. . . . My wife & my mother, believing (unfortunately) what you wrote me, called, as is duty bound & like other American ladies living in Rome, to pay their respects to Mrs. Schuyler at her regular weekly reception. I hardly need to repeat what occurred. In the presence of a crowded room, before friends & acquaintances of ours, the ladies of my family were treated by your wife with marked & intentional discourtesy. And this was no *private* party given to your personal friends, but the *public* & *regular* reception which as the Consul's wife Mrs. Schuyler is bound to give. The following week came the two official evening receptions which you offerred [*sic*] to the American colony of Rome, & to which you invited every American in the city, without reference to his or her antecedents, excepting only my family excluded for the crime of having mixed blood in their veins.

The Roman expatriate community included some "whose amusement it is," Putnam wrote, "to persecute though unsuccessfully my family & self because we dare to assert our rights."[55] In other words, they personally knew the other American expatriates who were residing in Italy, where, unfortunately, they had to continue their relentless campaign for social justice.

Putnam had prepared a statement of the consul's behavior to which he had added their correspondence and was about to send it to Washington "to the proper authorities." As he stated in the letter, he was entitled to "the same formal courtesy" that Schuyler "would as U.S. Consul freely accord to the humblest American citizen, provided he had a white face" ("white face" is underlined twice). He further accused the official American representative of attempts to enforce a "colour line" and the *Dred Scott* decision in Rome, on foreign soil. Putnam pointed out that the consul's "persecution" of him and his family was in direct contrast to the courtesy and politeness of the Marshes, whose friendship dated back many years to their first meeting in Florence.[56] Putnam expected the same courtesy that American official representatives showed to white American citizens.

In December 1882, Edmund was back in Rome, where he was in charge of the hotel he managed with Gertie, who had gone to San Remo to take care of her father. In one of her letters to Mignaty, Gertie complained about not having heard from her mother-in-law or from Sargent since October when they had spent three weeks together in San Remo. Gertie was unable to join the others in Rome for Christmas, because her father was "so helpless & poorly." Edmund, instead, could have traveled to San Remo, as Gertie wrote, "if Pal[azzo] Moroni could have been let. . . . No such luck however[.] they are at home & will spend Xmas without me & I am sorry."[57] Frederick Douglass, among others, visited the Putnams at the hotel they ran, the Palazzo Moroni, during the 1880s.

The sixteenth-century building, at the time owned by Duke Giuseppe Caffarelli Negroni, was located right next to St. Peter's Basilica, on 165 Borgo Vecchio (now 51 Via della Conciliazione), which leads from Castel St. Angelo to St. Peter's. Palazzo Moroni was built at the same time as St. Peter's, which meant that artists and architects would go back and forth between the two buildings under construction. The magnificent frescoes in Palazzo Moroni that decorated the ceiling of what used to be an open loggia are attributed to the school of Pietro da Cortona, and some of the same scenes figure in St. Peter's, painted by Pietro da Cortona himself. In 1879, the building was sold by the Moroni family to Duke Negroni Caffarelli, who left it to his son. In 1881, the Salvatorians, a religious priesthood, started renting rooms in the Palazzo Moroni because the space they had in Piazza Farnese no longer was big enough for them. The Salvatorians offered their hospitality to pilgrims, which meant that the rooms they were in charge of were given to religious guests, whereas the rooms the Putnams were renting out were for lay people. In 1895, the Salvatorians bought the entire building.[58] The Putnams were in charge of the hotel from 1882 until at least 1887, as testified by Douglass.

On his extensive overseas tour of Italy, France, and Egypt with his second wife, Helen Pitts, Douglass stopped in Rome, where he toured the main sites—St. Peter's, the Roman Forum, Pincian Hill, the Vatican, and the Colosseum. In 1884, when Douglass married Helen, a white woman, his first wife of forty-four years, Anna Murray Douglass, had already been deceased for nearly two years. Pitts, who had taught free African Americans in Norfolk, Virginia, was an advocate of temperance and women's emancipation and had worked as a clerk in Douglass's office since 1882.[59] When the couple arrived in Rome, Caroline Putnam, through a friendship with a priest, had organized a special privileged visit for them to see the treasures of St. Peter's that included the costly vestments—covered with gold, silver, and other precious stones—that bishops, cardinals, and popes wore on great occasions.[60]

On Thursday, 25 January 1887, Douglass had lunch with the Remond sisters:

> After seeing the wonders of the Vatican went to lunch with the Putnams at their Hotel Palazzo Moroni 165 Borgo Vecchio, Roma.
>
> We spent here the remainder of the day and spent it very pleasantly. The elder Mrs Putnam, was formerly Miss Caroline Remond—sister to the late Charles Lenox Remond,—Her son Edmund married a Miss Elleson of Cheltenham England, a very pleasant lady who is now the Mistress of the house. We met here she that I knew forty years and more ago as Miss Sarah Remond, and also Maritcha Remond. A daughter of the late Rev. John Sargent is boarding with the Putnams. It was very delightful to meet this charming circle of Massachusetts people away off here in the city of Rome. Like myself the Remond sisters with exception of Caroline have grown quite old but in all of them I saw much of the fire of their eloquent brother Charles.[61]

Two days later, Douglass made a visit to see Edmonia Lewis, "who had loaned Helen some books." "She seems very cheerful and happy," Douglass wrote, "and successful. . . . She has resided in Rome twenty years and constantly speaking Italian has somewhat impaired her English."[62] She lived in a "very pleasant room with a commanding view," at 4 Via Venti Settembre. Like Remond, Lewis was fluent in Italian, marking her assimilation into her adoptive home where she was working on statues that often bore a political message of black liberation and gender emancipation.

The medium Lewis frequently used for her statues was white Carrara marble. Scholars have noted that the white marble "flesh" of bodies denoted the purity and innocence of the nude figures, women in particular. Moreover, art critics perceived white as an absence of color rather than an ideological stance.[63] And yet, by sculpting a slave woman in white marble, artists, consciously or unintentionally, linked the black female figure to the concept of ideal womanhood, which in the (white) cult of true womanhood was depicted as pure and pious. Since black women in the nineteenth-century United States were excluded from consideration in the cult of true womanhood, Lewis's white statues of black women conveyed powerful ideological messages.

In the company of Lewis and a Miss Gates, an artist and philanthropist who had done "a great deal for the colored people," Douglass then left for Naples.[64] The interracial party toured museums and other local attractions, and Douglass also visited Pompeii, Amalfi, and Salerno. In February he lectured "on John B[rown] to a fine audience."[65] On his return to Rome, after Douglass and his wife had visited Egypt, they first stayed at the Hotel de la Poste, where Victoria Woodhull, known for her radical views on women, came to visit on 15 April. As he wrote to Amy Post on 10 June 1887: "When in Rome at the Hotel De la Poste, there came to see me a handsome and elegantly dressed lady. She was refined in her manners and appearance, and made a favorable impression upon all who saw her. She called many names of persons with whom I am acquainted in America. . . . At last she told me 'I am she that was Victoria Woodhull.' "[66] She then told Douglass that she was married to a banker with whom she lived quietly in London.

On 18 April, Douglass left the Hotel de la Poste to move to the Putnams' Palazzo Moroni. At the time, Madame Remond Pintor, as Douglass identified her, lived in 6 Piazza Barberini.[67] It was a central location right along the piazza famous for the Tritone Fountain created by Gian Lorenzo Bernini. Among local sculptors, the Murray guide from 1888 advertised "Miss Edmonia Lewis (American)" at the same location, Piazza Barberini.[68] Douglass wrote to Amy Post about meeting the three sisters of Charles Remond in Rome: "It was very pleasant to meet so far away from home these dear people. Like Charles they detest prejudice of color and say they would not live in the U. States, if you could or would give them America!"[69]

In May Douglass was in Florence, where he went directly to the Protestant Cemetery to see the grave of Parker. Standing by the grave, Douglass mused, "I could but recall as I looked upon his grave, the many services rendered the cause of human freedom by him, freedom not only from physical chains but the chains of superstition, those which not only galled the limbs and tore the flesh, but those which marred and wounded the human soul." He realized that only a few feet away from the remains of Parker was the grave of Richard Hildreth, "another American who will never be forgotten by those who have read his book entitled Despotism in America and the White Slave." Of Hildreth, who had passed away in 1865, he wrote: "It is said [*sic*] to think that one with such talent as Richard Hildreth should have died in absolute poverty in a foreign [land], but such I am told was the fact."[70] He also found the grave of Barrett Browning, who had condemned slavery in her poems. He thus visited the graves of abolitionists who had contributed to the liberation of black Americans by raising awareness of the arbitrary nature of racial divides and the injustice of the system of slavery in their poems, speeches, and antislavery novels. They all lay buried in Italy.

Douglass's overall impression of Florence was positive: the city seemed full of life, the streets were crowded with people of all nationalities, and he observed that men were well dressed and women elegant. He toured the sites, including the Uffizi Gallery, San Marco, and the Medici Mausoleum.[71] He concluded that his stay in Florence had been all too brief. From there he traveled on to Venice, Milan, and Lucerne. Of his extensive tour abroad he concluded that "after my life of hardships in slavery and of conflict with race and color prejudice and proscription at home, there was left to me a space in life when I could and did walk the world unquestioned, a man among men."[72] The equality with others that Douglass valued was the fundamental reason for Remond and her sisters to remain in Europe. With Douglass Remond shared the same desire for racial justice and egalitarianism, both more readily available to her in Italy than in her native America.

Little is known of the last years of Remond's life. According to her death certificate, she passed away in Rome where she was buried in the Protestant Cemetery (now called the Non-Catholic Cemetery for Foreigners, Rome). Initially, she had a centrally located grave but subsequently her remains were removed to an ossuary. Her death certificate informs that "Remond, Sarah Parker," a "colored woman" ("donna di colore") from the United States, born on 6 June 1826, passed away on 13 December 1894 at 6:00 am at the Hospital of Sant'Antonio in Rome, at the age of seventy (actually, she was sixty eight). The cemetery documents indicate that she was still married to Lazzaro Pintor. Her residence is listed as Florence and her profession at the time of her death was surgeon ("medico chirurgo"). In other words, it seems that she had continued her studies, had become a surgeon, and had remained married to Pintor until her death, with a permanent residence in Florence. It also seems that her nephew Edmund Quincy Putnam had arranged for her burial. The grave of "Sara Remond Pintor, Americana," as listed in the cemetery's register, was in "the fifth row below the tomb of the poet Goethe" ("5 fila sotto la tomba del poeta Goethe") and was subsequently exhumed.[73]

Gertie, who passed away on 6 April 1901, was also buried at the Protestant Cemetery in Rome, where her funeral monument praises her as a woman with a kind soul and beautiful heart ("To the beloved memory / of / Gertrude Agnes Putnam / wife of / Edmund Quincy Putnam / and who died / in / Rome / Easter Sunday / 6 April 1901 / di anima gentile / di cuore bello"). She lies buried in the old section of the cemetery. Richard Dana Jr., Marsh, and many other prominent expatriates were also interred in the same cemetery. Caroline Putnam, instead, seems to have moved to England, where she became a British citizen in 1889.[74] She passed away on 6 November 1908 in her adopted home, where she had resided at 35b Clanricarde Gardens, Bayswater Road, in London.[75] Her residence was in a fashionable section of the city, close to Hyde Park. Her son Edmund lived in England until 1914 after which he moved back to the United States. He traveled to Shanghai, China, on 19 April 1919 to visit a niece, and temporarily lived there teaching languages from April 1919 to August 1920. He died in Bedfordshire at the age of eighty on 27 July 1927.[76]

Without a doubt, Remond and her family continued to influence people around them until the very end. In particular Remond was, and had always been, an intellectual leader who persevered in the vindication of her race and in striving to obtain the kind of education that was unavailable to her in the United States. She contributed to raising awareness of sociopolitical injustice and continuously questioned established social norms. By excelling first in her public role as an abolitionist lecturer, then in her career as a physician in a foreign country, she demonstrated her courage, racial pride, and self-esteem, and thus achieved her vindication. While initially socially marginalized, she triumphed in negotiating her social belonging, and she actively troubled the superior-inferior binary divide that characterized nineteenth-century United States. She pushed through the normative limits of oppression, beyond what her gender and race would conventionally have prescribed. Through her example, Remond articulated future possibilities for women and, in particular, for African Americans. As she debunked racist and sexist expectations, Remond moved beyond her racialized identity, which had been used to validate criteria for sustaining asymmetrical power relations. She powerfully propagated the message of social and political equality. Remond demonstrated to herself and others that she, like world leaders after her, came from different cultures and belonged to all of them.

Coda

"NO WORDS CAN EXPRESS THE MENTAL SUFFERING we are obliged to bear because we happen to have a dark complexion," Sarah Remond wrote in 1859. "No language can give one an idea of the spirit of prejudice which exists in the States," she continued.[1] Every chance Remond had, she fought against prejudice, challenging the false notions of black inferiority. She brought attention to the fact that race prejudice and discrimination affected every aspect of black lives. As a black intellectual and proto-feminist who belonged to an educated elite, she participated in changing the all-pervasive discrimination that she constantly contested in her private life and her public careers. Hence, Remond's experience calls for a change in interpreting power and powerlessness: she assumed control of her destiny and conceptualized a new, progressive black womanhood, which was in tension with the white cult of (submissive) true womanhood.

Remond ceaselessly resisted prejudiced assumptions and defied American society's arbitrary constructions of her gendered and racialized identity. She proved false the insistence on her inferiority as a woman and African American by first demonstrating her capabilities as an antislavery lecturer and women's rights advocate who fearlessly confronted discrimination during her abolitionist tours in the United States. She stood side by side with such white pioneers as Susan B. Anthony and Abby Kelley Foster with whom Remond fought against race and gender oppression.

Anthony, who seems to have remained in contact with the Remond family, followed Remond's progress in Europe; on 12 December 1876, Anthony was in Salem, where she visited Richie (Maritcha) Remond and in her diary noted that Charles Lenox Remond and his wife had passed away but that Richie and Susan still lived in Salem, whereas Caroline Putnam and Sarah Remond were in Florence.[2] Anthony, as well as many others, were inspired by Remond's triumph in Europe where her personal success story offered an alternative narrative of a black woman's experience, thus influencing the sociopolitical scene of her native America.

Although no doubts remain about Remond's significant contribution to race progress, studying further her views on peace movements, opinions concerning emancipation in other countries, and examining her contacts and correspondence with people she befriended or may have met in Britain and Italy may offer additional information about Remond herself while revealing more about her contributions to changing the world she inhabited. Her collaboration with such prominent feminists as Anthony would need further study in order to fully recover Remond's role in early women's rights movements. Presently, the history of American feminism tends to celebrate the victories of white women.

If paternalist racism and patronizing attitudes often characterized the racially mixed societies in the United States, in England racial and female solidarity was more clearly felt and expressed. During the decades between the 1850s and 1890s, when both white and black women struggled to gain a public voice to denounce oppression in all its varied forms, Remond participated in demanding more opportunities for self-expression, education, careers, and liberty both for black Americans and for women. Claims for equal rights were a central ideological concern for Remond, whose determination to realize race and gender equality gained force when she had an opportunity to express progress through lived experience in a more liberal Europe.

In her antislavery lectures in England, Ireland, and Scotland, Remond capitalized on the rivalry between Britain and the United States as she brought attention to sociopolitical injustice, realizing that the claim concerning the inferiority of black Americans was used as a justification for slavery, discrimination, and segregation. She boldly denounced Christianity and read excerpts from laws that prohibited the teaching of slaves. She addressed topics that other men or women feared to openly address, including sexual abuse of women slaves. Even American newspapers avoided directly discussing this topic, and as in the case of Margaret Garner, the slave woman's own voice was frequently silenced in newspaper reports. Such silencing highlights Remond's courage in giving a black voice to black women's tragedies.

With her travels and activism, Remond provided a different narrative of the African American experience. For women, travel was a liberating activity—physically, emotionally, and intellectually. As women refused to succumb to geographical and intellectual constraints, they moved out of the domestic confinements into international public platforms. Travel, as Mary Suzanne Schriber has suggested, "was transforming women from private into public actors on the world stage."[3] This was particularly applicable to Remond, who sought support and solidarity that enabled her to pursue her progressive goals. She demonstrated how gender dynamics functioned in organized activities that, to quote Nico Slate, "extended beyond racial roots to encompass a shared history of oppression."[4] In England, Remond joined forces with like-minded activists who were struggling to realize their enlightened views of emancipation and freedom from oppression. She excelled in her highly public career as a lecturer while continuing her studies, first at the Bedford Ladies College, where she studied humanities, followed by her training to become a nurse and subsequently graduation as a doctor. Unlike most women travelers, Remond embarked on a journey that was linear rather than circular. Her destination was Europe where she remained to validate her "race" through accelerated individual and collective success without ever returning to the United States.

Transnational empathy characterized Remond's activism, which embraced the oppressed, be they African American, women, poor, or those striving for national emancipation. Her abolitionist rhetoric was a conscious political act geared toward emancipation, and in her complex interplay among gender, class, and race, Remond negotiated the racialized and gendered world around her, rewriting boundaries, while she politicized the public and private spheres that surrounded her. During her stay in England and Italy, Remond remained involved in and concerned about issues relevant to nineteenth-century America but also in struggles of radicals and revolutionaries from other nations; her experience remained embedded in the historical and social changes of the period. In her lectures she campaigned against slavery and oppression of women; in her private life she fought to be recognized as a citizen, free to travel and strive for self-realization. As a fearless and progressive activist dedicated to abolishing slavery and racial discrimination as well as advancing women's rights, Remond participated in the rewriting of history as exemplified through her transatlantic travels whose objective was to promote her political and ideological agendas.

Remond's activism reveals the protagonism and central role of a black woman in the transatlantic history of activism, thus blurring conceptualizations of centrality and marginality. Her transnational efforts in promoting black solidarity laid a foundation for future collaboration between women working internationally to eradicate discrimination and oppression. Many associations with international membership and goals were established after Remond's pioneering work as a race leader. Her identity and belonging were removed from her national roots and transferred to Europe. Hers was a form of positive belonging, of being part of an intellectual collectivity that recognized Remond beyond any racial divides based on the color of her complexion, which in the United States was used as a marker of her marginalized national identity. By joining white American intellectuals on their Grand Tours of acculturation, she became an embodiment of nineteenth-century transatlantic cosmopolitanism; for black Americans, Remond offered an example of determination, success, and equality. As she fought against black injustice and journeyed toward personal success, Remond transformed individual and collective ideals into reality.

In one of her powerful and eloquent speeches, given in Dublin, Ireland, in March 1859, Remond reasoned that "the lives of good men are not lost when they die for justice sake; for so great is justice that she rewards all who suffer for her with greatness; and, though their heads are sodden in their gaze upon the scaffold or block—upon a tower high or city walls—and though their bones may strew the wilderness—the just cause for which they rendered up their lives give them immortality, and their spirits walk the earth."[5] Remond's powerful contribution to the goal of eliminating racial divides and the paradigm constructed on the notion of black inferiority laid a foundation on which to build justice. Her life was dedicated to striving for equality, and those who met Remond admired her courage and truthfulness: "She was not afraid to speak the truth, though it might give some offence."[6] Remond, thus, offered a courageous model of black womanhood, one of success and triumph, of independence and intellectuality, one that was in dramatic contrast to dominant, demeaning stereotypes constructed of black women. With her actions she participated in raising black consciousness and changing society. Sarah Remond was an example of emancipation and empowerment, and with her international activities she crossed borders—national, social, and racial.

NOTES

Introduction: Sarah Remond and the Black American Grand Tour

1. Sarah Parker Remond, "The Negro Race in America," *London Daily News*, 22 September 1866, dated Florence, Italy, 19 September 1866, www.britishnewspaperarchive.co.uk. Unless indicated otherwise, all subsequent information and quotations from nineteenth-century English, Irish, and Scottish newspapers have been accessed through www.britishnewspaper-archive.co.uk.
2. According to some sources, for example, Dorothy Sterling, ed., *We Are Your Sisters: Black Women in the Nineteenth Century* (New York: Norton, 1997), 175, and Dorothy Burnett Porter, "The Remonds of Salem, Massachusetts: A Nineteenth-Century Family Revisited," *American Antiquarian Society Proceedings* 95, no. 2 (1985): 281, Remond was born in 1824, while her marriage certificate confirms her birth in 1826 by indicating that she was fifty years old in April 1877.
3. Alan Rice, *Radical Narratives of the Black Atlantic* (London: Continuum, 2003), 175.
4. Sarah P. Remond, "Sarah P. Remond," in *Our Exemplars, Poor and Rich; Biographical Sketches of Men and Women Who Have, by an Extraordinary Use of Their Opportunities, Benefited Their Fellow-Creatures*, ed. Matthew Davenport Hill (London: Cassell, Petter, and Galpin, 1861), 277.
5. Arthur Riss, *Race, Slavery, and Liberalism in Nineteenth-Century American Literature* (Cambridge: Cambridge University Press, 2006), 1.
6. Hazel V. Carby, *Reconstructing Womanhood: The Emergence of the Afro-American Woman Novelist* (New York: Oxford University Press, 1987), 17.
7. Sterling, *We Are Your Sisters*, xiii.

8. Ibid., xviii. For more about the exclusion of black women from the cult of true womanhood, see Carby, *Reconstructing Womanhood.*
9. Richard Bardolph, "Social Origins of Distinguished Negroes, 1770–1865: Part I," *Journal of Negro History* 40, no. 3 (1955): 534–35.
10. See Kathryn Grover and Janine V. da Silva, "Historic Resource Study," 31 December 2012, Boston African American National Historic Site, www.nps.gov.
11. Sterling, *We Are Your Sisters,* xvi–xvii.
12. Margaret H. McFadden, *Golden Cables of Sympathy: The Transatlantic Sources of Nineteenth-Century Feminism* (Lexington: University Press of Kentucky, 1999), 110.
13. Susan Castillo, *American Literature in Context to 1865* (Chichester, Eng.: Wiley-Blackwell, 2011), 158.
14. Sterling, *We Are Your Sisters,* xvii.
15. Jennifer Bernhardt Steadman, *Traveling Economies: American Women's Travel Writing* (Columbus: Ohio State University Press, 2007), 4.
16. Paul Gilroy, *The Black Atlantic: Modernity and Double Consciousness* (Cambridge, Mass.: Harvard University Press, 1993), 6.
17. Steadman, *Traveling Economies,* 10.
18. Mary Suzanne Schriber, "Introduction," in *Telling Travels: Selected Writings by Nineteenth-Century American Women Abroad,* ed. Mary Suzanne Schriber (DeKalb: Northern Illinois University Press, 1995), xv–xvi.
19. Ibid., xix.
20. Paola Gemme, *Domesticating Foreign Struggles: The Italian Risorgimento and Antebellum American Identity* (Athens: University of Georgia Press, 2005), 8.
21. Ibid., 11.
22. Ibid., 11.
23. Luca Codignola, "The Civil War: The View from Italy," *Reviews in American History* 3, no. 4 (1975): 460.
24. William W. Stowe, *Going Abroad: European Travel in Nineteenth-Century American Culture* (Princeton, N.J.: Princeton University Press, 1994), xi.
25. See, for example, Paul R. Baker, *The Fortunate Pilgrims: Americans in Italy, 1800–1860* (Cambridge, Mass.: Harvard University Press, 1964); Attilio Brilli, *Quando viaggiare era un'arte: Il romanzo del Grand Tour* (Bologna: Mulino, 1995); Barbara Korte, *English Travel Writing from Pilgrimages to Postcolonial Explorations* (London: Macmillan, 2000); and Stowe, *Going Abroad.*
26. Nico Slate, *Colored Cosmopolitanism: The Shared Struggle for Freedom in the United States and India* (Cambridge, Mass.: Harvard University Press, 2012), 66.
27. For more about white marble and black bodies, see Charmaine A. Nelson, "White Marble, Black Bodies and the Fear of the Invisible Negro: Signifying Blackness in Mid-Nineteenth-Century Neoclassical Sculpture," *RACAR: Revue d'art canadienne / Canadian Art Review* 27, nos. 1–2 (2000): 87–101.
28. Charlotte Streifer Rubinstein, *American Women Sculptors: A History of Women Working in Three Dimensions* (Boston: G. K. Hall, 1990), 54.
29. Ibid., 54.
30. Levina Buoncuore Urbino, *An American Woman in Europe: The Journal of Two Years and a Half Sojourn in Germany, Switzerland, France, and Italy* (Boston: Lee and Shepard, 1869), 229.
31. Frances E. Willard, *Writing out My Heart: Selections from the Journal of Frances E. Willard, 1855–96,* ed. Carolyn De Swarte Gifford (Urbana: University of Illinois Press, 1995), 328–29.

32. R. J. M. Blackett, *Building an Antislavery Wall: Black Americans in the Atlantic Abolitionist Movement, 1830–1860* (Baton Rouge: Louisiana State University Press, 1983), xi, 3.
33. See Patrick C. Kennicott, "Black Persuaders in the Antislavery Movement," *Journal of Black Studies* 1, no. 1 (1970): 16–17.
34. McFadden, *Golden Cables,* 20.
35. Ibid., 3.
36. Ruth Y. Jenkins, "The Gaze of the Victorian Woman Traveler: Spectacles and Phenomena," in *Gender, Genre, and Identity in Women's Travel Writing,* ed. Kristi Siegel (New York: Peter Lang, 2004), 17, 27.
37. Schriber, "Introduction," xxx.
38. Gilroy, *Black Atlantic,* 6.
39. Jean Fagan Yellin, ed., *The Harriet Jacobs Family Papers,* vol. 1 (Chapel Hill: University of North Carolina Press, 2008), xxxiii.
40. Gilroy, *Black Atlantic,* 9.
41. Ibid., 122–23.
42. On the social and political significance of ethnic music in the black Atlantic, see Gilroy, *Black Atlantic,* 72–110.
43. See F. Michael Higginbotham, *Ghosts of Jim Crow: Ending Racism in Post-Racial America* (New York: New York University Press, 2013).
44. Ibid. 18–19.
45. For more about the elimination of the racial paradigm, see ibid., "Preface," 1–23.
46. Buoncuore Urbino, *American Woman,* 133.

1. Remond and Antebellum Free Black Communities

1. Ruth Bogin and Jean Fagan Yellin, "Introduction," in *The Abolitionist Sisterhood: Women's Political Culture in Antebellum America,* ed. Jean Fagan Yellin and John C. Van Horne (Ithaca, N.Y.: Cornell University Press, 1994), 19.
2. Sarah P. Remond, "Sarah P. Remond," in *Our Exemplars, Poor and Rich; Biographical Sketches of Men and Women Who Have, by an Extraordinary Use of Their Opportunities, Benefited Their Fellow-Creatures,* ed. Matthew Davenport Hill (London: Cassell, Petter, and Galpin, 1861), 276.
3. See Charlotte Forten Grimké, *The Journals of Charlotte Forten Grimké,* ed. Brenda Stevenson (Oxford: Oxford University Press, 1988), 554n17, and Dorothy Burnett Porter, "The Remonds of Salem, Massachusetts: A Nineteenth-Century Family Revisited," *American Antiquarian Society Proceedings* 95, no. 2 (1985): 289–92. The dates for Caroline and Sarah vary depending on the source but according to their passports, Caroline was born before Sarah (see chapter 4).
4. Register vol. A, pp. 45, 73, Salem City Hall, Salem, Mass.
5. "Massachusetts State Census, 1855," *FamilySearch,* https://familysearch.org, Edmund F. Putnam in household of George Putnam, Ward 04, Salem, Essex Co., Mass.; State Archives, Boston, digital folder number 004279395, GS film number 000953981, image number 00249, FHL microfilm 953,981.
6. Remond, "Sarah P. Remond," 276.
7. Shirley J. Yee, *Black Women Abolitionists: A Study in Activism, 1828–1860* (Knoxville: University of Tennessee Press, 1993), 2.

8. Ruth Bogin, "Sarah Parker Remond: Black Abolitionist from Salem," *Essex Institute Historical Collections* 110 (1974): 121; Laura Rundell and Emily A. Murphy, *African American Heritage Sites in Salem: A Guide to Salem's History* (Salem: Salem Maritime National Historic Site, 2008), 1, www.nps.gov.
9. Rundell and Murphy, *African American Heritage Sites,* 1.
10. Bogin, "Sarah Parker Remond," 122.
11. Matthew Frye Jacobson, *Whiteness of a Different Color: European Immigrants and the Alchemy of Race* (Cambridge, Mass.: Harvard University Press, 2002), 36.
12. See also Michael Kammen, *People of Paradox: An Inquiry concerning the Origins of American Civilization* (New York: Oxford University Press, 1980), 262.
13. Leon A. Higginbotham Jr. and Barbara K. Kopytoff, "Racial Purity and Interracial Sex in the Law of Colonial and Antebellum Virginia," in *Interracialism: Black-White Intermarriage in American History, Literature, and Law,* ed. Werner Sollors (Oxford: Oxford University Press, 2000), 89.
14. See ibid., 89–90, and Jacobson, *Whiteness of a Different Color,* 33.
15. Werner Sollors, "Introduction," in Sollors, *Interracialism,* 3.
16. Ibid., 6.
17. See Eve Allegra Raimon, *The Tragic Mulatta Revisited: Race and Nationalism in Nineteenth-Century Antislavery Fiction* (New Brunswick, N.J.: Rutgers University Press, 2004), 12.
18. Nico Slate, *Colored Cosmopolitanism: The Shared Struggle for Freedom in the United States and India* (Cambridge, Mass.: Harvard University Press, 2012), 4.
19. Dorothy B. Porter, "The Organized Educational Activities of Negro Literary Societies, 1828–1846," *Journal of Negro Education* 5, no. 4 (1936): 555.
20. For more about national identity, see also Paola Gemme, *Domesticating Foreign Struggles: The Italian Risorgimento and Antebellum American Identity* (Athens: University of Georgia Press, 2005), 108.
21. See, for example, Richard Bardolph, "Social Origins of Distinguished Negroes, 1770–1865: Part I," *Journal of Negro History* 40, no. 3 (1955): 211–49, and Yee, *Black Women Abolitionists,* 113.
22. Remond, "Sarah P. Remond," 276–77.
23. Hazel V. Carby, *Cultures in Babylon: Black Britain and African America* (London: Verso, 1999), 70.
24. Hazel V. Carby, *Reconstructing Womanhood: The Emergence of the Afro-American Woman Novelist* (New York: Oxford University Press, 1987), 39, 6.
25. Beth Maclay Doriani, "Black Womanhood in Nineteenth-Century America: Subversion and Self-Construction in Two Women's Autobiographies," *American Quarterly* 43, no. 2 (1991): 205.
26. Susan Castillo, *American Literature in Context to 1865* (Chichester, Eng.: Wiley-Blackwell, 2011), 154. See also Linda K. Kerber, *Women of the Republic: Intellect and Ideology in Revolutionary America* (Chapel Hill: University of North Carolina Press, 1997), 7–12, 35–36.
27. Paula Baker, "The Domestication of Politics: Women and Political Society, 1780–1920," in *Unequal Sisters: A Multicultural Reader in U.S. Women's History,* ed. Ellen Carol DuBois and Vicki L. Ruiz (New York: Routledge, 1990), 68.
28. Dorothy Sterling, ed., *We Are Your Sisters: Black Women in the Nineteenth Century* (New York: Norton, 1997), xix.
29. Remond, "Sarah P. Remond," 277.

30. Ibid., 279.
31. See Porter, "Remonds," 263.
32. For more information about John Remond, see Sibyl Ventress Brownlee, *Out of the Abundance of the Heart: Sarah Ann Parker Remond's Quest for Freedom* (Amherst: University of Massachusetts Press, 1997), 42–78.
33. Yee, *Black Women Abolitionists,* 52.
34. Remond Family Papers, MSS 271, Phillips Library, Peabody Essex Museum, Salem, Mass. (hereafter cited as Remond Family Papers); Porter, "Remonds," 265–66.
35. Sterling, *We Are Your Sisters,* xviii.
36. "Biographical Sketches," Remond Family Papers finding aid, 2; "Invoice of LaFayette Dinner," box 1, folder 4, Remond Family Papers.
37. Porter, "Remonds," 271–72.
38. Yee, *Black Women Abolitionists,* 49.
39. Paul Gilroy, *The Black Atlantic: Modernity and Double Consciousness* (Cambridge, Mass.: Harvard University Press, 1993), 123.
40. Published in the *Liberator* on 24 June 1854; qtd. in Arthur O. White, "The Black Leadership Class and Education in Antebellum Boston," *Journal of Negro Education* 42, no. 4 (1973): 515.
41. Remond, "Sarah P. Remond," 278.
42. Ibid., 280.
43. Ibid., 279.
44. Ibid., 279, 280.
45. Ibid., 280.
46. "Sixteenth Anniversary of the Pennsylvania Anti-Slavery," *National Anti-Slavery Standard,* 12 November 1853.
47. See, for example, Porter, "Organized Educational Activities."
48. Yee, *Black Women Abolitionists,* 58.
49. Ibid., 5–12.
50. Remond, "Sarah P. Remond," 282.
51. Advertisement label for "John Remond, Perfumery & Dressing Room," box 1, folder 5, Remond Family Papers.
52. Remond, "Sarah P. Remond," 282.
53. Mary Harrod Northend, *American Homes and Their Furnishings in Colonial Times* (Boston: Little, Brown, 1912), 166.
54. Mary Harrod Northend, "Cassell, of Old Salem," *Good Housekeeping,* February 1909, 191, http://hearth.library.cornell.edu.
55. See Rundell and Murphy, *African American Heritage Sites.*
56. Yee, *Black Women Abolitionists,* 54.
57. Sterling, *We Are Your Sisters,* 97.
58. "Remond, Sarah Parker (6 June 1826–13 Dec. 1894)," in *American National Biography,* ed. John A. Garraty and Mark C. Carnes, vol. 18 (Oxford: Oxford University Press, 1999), 337; "Remond, Sarah Parker (June 6, 1826–post 1887)," in *Notable American Women, 1607–1950: A Biographical Dictionary,* ed. Edward T. James, Janet Wilson James, and Paul S. Boyer, vol. 2 (Cambridge, Mass.: Belknap Press of Harvard University Press, 1971), 136; Sterling, *We Are Your Sisters,* 96.
59. Porter, "Remonds," 290.
60. "Biographical Sketches," Remond Family Papers finding aid, 2.

61. Yee, *Black Women Abolitionists,* 28.
62. "Biographical Sketches," Remond Family Papers finding aid, 2.
63. Yee, *Black Women Abolitionists,* 145.
64. Robert L. Johns, "Georgiana Putnam," in *Notable Black American Women, Book II,* ed. Jessie Garney Smith (Detroit: Gale, 1996), 533; Kathryn Grover and Janine V. da Silva, "Historic Resource Study," 31 December 2012, Boston African American National Historic Site, www.nps.gov.
65. See Grover and da Silva, "Historic Resource Study," and Yee, *Black Women Abolitionists,* 130–31.
66. Scott Hancock, "The Elusive Boundaries of Blackness: Identity Formation in Antebellum Boston," *Journal of Negro History* 84, no. 2 (1999): 125.
67. See, for example, White, "The Black Leadership Class," 512–15.
68. Remond, "Sarah P. Remond," 280.
69. Yee, *Black Women Abolitionists,* 2.
70. Ray Allen Billington, "A Social Experiment: The Port Royal Journal of Charlotte L. Forten, 1862–1863," *Journal of Negro History* 35, no. 3 (1950): 233; Yee, *Black Women Abolitionists,* 16.
71. Yee, *Black Women Abolitionists,* 13.
72. Forten Grimké, *Journals,* 557nn31, 69.
73. See Forten Grimké, *Journals;* Rundell and Murphy, *African American Heritage Sites;* Kay Anne Taylor, "Mary S. Peake and Charlotte L. Forten: Black Teachers during the Civil War and Reconstruction," *Journal of Negro Education* 74, no. 2 (2005): 131–33; Billington, "Social Experiment," 234; and Yee, *Black Women Abolitionists,* 16.
74. See Forten Grimké, *Journals,* for example 68–69, 93, 100–101, 111, 118, 123, 128–30, 147, 152.
75. Ibid., 54, 267.
76. Qtd. in Brenda Stevenson, "Introduction," in Forten Grimké, *Journals,* 32–33.
77. Yee, *Black Women Abolitionists,* 2.
78. See Forten Grimké, *Journals,* and Billington, "Social Experiment," 234.
79. Raimon, *Tragic Mulatta,* 12.
80. Castillo, *American Literature in Context,* 160.
81. William and Ellen Craft, *Running a Thousand Miles for Freedom: The Escape of William and Ellen Craft from Slavery* (Athens: University of Georgia Press, 1999), 90.
82. Barbara McCaskill, "Introduction," in ibid., xiii.
83. Qtd. in Arthur Riss, *Race, Slavery, and Liberalism in Nineteenth-Century American Literature* (Cambridge: Cambridge University Press, 2006), 2.
84. Castillo, *American Literature in Context,* 164.
85. Remond, "Sarah P. Remond," 283–84.
86. Brownlee, *Out of the Abundance,* 68.
87. "Opera Eibotion [*sic*] Case," *Liberator,* 10 June 1853.
88. "American Equality," *Dundee Courier* (Angus, Scotland), 8 June 1853.
89. "Remond, Sarah Parker (6 June 1826–13 Dec. 1894)," 18:337; Remond, "Sarah P. Remond," 281; Porter, "Remonds," 283.
90. "Speech by Sarah P. Remond," in *The Black Abolitionist Papers: The British Isles, 1830–1865,* ed. Peter C. Ripley, vol. 1 (Chapel Hill: University of North Carolina Press, 1985), 440–41.
91. Forten Grimké, *Journals,* 230.
92. Ibid., 232.
93. Ibid., 98.

2. Early Activism in the United States

1. Sarah P. Remond, "Sarah P. Remond," in *Our Exemplars, Poor and Rich; Biographical Sketches of Men and Women Who Have, by an Extraordinary Use of Their Opportunities, Benefited Their Fellow-Creatures,* ed. Matthew Davenport Hill (London: Cassell, Petter, and Galpin, 1861), 286.
2. Susan Castillo, *American Literature in Context to 1865* (Chichester, Eng.: Wiley-Blackwell, 2011), 154–55.
3. Hazel V. Carby, *Cultures in Babylon: Black Britain and African America* (London: Verso, 1999), 73.
4. John Hope Franklin and Alfred A. Moss Jr., *From Slavery to Freedom: A History of African Americans* (New York: Knopf, 1994), 178.
5. Beverly Guy-Sheftall, "African American Women: The Legacy of Black Feminism," in *Sisterhood Is Forever: The Women's Anthology for a New Millennium,* ed. Robin Morgan (New York: Washington Square Press, 2003), 179.
6. Ibid.
7. Marilyn Richardson, *Maria W. Stewart: America's First Black Woman Political Writer* (Bloomington: Indiana University Press, 1987), xiv.
8. Joycelyn Moody, *Sentimental Confessions: Spiritual Narratives of Nineteenth-Century African American Women* (Athens: University of Georgia Press, 2003), 44, 27.
9. Ruth Bogin and Jean Fagan Yellin, "Introduction," in *The Abolitionist Sisterhood: Women's Political Culture in Antebellum America,* ed. Jean Fagan Yellin and John C. Van Horne (Ithaca, N.Y.: Cornell University Press, 1994), 7.
10. Castillo, *American Literature in Context,* 155.
11. Rodney D. Coates, "Social Action, Radical Dialectics, and Popular Protests: Treatment of African American Leaders and Intellectuals by the Press," *Journal of Black Studies* 30, no. 1 (1999): 87.
12. Bogin and Yellin, "Introduction," 9.
13. Salem Female Anti-Slavery Society Records, 1, MSS 34, Phillips Library, Peabody Essex Museum, Salem, Mass.
14. Shirley J. Yee, *Black Women Abolitionists: A Study in Activism, 1828–1860* (Knoxville: University of Tennessee Press, 1993), 16; Dorothy Sterling, ed., *We Are Your Sisters: Black Women in the Nineteenth Century* (New York: Norton, 1997), 175.
15. Lee V. Chambers, *The Weston Sisters: An American Abolitionist Family* (Chapel Hill: University of North Carolina Press, 2014), xxiv.
16. Barbara Bingham Van Broekhoven, "Needles, Pens, and Petitions: Reading Women into Antislavery History," in *The Meaning of Slavery in the North,* ed. David Roediger and Martin H. Blatt (New York: Garland, 1998), 134–41, 144.
17. Ibid., 146.
18. F. K. Prochaska, *Women and Philanthropy in Nineteenth-Century England* (Oxford: Clarendon Press, 1980), 56.
19. Ibid., 57, 63.
20. Salem Female Anti-Slavery Society Records, 2.
21. Bogin and Yellin, "Introduction," 6.
22. Ibid., 7.
23. Van Broekhoven, "Needles," 143.
24. For the complex controversies that characterized the African American convention

movement from the 1830s to 1850s, see, for example, Stanley Harrold, *American Abolitionists* (Essex, Eng.: Pearson Education, 2001); Charles H. Wesley, "The Participation of Negroes in Anti-Slavery Political Parties," *Journal of Negro History* 29, no. 1 (1944): 32–74; Patrick C. Kennicott, "Black Persuaders in the Antislavery Movement," *Journal of Black Studies* 1, no. 1 (1970): 5–20; Howard H. Bell, "National Negro Conventions of the Middle 1840's: Moral Suasion vs. Political Action," *Journal of Negro History* 42, no. 4 (1957): 247–60; and Benjamin Quarles, "The Breach between Douglass and Garrison," *Journal of Negro History* 23, no. 2 (1938): 144–54.

25. Jane H. Pease and William H. Pease, "Negro Convention and the Problem of Black Leadership," *Journal of Black Studies* 2, no. 1 (1971): 40.
26. Wesley, "Participation," 33–46, 61, 68.
27. Harrold, *American Abolitionists*, 47–48.
28. Sterling, *We Are Your Sisters*, 127–32.
29. Ibid., 176.
30. Margaret H. McFadden, *Golden Cables of Sympathy: The Transatlantic Sources of Nineteenth-Century Feminism* (Lexington: University Press of Kentucky, 1999), 16.
31. Peter C. Ripley, ed., *The Black Abolitionist Papers: The United States, 1830–1846*, vol. 3 (Chapel Hill: University of North Carolina Press, 1991), 26–27.
32. Hazel V. Carby, *Reconstructing Womanhood: The Emergence of the Afro-American Woman Novelist* (New York: Oxford University Press, 1987), 66.
33. See, for example, Margaret Hope Bacon, "'One Great Bundle of Humanity': Frances Ellen Watkins Harper (1825–1911)," *Pennsylvania Magazine of History and Biography* 113, no. 1 (1989): 22–33.
34. Sterling, *We Are Your Sisters*, 414.
35. Ibid., 414.
36. Wesley, "Participation," 32.
37. Richard Bardolph, "Social Origins of Distinguished Negroes, 1770–1865: Part I," *Journal of Negro History* 40, no. 3 (1955): 230.
38. Yee, *Black Women Abolitionists*, 17, 21.
39. Bogin and Yellin, "Introduction," 16.
40. See "Abby Kelley Foster: Anti-Slavery, Women's Rights, and Seneca Falls," National Park Service, U.S. Department of the Interior, Women's Rights National Historical Park, www.nps.gov.
41. Qtd. in Alexandra Gripenberg, *A Half Year in the New World*, trans. Ernest J. Moyne (1889; Newark: University of Delaware Press, 1954), 15.
42. Bogin and Yellin, "Introduction," 10–11.
43. Ibid., 2.
44. Castillo, *American Literature in Context*, 158–59.
45. Diane Barnes, ed., *Frederick Douglass: A Life in Documents* (Charlottesville: University of Virginia Press, 2013), 170.
46. McFadden, *Golden Cables*, 109.
47. See, for example, Benjamin Quarles, "Frederick Douglass and the Woman's Rights Movement," *Journal of Negro History* 25, no. 1 (1940): 35–44.
48. Leila J. Rupp, *Worlds of Women: The Making of an International Women's Movement* (Princeton, N.J.: Princeton University Press, 1997), 15–21.
49. Bogin and Yellin, "Introduction," 10.

50. Ibid.
51. Bacon, "One Great Bundle," 34–35.
52. Carby, *Reconstructing Womanhood,* 68.
53. Qtd. in "American Slavery: Lecture by a Lady," *Paisley Herald and Renfrewshire Advertiser,* 12 January 1861.
54. Michael Kammen, *People of Paradox: An Inquiry Concerning the Origins of American Civilization* (New York: Oxford University Press, 1980), 256.
55. Alan Rice, *Radical Narratives of the Black Atlantic* (London: Continuum, 2003), 183.
56. Carby, *Cultures in Babylon,* 69.
57. Yee, *Black Women Abolitionists,* 93.
58. Charles L. Blockson, *The Underground Railroad* (New York: Prentice Hall, 1987), 260.
59. Arthur Riss, *Race, Slavery, and Liberalism in Nineteenth-Century American Literature* (Cambridge: Cambridge University Press, 2006), 15.
60. Ibid., 16.
61. See, for example, ibid., 18.
62. R. J. M. Blackett, *Building an Antislavery Wall: Black Americans in the Atlantic Abolitionist Movement, 1830–1860* (Baton Rouge: Louisiana State University Press, 1983), 26.
63. Fredrika Bremer, *The Homes of the New World; Impressions of America,* vol. 1 (New York: Harper and Brothers, 1853), 583.
64. Ibid., 585.
65. Sarah P. Remond, "Why Slavery Is Still Rampant," in *The Rhetoric of Struggle: Public Address by African American Women,* ed. Robbie Jean Walker (New York: Garland, 1992), 45.
66. Rice, *Radical Narratives,* 14.
67. Barbara McCaskill, "Introduction," in William and Ellen Craft, *Running a Thousand Miles for Freedom: The Escape of William and Ellen Craft from Slavery* (Athens: University of Georgia Press, 1999), ix, xi.
68. Ibid., viii.
69. Pauline Elizabeth Hopkins, *Winona: A Tale of Negro Life in the South and Southwest* (1902; La Vergne, Tenn.: Dodo Press, 2002), 90.
70. "Remond, Sarah Parker (6 June 1826–13 Dec. 1894)," in *American National Biography,* ed. John A. Garraty and Mark C. Carnes, vol. 18 (Oxford: Oxford University Press, 1999), 337.
71. "Contemptible Conduct at Ogdensburg," *Liberator,* 26 December 1856.
72. Sibyl Ventress Brownlee, *Out of the Abundance of the Heart: Sarah Ann Parker Remond's Quest for Freedom* (Amherst: University of Massachusetts Press, 1997), 110.
73. William Lloyd Garrison, *The Letters of William Lloyd Garrison: From Disunionism to the Brink of War, 1850–1860,* vol. 4, ed. Louis Ruchames (Cambridge, Mass.: Belknap Press of Harvard University Press, 1975), 425.
74. Ibid., 434.
75. "Western Anti-Slavery Society," *Liberator,* 18 September 1857.
76. William Lloyd Garrison to Helen Eliza Garrison, 12 February 1857, Boston Public Library, Boston, Mass., https://archive.org.
77. Ruth Bogin, "Sarah Parker Remond: Black Abolitionist from Salem," *Essex Institute Historical Collections* 110 (1974): 130; Charlotte Forten Grimké, *The Journals of Charlotte Forten Grimké,* ed. Brenda Stevenson (Oxford: Oxford University Press, 1988), 185–96.
78. See Sarah Parker Remond to Amy Post, 15 March 1857, "Remond, Sarah Parker, Letter to Amy Kirby Post," Post Family Papers Project, http://rbsc.library.rochester.edu,

and William Lloyd Garrison to Helen Eliza Garrison, 12 February 1857, Boston Public Library.

79. Forten Grimké, *Journals,* 200.
80. Lillie Buffum Chace Wyman and Arthur Crawford Wyman, *Elizabeth Buffum Chace, 1806–1899: Her Life and Its Environment,* vol. 1 (Boston: W. B. Clark, 1914), 196.
81. Sterling, *We Are Your Sisters,* 177.
82. Ibid.
83. "Miss Sarah P. Remond," *Liberator,* 5 November 1858.
84. Garrison, *Letters,* 4:600.
85. Ibid.
86. Castillo, *American Literature in Context,* 168.

3. England, 1858–1866

1. Amanda Claybaugh, "Toward a New Transatlanticism: Dickens in the United States," *Victorian Studies* 48, no. 3 (Spring 2006): 439.
2. Ruth Y. Jenkins, "The Gaze of the Victorian Woman Traveler: Spectacles and Phenomena," in *Gender, Genre, and Identity in Women's Travel Writing,* ed. Kristi Siegel (New York: Peter Lang, 2004), 15.
3. William W. Stowe, *Going Abroad: European Travel in Nineteenth-Century American Culture* (Princeton, N.J.: Princeton University Press, 1994), xi.
4. Paul Gilroy, *The Black Atlantic: Modernity and Double Consciousness* (Cambridge, Mass.: Harvard University Press, 1993), 95.
5. Claybaugh, "Toward a New Transatlanticism," 444.
6. See ibid., 444.
7. Other Remond women, who may have been relatives, traveled to England in July. On 6 July 1858, the *New York Times* published a passenger list of the steamship *Vanderbilt* heading from New York for Southampton and Havre, carrying onboard a Mrs. N. (Nancy?) Remond and daughter, and a Miss Remond.
8. "From the London Anti-Slavery Advocates," *London Anti-Slavery Advocate,* reprinted in the *Liberator,* 19 November 1858.
9. Sarah P. Remond, "Sarah P. Remond," in *Our Exemplars, Poor and Rich; Biographical Sketches of Men and Women Who Have, by an Extraordinary Use of Their Opportunities, Benefited Their Fellow-Creatures,* ed. Matthew Davenport Hill (London: Cassell, Petter, and Galpin, 1861), 286.
10. Qtd. in Dorothy Sterling, ed., *We Are Your Sisters: Black Women in the Nineteenth Century* (New York: Norton, 1997), 176.
11. "From the London Anti-Slavery Advocates," *Liberator,* 19 November 1858.
12. "Our European Correspondence," *National Anti-Slavery Standard,* 17 August 1861.
13. Giuseppe Mazzini, *Edizione nazionale di scritti editi ed inediti di Giuseppe Mazzini* (Imola, Italy: Cooperativa tipografico-editrice Paolo Galeati, 1936–39), 82:296.
14. Mary Suzanne Schriber, *Writing Home: American Women Abroad, 1830–1920* (Charlottesville: University Press of Virginia, 1997), 7.
15. Remond, "Sarah P. Remond," 286; "Sarah P. Remond and the Passport Issue," in *The Black Abolitionist Papers: The British Isles, 1830–1865,* ed. Peter C. Ripley, vol. 1 (Chapel Hill, University of North Carolina Press, 1985), 470.
16. "Coloured Persons and Cunard Steamers," *Lloyd's Weekly Newspaper,* 8 July 1860. See also

"Coloured Persons and Cunard Steamers," *Western Daily Press*, 4 July 1860. The material in the next two paragraphs also comes from this source.

17. R. J. M. Blackett, *Building an Antislavery Wall: Black Americans in the Atlantic Abolitionist Movement 1830–1860* (Baton Rouge: Louisiana State University Press, 1983), 39.
18. "Coloured Persons and Cunard Steamers," *Lloyd's*.
19. Ibid.
20. "To Sir Samuel Cunaed [*sic*], Bart," *London Weekly Dispatch*, reprinted in the *Liberator*, 14 September 1860.
21. See, for example, Lee V. Chambers, *The Weston Sisters: An American Abolitionist Family* (Chapel Hill: University of North Carolina Press, 2014), xxiii–xxiv.
22. Shirley J. Yee, *Black Women Abolitionists: A Study in Activism, 1828–1860* (Knoxville: University of Tennessee Press, 1993), 34.
23. Blackett, *Building an Antislavery Wall*, 80.
24. Douglas H. Maynard, "The World's Anti-Slavery Convention of 1840," *Mississippi Valley Historical Review* 47, no. 3 (1960): 452.
25. Ibid., 456–60.
26. Clare Midgley, *Women against Slavery: The British Campaign, 1780–1870* (London: Routledge, 1995), 12.
27. Maynard, "World's Anti-Slavery Convention," 467.
28. Ibid., 469.
29. See, for example, Ellen Carol DuBois, "Outgrowing the Compact of the Fathers: Equal Rights, Woman Suffrage, and the United States Constitution, 1820–1878," *Journal of American History* 74, no. 3 (Dec. 1987): 836–62.
30. Blackett, *Building an Antislavery Wall*, xi.
31. Ibid., 17, 79.
32. Ibid., 75.
33. Teresa Zackodnik, *Press, Platform, Pulpit: Black Feminist Publics in the Era of Reform* (Knoxville: University of Tennessee Press, 2011), 58.
34. Qtd. in Blackett, *Building an Antislavery Wall*, 6.
35. Lee Jenkins, "Beyond the Pale: Frederick Douglass in Cork," *Irish Review* 24 (1999): 87–88.
36. Harriet Beecher Stowe, *Lady Byron Vindicated: A History of the Byron Controversy from Its Beginning in 1816 to the Present Time* (Boston: Fields, Osgood, 1870), 145–50, 151.
37. Blackett, *Building an Antislavery Wall*, 40.
38. Alan Rice, *Radical Narratives of the Black Atlantic* (London: Continuum, 2003), 177.
39. Blackett, *Building an Antislavery Wall*, 41.
40. See also Rice, *Radical Narratives*, 174–81.
41. Frederick Douglass, "The Color Line," *North American Review*, June 1881, 571, 568.
42. Ibid., 568.
43. Ibid., 572, 573.
44. William G. Allen et al., "Letters to Antislavery Workers and Agencies [Part 6]," *Journal of Negro History* 10, no. 3 (1925): 468–69.
45. William G. Allen, *The American Prejudice against Color by William G. Allen, a Refugee from American Despotism* (London: W. and F. G. Cash, 1853), 23–27; Benjamin Quarles, "Antebellum Free Blacks and the 'Spirit of '76,'" *Journal of Negro History* 61, no. 3 (1976): 234.
46. Blackett, *Building an Antislavery Wall*, 11; Richard Bardolph, "Social Origins of Distinguished Negroes, 1770–1865: Part I," *Journal of Negro History* 40, no. 3 (1955): 234n40.

47. Rice, *Radical Narratives,* 177.
48. Ibid., 177–78.
49. See Blackett, *Building an Antislavery Wall,* 158.
50. See, for example, F. S. Schwarzbach, "'*Terra Incognita*'—An Image of the City in English Literature, 1820–1855," in *The Art of Travel: Essays on Travel Writing,* ed. Philip Dodd (London: Frank Cass, 1982), 78–80.
51. Allen et al., "Letters to Antislavery Workers," 469.
52. "Personal," *Harper's Bazaar,* 18 January 1879, 39.
53. Ibid.; emphasis added.
54. Charmaine A. Nelson, *The Color of Stone: Sculpting the Black Female Subject in Nineteenth-Century America* (Minneapolis: University of Minnesota Press, 2007), 35.
55. Blackett, *Building an Antislavery Wall,* 106.
56. Ibid., 124.
57. Ibid., 125.
58. Barbara McCaskill, "Introduction," in William and Ellen Craft, *Running a Thousand Miles for Freedom: The Escape of William and Ellen Craft from Slavery* (Athens: University of Georgia Press, 1999), xv.
59. See "American Slavery," *Essex Standard,* 5 August 1859.
60. See McCaskill, "Introduction," xix.
61. "Remarkable Return in the Census, Disgrace to America," *Hereford Journal,* 30 April 1851.
62. Blackett, *Building an Antislavery Wall,* 14–16; "Introduction," in Ripley, *Black Abolitionist Papers,* 1:22.
63. Craft, *Running a Thousand Miles,* 68–69.
64. McCaskill, "Introduction," xvii.
65. Harriet Ritvo, *The Platypus and the Mermaid and Other Figments of the Classifying Imagination* (Cambridge, Mass.: Harvard University Press, 1997), 125, 134.
66. "Leeds Young Men's Anti-Slavery Society," *Leeds Times,* 17 December 1859.
67. "Anti-Slavery Demonstrations in England; Fred. Douglass on the Harper's Ferry Business," *New York Times,* 16 January 1860; "Leeds Young Men's Anti-Slavery Society," *Liberator,* 27 January 1860.
68. See "Anti-Slavery Meeting in Wakefield," *Leeds Mercury,* 14 January 1860.
69. Margaret H. McFadden, *Golden Cables of Sympathy: The Transatlantic Sources of Nineteenth-Century Feminism* (Lexington: University Press of Kentucky, 1999), 185.
70. Qtd. in Blackett, *Building an Antislavery Wall,* 6.
71. Craft, *Running a Thousand Miles,* 69; Dorothy B. Porter, "Sarah Parker Remond, Abolitionist and Physician," *Journal of Negro History* 20, no. 3 (1935): 291.
72. "Introduction," in Ripley, *Black Abolitionist Papers,* 1:3–4, 7–8; Blackett, *Building an Antislavery Wall,* 19.
73. McCaskill, "Introduction," xxiii.
74. "Anti-Slavery Movement in England," *Derbyshire Times* and *Chesterfield Herald,* both 19 February 1859.

4. Advocate for Racial and Gender Emancipation

1. Dorothy Burnett Porter, "The Remonds of Salem, Massachusetts: A Nineteenth-Century Family Revisited," *American Antiquarian Society Proceedings* 95, no. 2 (1985): 285.

2. "Lecture on American Slavery by a Colored Lady," *Warrington Times,* 29 January 1859, reprinted in the *Liberator,* 11 March 1859.
3. "Speech by Sarah P. Remond," in *The Black Abolitionist Papers: The British Isles, 1830–1865,* ed. Peter C. Ripley, vol. 1 (Chapel Hill: University of North Carolina Press, 1985), 438.
4. Ibid., 1:439–40.
5. R. J. M. Blackett, *Building an Antislavery Wall: Black Americans in the Atlantic Abolitionist Movement, 1830–1860* (Baton Rouge: Louisiana State University Press, 1983), 8, 11.
6. P. Gabrielle Foreman, *Activist Sentiments: Reading Black Women in the Nineteenth Century* (Urbana: University of Illinois Press, 2009), 24.
7. "The Lecture at the Lion Hotel," *Warrington Times,* reprinted in the *Liberator,* 11 March 1859.
8. Ibid.
9. Ibid.
10. "Remond, Sarah Parker (June 6, 1826–post 1887)," in *Notable American Women, 1607–1950: A Biographical Dictionary,* ed. Edward T. James, Janet Wilson James, and Paul S. Boyer, vol. 2 (Cambridge, Mass.: Belknap Press of Harvard University Press, 1971), 136.
11. Qtd. in Audrey A. Fisch, *American Slaves in Victorian England: Abolitionist Politics in Popular Literature and Culture* (Cambridge: Cambridge University Press, 2000), 123n22.
12. Paul Gilroy, *The Black Atlantic: Modernity and Double Consciousness* (Cambridge, Mass.: Harvard University Press, 1993), 19.
13. "A Second Lecture by Miss Remond," *Warrington Times,* reprinted in the *Liberator.* 11 March 1859.
14. "Miss Remond's Anti-Slavery Lecture," *Freeman's Journal,* 15 March 1859.
15. "American Slavery: Lecture by a Lady," *Paisley Herald and Renfrewshire Advertiser,* 12 January 1861.
16. Sarah Parker Remond to Maria Weston Chapman, 6 October 1859, Boston Public Library, Boston, Mass., https://archive.org.
17. "Miss Remond's Anti-Slavery Lecture," *Freeman's Journal,* 15 March 1859.
18. Carla Peterson, *"Doers of the Word": African-American Women Speakers and Writers in the North (1830–1880)* (Oxford: Oxford University Press, 1995), 119.
19. Ibid.
20. For separate sphere ideology, see, for example, ibid., 126.
21. "Miss Remond and the London First of August Meeting," *National Anti-Slavery Standard,* 12 November 1859; "Our European Correspondence," *National Anti-Slavery Standard,* 31 December 1859.
22. Qtd. in Sibyl Ventress Brownlee, *Out of the Abundance of the Heart: Sarah Ann Parker Remond's Quest for Freedom* (Amherst: University of Massachusetts Press, 1997), 133, 134.
23. "Lecture on American Slavery by a Colored Lady," *Warrington Times,* 29 January 1859.
24. From the *Liverpool Mercury,* reprinted in the *Liberator,* 18 February 1859, with the title "Miss Sarah P. Remond in Liverpool."
25. Blackett, *Building an Antislavery Wall,* 201.
26. "Miss Remond's Anti-Slavery Lecture," *Freeman's Journal,* 15 March 1859.
27. Foreman, *Activist Sentiments,* 5.
28. "Miss Remond's Anti-Slavery Lecture," *Freeman's Journal,* 15 March 1859.
29. "Speech by Sarah P. Remond," in Ripley, *Black Abolitionist Papers,* 1:457–58, 459.
30. Sarah P. Remond, "Why Slavery Is Still Rampant," in *The Rhetoric of Struggle: Public Address by African American Women,* ed. Robbie Jean Walker (New York: Garland, 1992), 43.
31. "American Slavery," *Huddersfield Chronicle,* 7 January 1860.

32. "Lecture on Slavery by Miss Remond," *Birmingham Journal,* 26 January 1861; "Lecture on Slavery by Miss Remond," *Birmingham Daily Post,* 25 January 1861.
33. "Temperance Demonstration at Leeds," *London Daily News,* 28 December 1859.
34. See "Leeds Temperance Union," *Leeds Mercury,* 27 December 1859.
35. Shirley J. Yee, *Black Women Abolitionists: A Study in Activism, 1828–1860* (Knoxville: University of Tennessee Press, 1993), 84.
36. "Lecture on Slavery by Miss Remond," *Birmingham Journal,* 26 January 1861.
37. Qtd. in Blackett, *Building an Antislavery Wall,* 179.
38. See, for example, Beverly Guy-Sheftall, "African American Women: The Legacy of Black Feminism," in *Sisterhood Is Forever: The Women's Anthology for a New Millennium,* ed. Robin Morgan (New York: Washington Square Press, 2003), 179.
39. Gilroy, *Black Atlantic,* 65.
40. See ibid., 64–65; Mark Reinhardt, "Who Speaks for Margaret Garner? Slavery, Silence, and the Politics of Ventriloquism," *Critical Inquiry* 29, no. 1 (2002): 91–92, 102.
41. Reinhardt, "Who Speaks," 93, 111.
42. Ibid., 91.
43. "American Freedmen's Relief Association," *Islington Gazette,* 16 June 1865.
44. Sarah Agnes Wallace and Frances Elma Gillespie, eds., *The Journal of Benjamin Moran 1857–1865,* vol. 1 (Chicago: University of Chicago Press, 1948), 608; "Sarah P. Remond and the Passport Issue," in Ripley, *Black Abolitionist Papers,* 1:469.
45. Wallace and Gillespie, *Journal,* 1:608.
46. Ibid., 1:608, 610.
47. "Refusal of American Passports to Persons of Color," *New Orleans Daily Crescent,* 2 February 1860.
48. "Sarah P. Remond and the Passport Issue," in Ripley, *Black Abolitionist Papers,* 1:469.
49. Wallace and Gillespie, *Journal,* 1:613, 616.
50. Ibid., 1:627.
51. "The Land of Liberty," *Lancaster Gazette,* 14 January 1860.
52. "American Freedom," *Bucks Herald,* 14 January 1860.
53. Wallace and Gillespie, *Journal,* 1:642.
54. "Disabilities of American Persons of Color," *New York Times,* 24 January 1860; "Colored Persons and Passports," *New York Times,* 25 January 1860; "The Question of Passports," *New York Times,* 25 January 1860.
55. Leon F. Litwack, "The Federal Government and the Free Negro, 1790–1860," *Journal of Negro History* 43, no. 4 (1958): 261.
56. See, for example, ibid.
57. Ifeoma Kiddoe Nwankwo, *Black Cosmopolitanism: Racial Consciousness and Transnational Identity in the Nineteenth-Century Americas* (Philadelphia: University of Pennsylvania Press, 2005), 175.
58. See ibid., 18, 114. For "double consciousness," see also Gilroy, *Black Atlantic.*
59. *Annual Report of the American Anti-Slavery Society, by the Executive Committee for the Year Ending May 1, 1860* (New York: American Anti-Slavery Society, 1861), 220.
60. Sarah Parker Remond to Maria Weston Chapman, 6 October 1859, Boston Public Library, https://archive.org.
61. "Our European Correspondence," *National Anti-Slavery Standard,* 30 June 1860.
62. For more about Reid, see Lee V. Chambers, *The Weston Sisters: An American Abolitionist*

Family (Chapel Hill: University of North Carolina Press, 2014).

63. Bedford College Papers, Bedford College Registry, BC AR/200–299, Session 1859–1860, No. 12, Miss Remond, Bedford College Archives, Bedford College, London.
64. Henry Crabb Robinson Diary, RF 104/1; Miss Bostock to Elizabeth Jesser Reid, RF 103/2/36, both Papers of Elizabeth Jesser Reid, Bedford College Archives.
65. See Henry Crabb Robinson Diary, 13 March 1859, RF 104/1, Papers of Elizabeth Jesser Reid.
66. Florence Kelly to Elizabeth Jesser Reid, 16 August 1864, RF 103/8/18, Papers of Elizabeth Jesser Reid.
67. Sarah P. Remond, "The Negroes in the United States of America," *Journal of Negro History* 27, no. 2 (1942): 218.
68. Ibid., 218.
69. "Miss Sarah P. Remond," *Liberator,* 23 September 1859.
70. Margaret H. McFadden, *Golden Cables of Sympathy: The Transatlantic Sources of Nineteenth-Century Feminism* (Lexington: University Press of Kentucky, 1999), 165.
71. F. K. Prochaska, *Women and Philanthropy in Nineteenth-Century England* (Oxford: Clarendon Press, 1980), 178.
72. "Two Days Later from Europe," *New York Times,* 3 September 1861.
73. Qtd. in Dorothy Sterling, ed., *We Are Your Sisters: Black Women in the Nineteenth Century* (New York: Norton, 1997), 179; qtd. in Brownlee, *Out of the Abundance,* 147.
74. Clare Midgley, *Women against Slavery: The British Campaign, 1780–1870* (London: Routledge, 1995), 173.
75. See Esther Sturge to Caroline Weston, 13 April 1863, Boston Public Library, https://archive.org.
76. Midgley, *Women against Slavery,* 133.
77. "Remond, Sarah Parker (6 June 1826–13 Dec. 1894)," in *American National Biography,* ed. John A. Garraty, and Mark C. Carnes, vol. 18 (Oxford: Oxford University Press, 1999), 338.
78. Sarah P. Remond, *Negroes and Anglo-Africans as Freedmen and Soldiers* (London: Emily Faithfull, 1864), 218.
79. Sarah Parker Remond to William Lloyd Garrison, 25 July 1864, Boston Public Library, https://archive.org.
80. Giuseppe Mazzini, *Edizione nazionale di scritti editi ed inediti di Giuseppe Mazzini* (Imola, Italy: Cooperativa tipografico-editrice Paolo Galeati, 1936–39), 79:188.
81. Ibid., 80:76.
82. Ibid., 80:13.
83. Frances Cobbe, *Life of Frances Power Cobbe by Herself,* vol. 1 (New York: Houghton, Mifflin, 1894), 283.
84. "Remond, Sarah Parker (6 June 1826–13 Dec. 1894)," 18:338.
85. Qtd. in Brownlee, *Out of the Abundance,* 149.
86. John Hope Franklin, *Racial Equality in America* (Chicago: University of Chicago Press, 1976), 58, 61.
87. Sarah Parker Remond, "The Negro Race in America," *London Daily News,* 22 September 1866.
88. Blackett, *Building an Antislavery Wall,* 155.
89. Remond, "Negro Race in America."
90. "Breakfast to Mr. Lloyd Garrison," *Manchester Times,* 6 July 1867.
91. William Lloyd Garrison to Helen Eliza Garrison, 26 July 1867, Boston Public Library, https://archive.org.

5. Abolitionists for Italian Risorgimento

1. Nico Slate, *Colored Cosmopolitanism: The Shared Struggle for Freedom in the United States and India* (Cambridge, Mass.: Harvard University Press, 2012), 5.
2. James Fenimore Cooper, *Excursions in Italy* (Paris: Baudry's European Library, 1838), 329.
3. Samuel Longfellow, *Final Memorials of Henry Wadsworth Longfellow* (Boston: Ticknor, 1887), 90.
4. Giuseppe Mazzini, *Edizione nazionale di scritti editi ed inediti di Giuseppe Mazzini* (Imola, Italy: Cooperativa tipografico-editrice Paolo Galeati, 1936–39), 78:27n1.
5. Emma Detti, *Margaret Fuller Ossoli e i suoi corrispondenti* (Florence: Le Monnier, 1942), 178–81. "Vous avez raison d'être blessée de l'indifférence avec laquelle on a accueilli ce noble témoignage de sympathie de votre Patrie. . . . Oui, ma chère amie, on n'a pas encore tout à fait rendu justice à l'Amérique dans la vieille Europe, on la regarde encore toujours un peu de haut en bas." Costanza Arconati to Margaret Fuller, 24 January 1848, ibid., 294.
6. R. J. M. Blackett, *Building an Antislavery Wall: Black Americans in the Atlantic Abolitionist Movement, 1830–1860* (Baton Rouge: Louisiana State University Press, 1983), 199.
7. Qtd. in ibid.
8. Karen Sánchez-Eppler, "Bodily Bonds: The Intersecting Rhetorics of Feminism and Abolition," in *Interracialism: Black-White Intermarriage in American History, Literature, and Law*, ed. Werner Sollors (Oxford: Oxford University Press, 2000), 415.
9. F. K. Prochaska, *Women and Philanthropy in Nineteenth-Century England* (Oxford: Clarendon Press, 1980), 27, 30, 47–53.
10. Meg McGavran Murray, *Margaret Fuller: Wandering Pilgrim* (Athens: University of Georgia Press, 2008), 285.
11. See Eugenio F. Biagini, "'The Principle of Humanity': Lincoln in Germany and Italy, 1859–1865," in *The Global Lincoln*, ed. Richard Carwardine and Jay Sexton (Oxford: Oxford University Press, 2011), 81, 77.
12. Murray, *Margaret Fuller*, 296.
13. See Blackett, *Building an Antislavery Wall*, 199.
14. "The Neapolitan Exiles," *Liberator*, 13 May 1859.
15. The same information was reprinted in the *National Anti-Slavery Standard*, 30 April 1859.
16. Blackett, *Building an Antislavery Wall*, 4.
17. See ibid., 8–9, 36, 39, 46.
18. Qtd. in ibid., 46.
19. Salvo Mastellone, *Mazzini scrittore politico in inglese: "Democracy in Europe" (1840–1855)* (Florence: Olschki, 2004), 25.
20. Ibid., 132.
21. Biagini, "Principle of Humanity," 76.
22. See ibid., 77.
23. Mazzini, *Edizione nazionale di scritti*, 78:244–45.
24. Elizabeth Barrett Browning, *The Letters of Elizabeth Barrett Browning*, vol. 2, ed. Frederic G. Kenyon (London: Smith, Elder, 1898), to Miss Mitford, dated Welbeck Street, Friday, 31 July 1852, n.p.
25. Ibid., to Mrs. Jameson, dated Casa Guidi, Florence, 17 March 1853, n.p.
26. Qtd. in Mastellone, *Mazzini*, 307.

27. Ibid., 279, 301.
28. Barrett Browning, *Letters,* to Miss Browning, dated Rome, 11 May 1861, n.p.
29. Luca Codignola, "The Civil War: The View from Italy," *Reviews in American History* 3, no. 4 (1975): 457.
30. Paola Gemme, *Domesticating Foreign Struggles: The Italian Risorgimento and Antebellum American Identity* (Athens: University of Georgia Press, 2005), 31.
31. Ibid., 20–27.
32. Qtd. in Biagini, "Principle of Humanity," 78.
33. Ibid., 78–79.
34. James Jackson Jarves to Margherita Mignaty, Paris, 29 September 1861, ms. C.V. 196.94, Biblioteca Nazionale Centrale di Firenze, Florence, Italy.
35. Mazzini, *Edizione nazionale di scritti,* 78:73.
36. "Lecture on Slavery by Miss Remond," *Birmingham Daily Post,* 25 January 1861.
37. Ibid.
38. Qtd. in Blackett, *Building an Antislavery Wall,* 179.
39. Mazzini, *Edizione nazionale di scritti,* 76:259–60.
40. Ibid., 78:75.
41. See ibid., 72:205–6.
42. Ibid., 72:208.
43. Ibid., 72:208, 325–26, 384.
44. Ibid., 74:66.
45. Ibid., 74:224.
46. Ibid., 76:124.
47. Ibid., 78:246–47.
48. Ibid., 78:247.
49. See, for instance, ibid., letters dated 23 December 1861, 72:131; 10 April 1862, 72:273; May 1863, 74:249; and 11 September 1864, 79:47.
50. Ibid., 79:86.
51. Prochaska, *Women and Philanthropy,* 216–17.
52. Elizabeth Crawford, *The Women's Suffrage Movement: A Reference Guide, 1866–1928* (London: University College London Press, 1999), 367.
53. For more information, see, for example, Paul McHugh, *Prostitution and Victorian Social Reform* (New York: Routledge, 2013).
54. Mazzini, *Edizione nazionale di scritti,* 81:207.
55. Ibid., 81:208.
56. Ibid., 84:265.
57. See, for example, "Mazzini," *Dundee Advertiser,* 23 March 1866.
58. Mazzini, *Edizione nazionale di scritti,* 80:230.
59. Susan Castillo, *American Literature in Context to 1865* (Chichester, Eng.: Wiley-Blackwell, 2011), 170.
60. John Hope Franklin, *Racial Equality in America* (Chicago: University of Chicago Press, 1976), 56.
61. "Mazzini," *Dundee Advertiser,* 23 March 1866.
62. Qtd. in Blackett, *Building an Antislavery Wall,* 179.
63. Ibid.
64. See also ibid., 11–12.

65. Gemme, *Domesticating Foreign Struggles,* 1–2.
66. Ibid., 12.
67. Rolando Anzilotti, "L'Italia e il Risorgimento nell'opera di Henry Theodore Tuckerman," in *Italia e Stati Uniti nell'età del Risorgimento e della Guerra Civile,* ed. Agostino Lombardo et al. (Florence: La Nuova Italia, 1969), 55, 64–65n26.
68. Biagini, "Principle of Humanity," 78.
69. Aldo Celli, "Il Risorgimento nella poesia Americana," in Lombardo et al., *Italia,* 34–35.
70. Anne Longfellow Pierce, unpublished journal, 14 December, Longfellow Family Papers, LONG 16173, Longfellow House–Washington's Headquarters National Historic Site Archives, Cambridge, Mass. (hereafter cited as Longfellow Family Papers).
71. Ibid.; see also Alice Mary Longfellow, unpublished journal, Longfellow Family Papers.
72. Gemme, *Domesticating Foreign Struggles,* 4.
73. For a discussion of the difference between the attitudes of white antislavery advocates, who often revealed paternalist racism in their depictions of slaves as helpless victims, and black abolitionists, who tended to present slaves as rebels against tyranny, see ibid., 7, 116, 120–21.
74. Biagini, "Principle of Humanity," 78.
75. Mary Somerville, *Personal Recollections, from Early Life to Old Age of Mary Somerville with Selections from Her Correspondence by Her Daughter Martha Somerville* (London: John Murray, 1874), 305.
76. Ibid.
77. Ibid., 306.
78. Anne Longfellow Pierce, unpublished journal, 1 December, Longfellow Family Papers.
79. "Art Matters in Florence: The American Sculptors, Greenough, Crawford, and Bartholomew, and Their Successors Works Now in Progress," written in October, published in the *New York Times,* 7 November 1860.
80. "American Art Abroad; Art-Artists in Italy Powers, Mead and Jackson in Florence Rogers, Story, Mozier and Others in Rome. Powers and His Studio. Mead and His 'Echo.' The Battle Story. Jackson and His Eve and Abel. American Artists at Rome. A Monumental Sculpture. A Collection of Attractions. Sculptors Rhineheart and Handley. American Painters at Rome," written in February, published in the *New York Times,* 6 March 1864.
81. See, for example, Marilyn Richardson, "Friends and Colleagues: Edmonia Lewis and Her Italian Circle," in *Sculptors, Painters, and Italy: Italian Influence on Nineteenth-Century American Art,* ed. Sirpa Salenius (Padova, Italy: Il Prato, 2009), 100–101.
82. "Miss Edmonia Lewis," *Gloucester Journal,* 10 March 1866.
83. "Miss Lewis," *Leeds Mercury,* 12 February 1867.

6. Firenze "La Bella"

1. Mary Suzanne Schriber, *Writing Home: American Women Abroad, 1830–1920* (Charlottesville: University Press of Virginia, 1997), 20.
2. William W. Stowe, *Going Abroad: European Travel in Nineteenth-Century American Culture* (Princeton, N.J.: Princeton University Press, 1994), xi.
3. See obituary in William Cooper Nell, *William Cooper Nell: Selected Writings, 1832–1874,* ed. Dorothy Porter Wesley and Constance Porter Uzelac (Baltimore: Black Classic Press, 2002), 517.
4. Marriage of Edmund Quincy Putnam and Gertrude Elliston, 24 May 1868, England and

Wales Marriage Registration Index, vol. 6, p. 702, line 267, National Archives, Kew, England, www.nationalarchives.gov.uk.

5. Dorothy Burnett Porter, "The Remonds of Salem, Massachusetts: A Nineteenth-Century Family Revisited," *American Antiquarian Society Proceedings* 95, no. 2 (1985): 292.
6. Jennifer Bernhardt Steadman, *Traveling Economies: American Women's Travel Writing* (Columbus: Ohio State University Press, 2007), 4.
7. Stowe, *Going Abroad,* 5.
8. For other travel writers, see Kristi Siegel, "Intersections: Women's Travel and Theory," in *Gender, Genre, and Identity in Women's Travel Writing,* ed. Kristi Siegel (New York: Peter Lang, 2004), 5–8.
9. Kwame Anthony Appiah, *Cosmopolitanism: Ethics in a World of Strangers* (New York: Norton, 2006), xiv.
10. See ibid., xiii, 137.
11. Gillian Brock, "Rethinking the Cosmopolitanism versus Non-Cosmopolitanism Debate: An Introduction," in *Cosmopolitanism versus Non-Cosmopolitanism: Critiques, Defenses, Reconceptualizations,* ed. Gillian Brock (Oxford: Oxford University Press, 2013), 3.
12. Ibid., 11.
13. James Jackson Jarves, *Italian Sights and Papal Principles, Seen through American Spectacles* (New York: Harper, 1856), 51.
14. See, for example, Douglas Tallack, *Twentieth-Century America: The Intellectual and Cultural Context* (London: Longman, 1991), 159, and T. J. Jackson Lears, *No Place of Grace: Antimodernism and the Transformation of American Culture, 1880–1920* (Chicago: University of Chicago Press, 1994), xvi.
15. Lears, *No Place of Grace,* xvi.
16. Jarves, *Italian Sights,* 44–46. For Pergola, see Pier Francesco Listri and Maurizio Naldini, *La Grande Storia di Firenze* (Florence: Ponte alle Grazie editori, 1992), 742–43.
17. Listri and Naldini, *Grande Storia,* 893; Ugo Pesci, *Firenze Capitale (1865–1870)* (Florence: R. Bemporad and Figlio, 1904), 65–67.
18. Listri and Naldini, *Grande Storia,* 928–30.
19. *Firenze in tasca: Una gita di piacere alla Capitale* (1867; Sesto Fiorentino, Italy: Apice libri, 2014), 12.
20. Pesci, *Firenze Capitale,* 320.
21. Listri and Naldini, *Grande Storia,* 880–81, 957–62, 901 (a list of mayors); Pesci *Firenze Capitale,* 338.
22. For more about the Peruzzi, see Vilfredo Pareto, *Lettere ai Peruzzi (1872–1900),* vol. 27 (Rome: Edizioni di storia e letteratura, 1968).
23. Jarves, *Italian Sights,* 34.
24. Ibid.
25. Jean Strouse, "J. Pierpont Morgan: Financier and Collector," *Metropolitan Museum of Art Bulletin* 1 (2000): 17.
26. Albert Ten Eyck Gardner, "The History of a Collection," *Metropolitan Museum of Art Bulletin* 5, no.8 (April 1947): 215–16.
27. Giuliana Artom Treves, *Anglo-Fiorentini di cento anni fa* (Florence: Sansoni, 1982), 187.
28. James Jackson Jarves to Margherita Mignaty, London, 2 May 1855, ms. C.V. 196.86, Biblioteca Nazionale Centrale di Firenze, Florence, Italy.

29. See Charmaine A. Nelson, *The Color of Stone: Sculpting the Black Female Subject in Nineteenth-Century America* (Minneapolis: University of Minnesota Press, 2007), 10.
30. Ibid., 7.
31. See also Sirpa Salenius, *Rose Elizabeth Cleveland: First Lady and Literary Scholar* (New York: Palgrave Macmillan, 2014), 58.
32. Giuseppe Mazzini, *Edizione nazionale di scritti editi ed inediti di Giuseppe Mazzini* (Imola, Italy: Cooperativa tipografico-editrice Paolo Galeati, 1936–39), 84:13, 19–20.
33. Fuller supposedly married Giovanni Ossoli in Florence as testified by letters of Costanza Arconati and Marchesa Angela De Andreis (see Emma Detti, *Margaret Fuller Ossoli e i suoi corrispondenti* [Firenze: Le Monnier, 1942]), but neither the names of Ossoli nor Fuller appears in any of the marriage registers of the Tuscan Grand Duchy in the years before, during, or right after the birth of their child ("atti di matrimonio" are on microfilm at the Archivio di Stato di Firenze, Florence, Italy).
34. Elizabeth Barrett Browning, *The Letters of Elizabeth Barrett Browning*, vol. 2, ed. Frederic G. Kenyon (London: Smith, Elder, 1898), to Miss E. F. Haworth, dated 126 Via Felice, Rome, about January 1861, n.p.
35. See Angelo DeGubernatis, *Dizionario Biografico degli scrittori contemporanei diretta da Angelo DeGubernatis*, vol. 1 (Florence: Le Monnier, 1879), 715.
36. See ibid.
37. Mrs. [Sophia] Hawthorne, *Notes in England and Italy* (New York: Putnam and Son, 1869), 489.
38. Nathaniel Hawthorne, *The French and Italian Notebooks*, ed. Thomas Woodson (1871; Columbus: Ohio State University Press, 1980), 496.
39. Sally Mitchell, *Frances Power Cobbe: Victorian Feminist, Journalist, Reformer* (Charlottesville: University of Virginia Press, 2004), 112.
40. Barrett Browning, *Letters*, n.p.
41. Mitchell, *Frances Power Cobbe*, 111.
42. Barrett Browning, *Letters*, to Miss E. F. Haworth, 28 Via Tritone, Rome, winter 1859, n.p.
43. Qtd. in Mitchell, *Frances Power Cobbe*, 112.
44. Ibid.
45. Ibid., 2, 116; Treves, *Anglo-Fiorentini*, 303.
46. Mitchell, *Frances Power Cobbe*, 121.
47. Charles Eliot Norton to Margherita Mignaty, Shady Hill, Cambridge, Mass., 7 July 1877, ms. C.V. 199 72, Biblioteca Nazionale Centrale di Firenze.
48. Steadman, *Traveling Economies*, 8.
49. Nelson, *Color of Stone*, 7.
50. John Murray, *Murray's Hand-Book for Travellers in Central Italy* (London: John Murray, 1867), 85.
51. Levina Buoncuore Urbino, *An American Woman in Europe: The Journal of Two Years and a Half Sojourn in Germany, Switzerland, France, and Italy* (Boston: Lee and Shepard, 1869), 209.
52. See Luca Codignola, "The Civil War: The View from Italy," *Reviews in American History* 3, no. 4 (1975): 457–61.
53. See Bayard Taylor to George Perkins Marsh, Lausanne, 14 June 1868, George Perkins Marsh Correspondence, Special Collections and University Archives, University of Vermont Libraries, Burlington.
54. David Lowenthal, *George Perkins Marsh: Prophet of Conservation* (Seattle: University of Washington Press, 2000), 315, 319, 32, 332.

55. Mazzini, *Edizione nazionale di scritti*, 82:296.
56. Qtd. in Angelita Reyes, "Elusive Autobiographical Performativity," in *Loopholes and Retreats: African American Writers and the Nineteenth Century*, ed. John Cullen Gruesser and Hanna Wallinger, special issue of *Forecaast* 17 (2009): 159.
57. See, for example, Listri and Naldini, *Grande Storia*, 864–65.
58. Charlotte Forten Grimké, *The Journals of Charlotte Forten Grimké*, ed. Brenda Stevenson (Oxford: Oxford University Press, 1988), 495.
59. See Archivio Storico Dell'Università degli Studi di Firenze, Cancelleria degli Studi dell'Arcispedale di S. Maria Nuova, Affari Spediti, filza 74, anno 1866–67, affare 11.
60. Jarves, *Italian Sights*, 328.
61. Donatella Lippi and Laura Vannucci, "Maria Maddalena Petroncini Ferretti: Una chirurga nella Firenze di fine settecento," in *Atti e Memorie dell'accademia Toscana di scienze e lettere la Colombaria* (Florence: Leo S. Olschki Editore, 2012), 327–33.
62. Murray, *Hand-Book*, 191.
63. *Firenze in tasca*, 73.
64. Jarves, *Italian Sights*, 329.
65. Archivio Storico Dell'Università degli Studi di Firenze, Cancelleria degli Studi dell'Arcispedale di S. Maria Nuova, Affari Spediti, filza 74, anno 1866–67, affare 11.
66. Ibid.
67. 15 March; Mazzini, *Edizione nazionale di scritti*, 84:264–65.
68. William Lloyd Garrison to Helen Eliza Garrison, 31 May 1867, Boston Public Library, Boston, Mass., https://archive.org; Sibyl Ventress Brownlee, *Out of the Abundance of the Heart: Sarah Ann Parker Remond's Quest for Freedom* (Amherst: University of Massachusetts Press, 1997), 153.
69. See chapter 4.
70. Archivio Storico Dell'Università degli Studi di Firenze, Cancelleria degli Studi dell'Arcispedale di S. Maria Nuova, Affari Spediti, filza 77, anno 1867–68.
71. Sarah Parker Remond to Santa Maria Nuova Hospital School, 8 Via S. Spirito, Florence, Italy, 13 November 1867, Archivio Storico Dell'Università degli Studi di Firenze, Cancelleria degli Studi dell'Arcispedale di S. Maria Nuova, Affari Spediti, filza 79, anno 1867–68, affare 115.
72. Information obtained from Biblioteca Biomedica, Florence.
73. Archivio Storico Dell'Università degli Studi di Firenze, Cancelleria degli Studi dell'Arcispedale di S. Maria Nuova, Affari Spediti, filza 79, 1867–68, affare 119.
74. Archivio Storico Dell'Università degli Studi di Firenze, Cancelleria degli Studi dell'Arcispedale di S. Maria Nuova, Affari Spediti, 1867–68, filza 79, affare 100, and affare 115; 93, no 119 and response to a document dated 22 July, no. 119.
75. Qtd. in Reyes, "Elusive Autobiographical Performativity," 155.
76. Qtd. in Brownlee, *Out of the Abundance*, 154, and Reyes, "Elusive Autobiographical Performativity," 160.

7. Transatlantic Cosmopolitan in Italy

1. "Personal," *Harper's Bazaar*, 28 August 1869, 547.
2. "The Revolution," *Revolution*, 5 August 1869.
3. "Personal," *Christian Recorder*, 7 August 1869.
4. "The Revolution," *Revolution*, 7 October 1869.

5. See "Rapporto speciale al sindaco senatore Marchese L. Ginori ed alla giunta comunale sulla Amministrazione igienica e politico-sanitaria non chè sul servizio di Assistenza Medico-Chirurgico-Ostetrica per l'anno 1867" (Florence: Tipografia del Giglio, 1868), OP 14.35, Archivio del comune, Florence, Italy.
6. Sibyl Ventress Brownlee, *Out of the Abundance of the Heart: Sarah Ann Parker Remond's Quest for Freedom* (Amherst: University of Massachusetts Press, 1997), 155.
7. Tania Friedel, *Racial Discourse and Cosmopolitanism in Twentieth-Century African American Writing* (New York: Routledge, 2008), 2.
8. Kwame Anthony Appiah, *Cosmopolitanism: Ethics in a World of Strangers* (New York: Norton, 2006), 137, 144.
9. Gillian Brock, "Rethinking the Cosmopolitanism versus Non-Cosmopolitanism Debate: An Introduction," in *Cosmopolitanism versus Non-Cosmopolitanism: Critiques, Defenses, Reconceptualizations,* ed. Gillian Brock (Oxford: Oxford University Press, 2013), 13.
10. Ibid., 23.
11. Ibid.
12. Ibid., 24.
13. Michael Blake, "We Are All Cosmopolitans Now," in Brock, *Cosmopolitanism,* 49.
14. Paul Gilroy, *The Black Atlantic: Modernity and Double Consciousness* (Cambridge, Mass.: Harvard University Press, 1993), 126–27.
15. Qtd. in Friedel, *Racial Discourse,* 4.
16. Anne Longfellow Pierce, unpublished journal, H. W. Longfellow Family Papers, LONG 27930 (hereafter cited as Longfellow Family Papers), 2 December, Longfellow House–Washington's Headquarters National Historic Site Archives, Cambridge, Mass.
17. Anne Longfellow Pierce, unpublished journal, 7, 13 December, Longfellow Family Papers.
18. Anne Longfellow Pierce, unpublished journal, 13 December, Longfellow Family Papers.
19. Anne Longfellow Pierce, unpublished journal, 3 December 1868, Longfellow Family Papers.
20. Henry Wadsworth Longfellow to Margherita Mignaty, Cambridge, Mass., 11 July 1877, C.V. 196.116, fondo Mignaty Albana Margherita e Mignaty Giorgio, Biblioteca Nazionale Centrale di Firenze, Florence, Italy.
21. Ibid.
22. Gertie Putnam to Margherita Mignaty, Viareggio, Italy, 17 June 1871, C.V. 200.51, Putnam-Mignaty letters, fondo Mignaty Albana Margherita e Mignaty Giorgio, Biblioteca Nazionale Centrale di Firenze. Interestingly, Gertie hardly ever used punctuation in her letters.
23. Edmund Putnam to Margherita Mignaty, 19 June 1871, C.V. 200.49,. Putnam-Mignaty letters, fondo Mignaty Albana Margherita e Mignaty Giorgio, Biblioteca Nazionale Centrale di Firenze.
24. Gertie Putnam to Margherita Mignaty, Viareggio, Italy, 17 June 1871, C.V. 200.51, Putnam-Mignaty letters, fondo Mignaty Albana Margherita e Mignaty Giorgio, Biblioteca Nazionale Centrale di Firenze.
25. Edmund Putnam to Margherita Mignaty, 19 June 1871, C.V. 200.49, Putnam-Mignaty letters, fondo Mignaty Albana Margherita e Mignaty Giorgio, Biblioteca Nazionale Centrale di Firenze.
26. Ibid.
27. T. J. Jackson Lears, *No Place of Grace: Antimodernism and the Transformation of American Culture, 1880–1920* (Chicago: University of Chicago Press, 1994), 52.
28. Ibid., 48.

29. Monica Rico, *Nature's Noblemen: Transatlantic Masculinities and the Nineteenth-Century American West* (New Haven, Conn.: Yale University Press, 2013), 90–91.
30. Lears, *No Place of Grace*, 50–51.
31. Gertie Putnam to Margherita Mignaty, Viareggio, Italy, 17 June 1871, C.V. 200.51, Putnam-Mignaty letters, fondo Mignaty Albana Margherita e Mignaty Giorgio, Biblioteca Nazionale Centrale di Firenze.
32. Edmund Putnam to Margherita Mignaty, 19 June 1871, C.V. 200.49, Putnam-Mignaty letters, fondo Mignaty Albana Margherita e Mignaty Giorgio, Biblioteca Nazionale Centrale di Firenze.
33. Gertie Putnam to Margherita Mignaty, Felsberg, Luzerne, 4 August 1871, C.V. 200.48, Putnam-Mignaty letters, fondo Mignaty Albana Margherita e Mignaty Giorgio, Biblioteca Nazionale Centrale di Firenze.
34. Brownlee, *Out of the Abundance*, 154, 156.
35. Gertie Putnam to Margherita Mignaty, Woodford Lodge, Blackhead, England, 17 October 1872, C.V. 200.50, Putnam-Mignaty letters, fondo Mignaty Albana Margherita e Mignaty Giorgio, Biblioteca Nazionale Centrale di Firenze.
36. Ibid.
37. Ibid.
38. Ibid.
39. Lillie Buffum Chace Wyman and Arthur Crawford Wyman, *Elizabeth Buffum Chace, 1806–1899: Her Life and Its Environment*, vol. 1 (Boston: W. B. Clark, 1914), 42–43.
40. Ugo Pesci, *Firenze Capitale (1865–1870)* (Florence: R. Bemporad and Figlio, 1904), 467, 477.
41. See "il libro dei Soci," register, 22 January 1874, Gabinetto Scientifico Letterario G.P. Vieusseux, Florence, Italy, www.vieusseux.it.
42. The marriage may have been a facade, of respectability, to conceal homosexuality or for some other motive, because Pintor is not mentioned in any document after the marriage.
43. Manuscript ASDCA, Quinque Libri Cagliari–Santa Cecilia, 17, c. 146v. His certificate of baptism reads: "Il giorno 12 febbraio 1833 io infrascritto ho battezzato solennemente un bambino nato il giorno precedente alle ore dodici della mattina, dai coniugi: Vincenzo Pintor, dottore in diritto, della parrocchia di Sant'Anna, e Chiara Piccaluga, della parrocchia di Sant'Eulalia; al bambino è stato imposto il nome Lazzaro, Tommaso, Efisio, Bernardo. Furono padrini il dottore in diritto Tommaso Floris Palmas, del paese di Bonarcado, e in nome dello stesso il dottore in diritto Efisio Luigi Siotto Pintor." I am grateful to Monsignor Tonino Cabizzosu at Archivio Diocesano in Cagliari for this information.
44. *Firenze in tasca: Una gita di piacere alla Capitale* (1867; Sesto Fiorentino, Italy: Apice libri, 2014), 106.
45. John Murray, *Murray's Hand-Book for Travellers in Central Italy* (London: John Murray, 1867), 88; John Murray, *Murray's Hand-Book of Florence and Its Environs* (London: John Murray, 1863), x, ii.
46. Matilda Lucas, *Two Englishwomen in Rome, 1871–1900* (London: Methuen, 1938), 90.
47. Ibid., 99.
48. Ibid., 43.
49. Ibid., 99.
50. Francesco Sanvitale, *The Song of a Life: Francesco Paolo Tosti (1846–1916)*, trans. Nicola Hawthorne (Burlington, Vt.: Ashgate, 2004), 10.

51. Mary McAleer Balkun, *The American Counterfeit: Authenticity and Identity in American Literature and Culture* (Tuscaloosa: University of Alabama Press, 2006), 105.
52. Qtd. in Brownlee, *Out of the Abundance,* 156.
53. Pier Francesco Listri and Maurizio Naldini, *La Grande Storia di Firenze* (Florence: Ponte alle Grazie editori, 1992), 956.
54. Copy of a letter by Edmund Quincy Putnam, 30 May 1880, George Perkins Marsh Correspondence, carton 7, folders 29–40, Special Collections and University Archives, University of Vermont Libraries, Burlington.
55. Ibid.
56. Ibid.
57. Gertie Putnam to Margherita Mignaty, Hotel Paradiso, San Remo, Italy, 22 December 1882, C.V. 200.47, Putnam-Mignaty letters, fondo Mignaty Albana Margherita e Mignaty Giorgio, Biblioteca Nazionale Centrale di Firenze.
58. I am grateful to the Salvatorians in Rome for the information concerning the history of the building.
59. Diane Barnes, ed., *Frederick Douglass: A Life in Documents* (Charlottesville: University of Virginia Press, 2013), 167.
60. Frederick Douglass, *Frederick Douglass Diary (Tour of Europe and Africa),* 20–22, Frederick Douglass Papers, Manuscripts Division, Library of Congress, Washington, D.C., www.loc.gov.
61. Ibid., 24.
62. Ibid., 25.
63. For more about the use and significance of white marble, see Charmaine A. Nelson, "White Marble, Black Bodies and the Fear of the Invisible Negro: Signifying Blackness in Mid-Nineteenth-Century Neoclassical Sculpture," *RACAR: revue d'art canadienne / Canadian Art Review* 27, no. 1/2 (2000): 87–101.
64. Douglass, *Diary,* 26.
65. Ibid., 28.
66. Frederick Douglass to Amy Post, 10 June 1887, D.93, Post Family Papers, University of Rochester Frederick Douglass Project, Rochester, N.Y., www.lib.rochester.edu.
67. Douglass, *Diary,* 56.
68. John Murray, *A Handbook of Rome and Its Environs* (London: John Murray, 1888), 15.
69. Frederick Douglass to Amy Post, 10 June 1887, D.93, Post Family Papers, University of Rochester Frederick Douglass Project.
70. Douglass, *Diary,* 57–58.
71. Ibid., 59–60.
72. Frederick Douglass, *Life and Times of Frederick Douglass* (1892; New York: Collier Macmillan, 1962), 590.
73. I received a copy of the death certificate from the Non-Catholic Cemetery for Foreigners, Rome. I am grateful to Amanda Thursfield, Nicholas Stanley-Price, and Ornella Forte, who also informed me that this form of description was common prior to the introduction of the more precise system used presently that indicates the zone, row number, and plot. According to them, rather than a result of an individual request, Remond's grave may have been among the circa six hundred graves that were exhumed in the 1930s and 1940s after their concessions had lapsed and space was needed for other burials.
74. See Harry Henderson and Albert Henderson, *The Indomitable Spirit of Edmonia Lewis: A Narrative Biography* (Milford, Conn.: Esquiline Hill Press, 2012).

75. England and Wales Death Registration Index, 1837–2007, Registration Quarter Oct-Nov-Dec, vol. 1A, page 75, line 340, General Register Office, Southport, England.
76. See his passport application dated 6 August 1920, National Archives and Records Administration, Washington, D.C. Information provided by FamilySearch.

Coda

1. "Sarah P. Remond and the Passport Issue," in *The Black Abolitionist Papers: The British Isles, 1830–1865,* ed. Peter C. Ripley, vol. 1 (Chapel Hill: University of North Carolina Press, 1985), 471.
2. Tuesday, 12 December 1876. Ann D. Gordon, ed., *The Selected Papers of Elizabeth Cady Stanton and Susan B. Anthony,* vol. 3 (New Brunswick, N.J.: Rutgers University Press, 2003), 276–77.
3. Mary Suzanne Schriber, *Writing Home: American Women Abroad, 1830–1920* (Charlottesville: University Press of Virginia, 1997), 13.
4. Nico Slate, *Colored Cosmopolitanism: The Shared Struggle for Freedom in the United States and India* (Cambridge, Mass.: Harvard University Press, 2012), 70.
5. "Miss Remond's Anti-Slavery Lecture," *Freeman's Journal,* 15 March 1859.
6. "American Slavery," *Waterford Mail* (Ireland), 9 April 1859, reprinted in the *Liberator,* 13 May 1859.

Index

SIRPA SALENIUS, a native of Finland, taught at the University of Tokyo and at American university study abroad programs in Rome and Florence before assuming her position as senior lecturer at the University of Eastern Finland. She received her MA in foreign languages and cultures from the University of Florence and her PhD in English studies from the University of Joensuu (now University of Eastern Finland). Her publications focus on transatlantic studies, on American writers and artists in Italy, and on examining race and gender in the transatlantic context. Her recent books include *Rose Elizabeth Cleveland: First Lady and Literary Scholar* (2014) and, as coeditor, *Transatlantic Conversations: Nineteenth-Century American Women's Encounters with Italy and the Atlantic World* (forthcoming 2016). She is married to a Florentine and considers Italy her home.